PORTRAIT OF AN ARTIST

Interviews and Polaroids by
Hugo Huerta Marin

PRESTEL

This collection of original interviews and Polaroid photographs of almost 30 trailblazing women spans creative industries, nationalities and generations to bring together a never-before-published collection of leading voices. Featuring an astounding range of names including FKA Twigs, Isabelle Huppert and Rei Kawakubo, this book creates both a portrait of each individual woman and collectively, a powerful portrait of the impact of women on the creative industries.

£26.00
Hardcover
424 pages, 70 colour illustrations
ISBN: 978-3-7913-8748-2

PRESTEL

www.prestel.com

GRANTA

12 Addison Avenue, London W11 4QR | email: editorial@granta.com
To subscribe go to granta.com/subscriptions, or call +44 (0) 1371 851873

ISSUE 157: AUTUMN 2021

This selection copyright © 2021 Granta Trust.

Granta, ISSN 173231 (USPS 508), is published four times a year by Granta Trust, 12 Addison Avenue, London W11 4QR, United Kingdom.

The US annual subscription price is $50. Airfreight and mailing in the USA by agent named World Container Inc., 150–15, 183rd Street, Jamaica, NY 11434, USA. Periodicals postage paid at Brooklyn, NY 11256.

US Postmaster: Send address changes to *Granta*, World Container Inc., 150–15, 183rd Street, Jamaica, NY 11434, USA.

Subscription records are maintained at *Granta*, c/o ESco Business Services Ltd, Wethersfield, Essex, CM7 4AY.

Air Business Ltd is acting as our mailing agent.

Granta is printed and bound in Italy by Legoprint. This magazine is printed on paper that fulfils the criteria for 'Paper for permanent document' according to ISO 9706 and the American Library Standard ANSI/NIZO Z39.48-1992 and has been certified by the Forest Stewardship Council (FSC).

Granta is indexed in the American Humanities Index.

ISBN 978-1-909-889-43-9

Nan Shepherd
THE LIVING MOUNTAIN

With seven original paintings by Rose Strang
Introduced by Robert Macfarlane

'One of the most
brilliant works of modern
landscape literature'
Robert Macfarlane

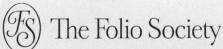
The Folio Society

CONTENTS

On Staying at Home

'Why do I travel so much when I am so terribly frightened
of traveling?' – Sven Lindqvist, *Exterminate All the Brutes*,
trans. Joan Tate

It's a good question. Some years ago, on the edge of the Taklamakan
Desert, in Xinjiang, China, a young Uyghur man asked me another one:
why, when I could travel 'anywhere', as he saw it, had I come to this place
of dust storms and surveillance, which he longed to escape? He couldn't
sleep, he said; whatever he tried, he couldn't sleep. China's network
of 're-education' camps, where as many as 1.5 million Uyghur people
are today enduring internment, forced labour, torture and rape, was
then in its infancy, but for him the 'autonomous region' was already
a nightmare of state harassment and incipient violence. He spoke in a
whisper, even in the desert. I had no reasonable answer to his question,
and felt, not for the first time, the self-disgust of the European travel
writer in a troubled place, who – journalistic pretexts aside – is neither
a news correspondent nor an international observer, but basically a
tourist with a book in mind: monitored, perhaps, but free to brush off
the sand and go home to his desk when he wishes. The feeling lingers.

This volume has evolved with such questions of travel in mind.
Since its tenth issue, published in 1984, *Granta* has been credited with
shaping, if not defining, what is blithely called 'travel writing'. *Granta*
10'scontents page is a catalogue of the genre's most influential, and
best-selling, modern practitioners, including Jan Morris, Bruce
Chatwin and Jonathan Raban. Its editor, Bill Buford, acknowledged
in his introduction that travel writing, as a genre which 'borrows from
the memoir, reportage and, most important, the novel', is hard to
pin down. We needn't persist with definitions, other than to wonder if
travel writing's resistance to them is one of the things that energises it.

The current volume exemplifies what Buford calls the 'generic
androgyny' of travel writing, but certain themes recur. Bathsheba
Demuth, in far-east Russia, and Eliane Brum (trans. Diane Grosklaus
Whitty), in the Antarctic, both write about environmental decline,
embodied in the whale and in humankind's treatment of this creature

we often profess to love. It's increasingly clear that the environmental crisis is inextricable from the crisis of human displacement, even while traditional drivers of exile persist. In her essay about the Afghan migrant community in Hamburg's Steindamm district, Taran N. Khan notes that 'when we talk of writing on travel, we are often describing borders'. It is partly in the hope of dealing with suppressed trauma that Javier Zamora drives with his friend Francisco Cantú to the US–Mexico border – the border he once crossed as an undocumented child migrant and Cantú once guarded as a Border Patrol agent.

They are not alone in *going back*, in memory or reality. 'When I thought about returning, it was only ever in my mother's language,' writes Jessica J. Lee, in her mapping of the alleys of Taipei, Taiwan, where her mother was born. Tiring of New York, Emmanuel Iduma returns to Nigeria, where he grew up, recalling the journeys of his father, an itinerant Presbyterian minister, and recognising in himself an inheritance of restlessness: 'From his impermanence I grew into mine.'

The American artist Roni Horn has been visiting Iceland since 1975, returning with what she calls 'migratory insistence and regularity'. She describes '16 Sheets from LOG' as a 'collection of notes, casual observations, facts, quotes, events of weather and private life, news, and anything otherwise notable that came to mind or hand each day'. There can be a feeling of liberation in surrendering to the complexity of any place – especially one that is not our home – and thus to its unknowability. 'I'm often asked but have no idea why I chose Iceland,' Horn writes, 'why I first started going, why I still go. In truth I believe Iceland chose me.'

It's been an interesting time to commission a volume of travel writing. The carbon implications were a consideration from the start – contributors were to be discouraged from flying – but in the event, the journeys they wrote about were by necessity journeys that had already been made. At first Covid was only an ominous whisper, but its spread can be traced across these pages. Aboard a Greenpeace ship, Brum hears of a virus that is 'devastating the whole world' and assumes the speaker is describing a disaster movie. Among the volcanoes of the Philippines' Cordillera Central, Ben Mauk registers rumblings of a 'novel virus in China that seemed at risk of spreading to other countries in Asia'. Then, around the world, cases erupt. In Kapka Kassabova's 'The Ninth Spring', seasonal workers returning to Bulgaria's Mesta basin bring Covid back with their pay cheques. Other journeys were abandoned altogether. Sinéad Gleeson's planned return to that ancient place of healing, Lourdes, had to be forgone in favour of a journey, compiled of fragments of memory, in the footsteps of the Ukrainian-born Brazilian writer Clarice Lispector. Both Khan's reflections on her status as an Indian passport holder and Carlos Manuel Álvarez's account (trans. Frank Wynne) of his interrogation by immigration officers in Cuba, meanwhile, are reminders that nonchalant global mobility has never been available to most of the world's population.

One response to Elizabeth Bishop's enquiry in her poem 'Questions of Travel' – 'Should we have stayed at home' – might be: 'It depends who you mean by *we*.' According to the writer Charles Sugnet, *Granta* 10 was nothing more than a 'highbrow version of the Banana Republic catalog', guilty of perpetuating 'colonialist discourse'. Hyperbole, perhaps, but the travel writer of myth – Bowie knife in one pocket, Moleskine in another, off to Patagonia – is a stubborn ghost, and even in the 1980s, often came across as a revenant of the 1890s: alarmingly erudite, unflappable, prone to affectionate generalisations, and indistinguishable in all but style from the emissaries of colonial power that went before.

The genre has lost some of its self-assurance, and that's a relief. The bluff tone has abated – prompted partly by an overdue postcolonial reckoning, partly by a greater plurality of perspectives, and partly by what scholars of the genre call 'belatedness'. Tim Hannigan, in his recent book *The Travel Writing Tribe*, describes this phenomenon as 'the nagging suspicion that all the truly worthwhile journeys have already been done'. The world having been well and truly 'discovered', and thus despoiled, the modern travel writer's task is to pick sagaciously over its bones. The Amazon basin is a smoking ruin; the sands of the Arabian Empty Quarter are as footprint-riddled as Clacton-on-Sea; the throat singers of Tuva are doing numbers on Instagram. But grief can easily become a posture of art, or lapse into colonialist nostalgia. It's hard to imagine a future, or even see the present clearly, when we are entranced by dreams of the past.

A second response to Bishop's question can be found in these words attributed to another American poet, Gary Snyder: *the most radical thing you can do is stay at home.* Stay at home and it's hard to colonise, enslave, pillage or fight a war, as Bishop recognised. Had *we* stayed at home, the human race might not be reeling from a global pandemic, and the globe itself might not be in the state it's in, with grey whales 'eating themselves from the inside out', as Demuth describes. When any long-haul flight can plausibly be described as an act of violence, we'd all do well to learn to dwell better, to know and love our own patch more deeply. And yet precisely because of the peril we face as a species, there remains value in venturing – carefully, reverently – beyond the horizon, as these pieces show, even if we reject the modes of travel that brought the world to this pass in the first place.

One of the contributors to *Granta* 10, Jan Morris, told the *Paris Review* that travel, for her, had been a search for reconciliation: 'with nature but with people too . . . a pursuit [of] unity and even an attempt to contribute to a sense of unity'. Putting together this volume has confirmed to me that conscious, conscientious travel (and writing about it) goes hand in hand with an ethos of hospitality. If the following pieces can be said to have an overriding characteristic, it is that they take seriously the experience of being a stranger. What does it mean to be an outsider, wherever we call home? How do we react when stripped of everything familiar? Who *are* we, removed from hearth and loved ones? And how can we, in turn, offer the stranger '[a] helping hand, a feeling of safety', in Zamora's words? Only by doing so, as we continue to go out to meet the world on its own terms, can we begin to imagine an equitable future. ■

William Atkins

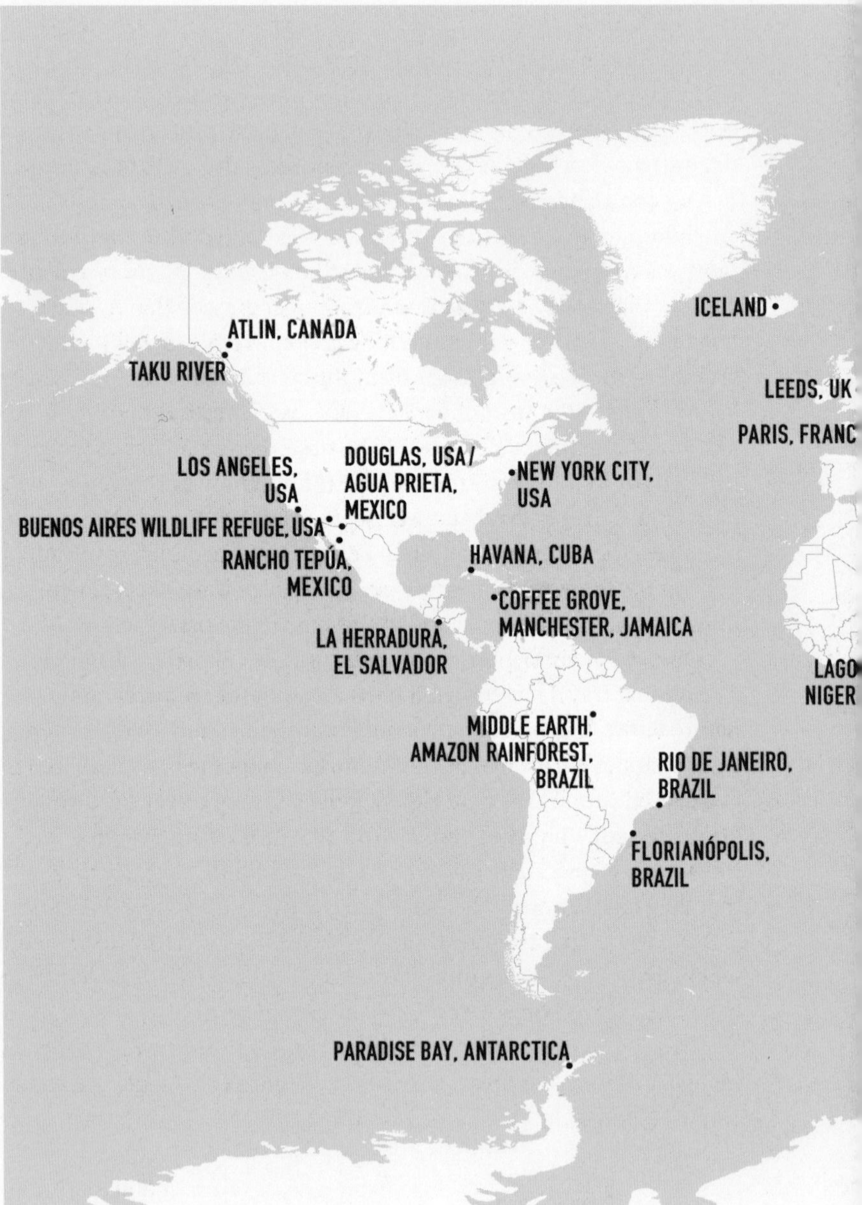

ICELAND •

ATLIN, CANADA

TAKU RIVER

LEEDS, UK

PARIS, FRANC

LOS ANGELES,
USA

DOUGLAS, USA /
AGUA PRIETA,
MEXICO

• NEW YORK CITY,
USA

BUENOS AIRES WILDLIFE REFUGE, USA •

RANCHO TEPÚA,
MEXICO

HAVANA, CUBA

• COFFEE GROVE,
MANCHESTER, JAMAICA

LA HERRADURA,
EL SALVADOR

LAGO
NIGER

MIDDLE EARTH,
AMAZON RAINFOREST,
BRAZIL

RIO DE JANEIRO,
BRAZIL

FLORIANÓPOLIS,
BRAZIL

PARADISE BAY, ANTARCTICA

CHUKOTKA, RUSSIA•

AMBURG, GERMANY

YAKORUDA, BULGARIA
•

BANDHAVGARH
NATIONAL PARK,
MADHYA PRADESH
INDIA

KABUL,•
AFGHANISTAN

•TAIPEI, TAIWAN

•LUZON, PHILIPPINES

UJA, NIGERIA
•

MUMBAI,•
INDIA

RT HARCOURT,
GERIA

KAURNA NATION,•
AUSTRALIA

Ivory Engraving of Chukchi Hunters

ON MISTAKING WHALES

Bathsheba Demuth

Before a gray whale becomes a home, or a barrel of oil, or a metaphor, before she enters the realm of human meaning, she is a being complete in herself. Born as most gray whales are on an early January day off northwestern Mexico's Baja Peninsula, her mother swims upside down, tail lifted, straining up, up, and she emerges head first not into water but into the air. Two thousand pounds of smooth pewter muscle born facing the sky. For the next three months, she practices pacing her breaths, the rise to the surface that keeps her from drowning in the water that is her home. In the calm lagoons, she grows more than a ton each month.

In April, the gray whale and her mother begin traveling north. They are often in sight of land, desert scrub becoming grassland, grassland turning to redwood groves and temperate rainforest as they move up the long arc of the North American continent. Their nearshore waters are punctuated by din: the ports of Los Angeles, Oakland, Seattle and Vancouver, each calling in its braided lanes of shipping traffic. In June, as they reach Unimak Pass in the Aleutian Islands, there is less clamor. They have swum more than 4,000 miles not for quiet but for the Bering Sea's pastures of clams and tube worms below them in the muck, creatures that have rounded generations of the whale's kin in blubber. As mother and calf scoop up the benthic riches, muddy blooms rise and trace across the sea's surface.

In midsummer, the feeding path of the gray whale and her mother turns west toward Russia, toward good eating and shelter amid the bays and inlets of the Chukchi Peninsula. Their route meanders across the International Date Line, between today and tomorrow, yesterday and today. A demarcation as meaningless to a whale as a day – that contained pulse of light and dark – is to a human being in the endless sun of an Arctic summer.

In one such Arctic summer, I go to Chukotka, crossing the Date Line to the Bering Sea to look for whales. A historian by training, I had for several years been gathering records about gray whales and their meanings: Indigenous Yupik and Chukchi histories transcribed in St Petersburg; whalers' logbooks in New Bedford, Massachusetts; Soviet economic plans on onion-skin paper in Vladivostok; the minutes of International Whaling Commission meetings in Washington DC. I spent that time imagining a whale, the contours of her life. Arriving in Chukotka, what I have are fragments. I am here, in the easternmost region of Russia, out of a kind of compulsive hope that in visiting the origin of these fragments, the place that has hosted centuries of varying relations between my species and the gray whale, I might find the line of a story. I am on the dawn-land edge of Eurasia looking for the plot.

I have a temporary apartment in Provideniya, a Soviet-era concrete town in the middle of Beringia National Park, its bays and beaches thick with whales and whaling sites. Seeing them is not simple. Alaska is close enough to be visible from points along this coast, so the Russian government considers all 737,700 square kilometers of the Chukotka Autonomous Okrug to be a border zone. Foreigners can travel here only with a *propusk*, a pass stamped by the governor and the Federal Security Service, or FSB. My *propusk* lists whether I have a curfew and what settlements I can visit. I also require minding; for anything further afield than a stroll, I am supervised by Nikolai Ettyne, a park guide. He makes our plans based on the weather and places in the park he has the vehicles and need to go. Or to avoid; one plan was scrapped because thousands of walruses had hauled themselves out onto the beach we were to see, and our presence might have caused them to stampede, crushing their young in a panicked heave toward the safety of the sea.

On a morning with fast-moving clouds and no rain, Nikolai collects me at my apartment. He is Chukchi, his ancestors native to this peninsula for generations, but not from *here*, he explains, as he was born 160 kilometers north in Lavrentiya. So it is good to travel with locals. Today, Alexei comes with us, driving the park's Trekol. It is clear, once we are outside town, why we need the vehicle's four-foot tires. Our way is along a narrow lake held by parallel ridges, their lichen-dark tops snow-boned, with barely a track ahead and no gentling of the incline where hill becomes lake. Americans, Alexei explains as water splashes over our hood, make roads. Russians make vehicles that do not require roads.

After a jolting hour, Alexei turns east. The Bering Sea is immediately on our left, the lake to the right; once, I think, the lake was a fjord, open to the sea, but the waves chose over some years to close the mouth with sand. Ahead is a low grassy hill, radiant green and rippling silver where the wind flips over the larkspur leaves. Clusters of beams rise pale and weathered. I take them to be wood, the edges worn ovoid and organic, but the beams are arrayed with the kind of order that marks to the eye things made by people.

As we walk up among them, I see that the beams were born. Slipped into the sea as the internal architecture of whales. The largest, ribs wide as I am, grew inside bowheads, the smaller come from grays. As we walk among them, I can see the bones are the ceilings of half-underground spaces. Many are sunk now below the larkspurs and monkshood, their sentinel ribs fallen to earth. These were houses, Nikolai says. This was the village of Eunmyn, that's the Chukchi name. In Yupik, they call it Avan.

Avan: a name I know from libraries. People have made houses from whale along the Bering Strait for thousands of years; the practice is more recent in Avan, starting perhaps a millennia ago. Over the subsequent centuries, waves of inhabitants, drawn to this place because of its vantage for hunting whales, left strata of tools and dwellings. At a museum in St Petersburg, I saw photographs from the 1920s, when this was a Yupik settlement. The Avatmiit, the Yupik of Avan, lived in walrus-hide tents, not these bone homes, and did not trace their ancestry to the builders. When Vasilii Ankatagin, born here in 1924 or 1925, gave an account of Avan to anthropologist Igor Krupnik in the 1970s, he described it as 'a good place: good hunting, many sea animals, fish, birds. To live here was good.'

There is a thrumming life still, among the houses where Vasilii must have run as a child, trampling the grasses as we do, hearing peregrine falcons keen as they ride the thermals high above. Perhaps he also touched the old whale bone, feeling how pliant it is with age. Or perhaps the sense of retained memories echoing up from these pits was too acute. I approach one house by crawling on my belly to peer down. In the dimness, the pale heavy brow of a whale's skull holds back the earth. A bone wall. The people who lived here lived in the heads of whales.

In twenty-first-century New England, the time and place that I live, whales are usually the subject of awe and benevolence. I have had neighbors tell me they love them, sentiments that do not require regular observation or even the precision of a species. Here whales have been homes. A practical space, shelter and host to meals and births and deaths. Host to the least abstract kinds of love. Familial, romantic, parental. Here whales have made those intimacies, by giving people the capacity to live.

I pick myself up and walk with Nikolai down to the gray sandy beach. The sea, which is constrained less and less each year by the tempering presence of sea ice, is eroding the embankment that separates Avan from the water, exposing the skull foundations of another house. At my feet are pieces of bone. Some were clearly tools, things worked by human hands. Among them, incongruously bright, is a Yoplait yogurt container, the English on the sea-worn plastic still legible: fat-free strawberry.

We turn and look for whale spouts. You can tell the species by their plumes of breath, Nikolai tells me. Gray whales exhale in heart-shapes. The horizon is a clean line between blue-green water and a sky purpling with more rain. We see no whales.

I had seen whales on my way to Provideniya, the week before. I was in Nikolai's village, Lavrentiya, waiting for the *Kapitan Sotnikov*, a small cargo ship heading for Provideniya, to set off. Young men in jeans and black windbreakers lashed bags of reindeer antlers onto the deck. Gathered from the inland herds and bound for China, Gena Zelensky told me. I had known Gena for some years; he is a master of Chukotkan logistics, fixer of my *propusk* and first port of call if things go awry. And they had. My plan was to fly straight to Provideniya from the regional capital of Anadyr, but there was an issue with my ticket – the sort of Russian bureaucratic problem that is never clear except in its outcome – and no empty seats for weeks. Gena improvised: I could go via Lavrentiya, where he lives in the summer, then take the *Kapitan Sotnikov* thirteen hours down the coast.

Lavrentiya was not listed on my *propusk*, however. As we waited for the ship, two plainclothes men from the security services asked me questions. We spoke in Russian. They mentioned my husband by name, casually, but also to make clear they knew things about me, things written in a file somewhere that I had not told them. After they left, Gena grumbled: what do they think you're going to do, steal the damn reindeer? Spy on the whales?

That evening I climbed from the diesel-scented passenger area of the *Kapitan Sotnikov*, in search of a horizon. The view through the portholes kept moving up and sideways or down and backward, leaving my stomach in transit between. I tried focusing on the flat-screen television playing a dubbed version of *Air Force One* on a continual loop, which was worse. On deck the cold wind knocked me breathless but took the nausea with it. The evening was silvery, the late sun filtering through low clouds and breaking through, here and there, in streamers of light.

I thought about the FSB men. A century and a half ago, a person in Chukotka from New England was a kind of robber. They sailed from New Bedford and Nantucket and other port cities to skin the fat off of whales and refine it into lamp oil. The want for light decimated Atlantic whales, sending hunters to harrow the Pacific. In 1845, commercial ships reached Baja California, where gray whales give birth in sheltered inlets each winter, the southerly reach of a migration that brings them north to the Bering Sea in summer. Gray whales gave little oil, of poor quality. But whalers were paid their share of a voyage's take only after its sale back in port. Every hand aboard knew the fastest way home was through killing any animal they could. So they lowered their small boats with the long harpoons into the nursery lagoons.

Within a few years, the whalers' pursuit of oil trailed the grays north to the Bering Sea. Gray whales learned that the ships brought danger and attacked their tormenters. Whalers feared and hated them for it, calling them devil fish or scrags. In waters not far from the *Kapitan Sotnikov*'s route, one ship's mate described 'chasing devil fish' only to have 'the head of the boat knocked off'. So many meetings between whales and people took place in which the singular experience was terror. For such people, the meaning of a whale was reduced to present injury risked for future profit. And for the whale? As seen from the surface by her killers, she raged.

It did not stop the slaughter. Thirty years on from the first commercial kill, there were perhaps 4,400 gray whales left to migrate between Baja and the Bering Sea. The sea floor was littered with thousands of bones that never became houses. New England sailors did not even eat much whale. Many judged the Yupik and Chukchi who did as lacking 'habits of industry', as one captain wrote, in part because they killed few whales and did not sell the blubber. But the commercial fleet was aware that whale was to Chukotkans what grain was to New Englanders. In New Bedford newspapers, ship captains castigated themselves for the famines they had caused, for how commercial slaughter was 'taking bread out of [Yupik and Chukchi] mouths'.

On the deck of the *Kapitan Sotnikov*, I watched three crepuscular sunbeams touch the rocking surface. In the shadows between, a back rose and split wide the sea in blasting exhale. A second followed. A mother gray and calf, by their sizes, and distinct from humpbacks or bowheads for having no dorsal fins. They were two of the nearly 27,000 gray whales then alive, descendants of those who survived being known by commerce.

What is it Herman Melville wrote? Quoting Daniel Webster, early in *Moby-Dick*: whalers added 'largely every year to the National wealth by the boldest and most persevering industry'. Melville had spent long enough in the gore and fear of whaling ships that the quote was ironic, but not untrue; he knew how in New England, on streets lit by blubber, remorseless havoc was made into a story of triumph. Light by which to read an American plot of progress.

The whales swam for a time in and out of the luminescence, pooling and dispersing on the water, the tips of the small waves shattering into fragments of light.

In Avan, I think of Vasilii Ankatagin, and wonder how many whales he had seen, looking out on this same sea. The New England fleet was decades gone when he was a boy in the 1930s, but Norwegian ships were by then killing with new industrial precision in Baja. In the Bering Sea, the Soviet Union's first factory whaler, the *Aleut*, killed gray whales as they fattened themselves in summer. I had spent hours with the *Aleut*'s flaking, itchy newsprint reports, reading how Soviet whalers also disliked grays for their habits of 'swimming in zigzags, moving from one side to the other without any determined direction', making them difficult to harpoon.

The *Aleut* killed its first whale on the fifteenth anniversary of the Bolshevik Revolution. That revolution brought a new and very clear plot to Chukotka. Inspired by Marx and refined by Lenin, it made history into a ladder: human society moved from hunting and gathering to feudal agriculture to capitalist production, masterful in its technological sophistication but terrible in its human exploitation.

Socialism would overthrow capitalism's injustices with capitalism's industrial tools. The result would be utopia. These rules, like supply and demand, were supposed to work everywhere, meaning that, by the laws of history, Chukotka would come to look like anywhere in the Soviet Union.

When Vasilii was a child, this revolution was still distant from Avan. One of its signs might have been in the gray whales, or their absence; by the time Vasilii was a teenager, seeing the backs rise to breathe would have been a rare thing. There were some 2,000 gray whales left. The *Aleut* found few to slaughter, and they were smaller each year. The crew moved on to killing other whales.

In 1941, fearing Japanese attack, the Soviet Union built a line of defensive artillery on the sandspit by the village. The Avatmiit were exiled. 'We only left this village when they closed us,' Vasilii remembered, 'When the war started.' Vasilii, like many of his kin, was sent to Ureliki.

On the road back from Avan, Alexei drives Nikolai and me through Ureliki. It is empty now, one of the many towns in Chuktoka that collapsed with the Soviet Union. Its streets run parallel to the bay, with Provideniya on the opposite bank. Through empty windows I see yellow-flowered wallpaper in one apartment, the empty shelves of a library, the long tables of a cafeteria. A mechanic shop sits with its door open, as if awaiting cars. The oldest building, made of piled and grouted local stone rather than poured concrete, appears to be a prison, still rimmed in concertina wire. The only people we see are a group of Russian soldiers, smoking and tidying among olive drab tents pitched in the courtyard of an empty apartment building.

In the account told to Igor Krupnik, Vasilii did not say what it was like to be moved into this place, into an apartment with square walls and gas heat. He was never allowed to return to Avan. Valsilii's way of whaling also went into exile. Soviet authorities wanted death to be more rationalized, more like the industrial ideal of a factory. Hunting from shore, as Chukchi and Yupik had done for so many centuries, was replaced with a small motorized catcher ship called the *Zvezdnyi*. It killed gray whales at sea and towed the carcasses to villages along the coast.

As we leave Ureliki it begins to rain, the driving kind that comes in August so close to the Arctic Circle. Alexei turns on the headlights and the concrete buildings vanish into curtains of bright drops. I thought of the accounts of this place from archives, the New England sailors so quick to describe Yupik and Chukchi with words like primitive and archaic, the Soviets taking Chukotka as backward, a place outside the flow of history their revolution was creating. This place and its people needed to fit into a singular story. What is visible in Avan, in the bone houses and Vasilii's memories, is how Soviet attempts to realize a singular plot in this place did not hold. The Soviets made wealth here, for a time, but not a home. They traveled so far after whales but never arrived.

In the time and place where I was born, we were taught that the right way to consume a whale is with your eyes. In English this is called whale watching; you, the human being, bear the verb out over the water to the noun that is *whale*. An object containing a pedagogy of wonder. I have whale watched off the coasts of Massachusetts and Rhode Island, looking for humpbacks or right whales, although not grays; their migrations were ended in the Atlantic more than two centuries ago by European hunters, perhaps in concert with some unknown ecological shift. But even floating over this extinction, whale watching is part of a plot I learned to call civilization. Yes, industrial whalers had pushed multiple species nearly to extirpation, but with knowledge of that destruction we – always a general we – put aside such brutal things. Death is in the past.

Several days after Avan, Nikolai drives us north from Provideniya on a gravel road through rolling treeless hills. The land from the truck looks flat green. We stop often, sometimes to watch a ground squirrel busy in the undergrowth, or to examine an abandoned Soviet building. Separate from the truck's speed and distance, I can see the tundra is a mosaic, each plant its own green, their dozens of shades interrupted by pink moss campion, minute alpine azaleas, short pale-yellow poppies, white tufts of cotton grass. Once, among them, is a piece of whale bone. Nikolai tells me it does not belong here. To be so far from salt water disrespects the whale, who in death wants to be close to her sea.

The road passes through low hills and comes to a wide rocky shore, a place Nikolai calls Inachpyk. Across a channel of turquoise water is Itygran Island. Down the beach from where we stop, a group of men and several large Soviet-era trucks cluster around an element of the sea that for the second time I take to be terrestrial, to be a gray oblong stone. As we walk toward them, I see that the stone has died. The stone is a whale.

She is not large, perhaps twenty-five feet long. Two Chukchi men in rubber boots and olive rain slickers give a curious nod and continue cutting open the side of her. There is an iron and gut smell on the air. The butchering is solemn and hard, the men straining to lift sheets of skin-rimmed blubber into the trucks. I overhear one of them saying what a gift the fat will be for his grandmother. She doesn't do well with other food, he says. This is what makes her well.

When these men were children, the Soviet Union collapsed. Their fathers and grandfathers began whaling again out of necessity – there were no more Soviet supply ships filling the towns with food. The *Aleut* had departed the Bering Sea like the rest of the world's industrial whalers; after slaughtering 3 million whales in the twentieth century, the fleets submitted to a moratorium under the International Whaling Commission.

Nikolai said this hunt was also regulated by the Commission. Chukotkan whalers are allowed to kill 140 grays each year. There are not enough experienced hunters, he says, to always reach this number, although the villages need the meat.

I reach out and touch the barnacles this whale collected in life. They are the colors of old teeth, grown in swirling constellations across the whale and dying with her, their feathered cirri desiccating in the air. Her blood smells like any blood, like the nosebleeds I get in winter. Shanks of yellow baleen, maybe ten inches long, hang from the curve of her jaw. One of the men says something to Nikolai, who takes out his knife and cuts away a few pounds of the dark flesh. It is good meat, he said. This is not a stink whale.

I ask him what he means by *stink whale*. In the past decade, he explains, some grays have a strong smell, not one from the ocean but chemical, like iodine. Sometimes it is so strong they exhale the odor, and hunters avoid them. But other times it is just in the meat. People who eat them go numb in the mouth, or have terrible diarrhea. The meat is not even good for dogs because they refuse to eat it. No one has told us why, Nikolai says. Some of these old hunters say it is in the water, algae maybe, something the whales eat. He wraps the meat in a newspaper and hands it to me. A gift from them, he says, nodding to the men.

In Provideniya that evening, I cook the whale and eat it with dark sweet bread. It tastes like mild venison, with a slight edge of sea. From the window in the kitchen, I look down the hill, through apartments and administrative buildings, to the bay below. Other than a few dark ripples cast by seals, the water is so calm I am looking down onto my building and the whole town twinned on its surface, the reflection shuddering only slightly to indicate the version that is not land.

At a distance or without attention it is easier – not necessary, but easier – to make grand summations about human nature and history. I was taught to see in that ease not a position but a quality of knowledge: to be far off is to be objective, able to define *what is* or *what was* or *what is right* that covers over the fragmentary nature of being, of being a person attempting to see. It is the lure of being modern. It makes everything exist in one plot. People have brought such ideas to Chukotka for two centuries. Their attempts are so plainly at odds with the practical lived reality of place, with the needs given down by the particularities of land and sea.

I n January 2019, five months after I left Chukotka, gray whales entered what marine scientists call an 'extreme mortality event'. Dead or dying grays stranded on beaches and rocky coves from Mexico to Alaska. By the late fall of 2020, 384 corpses had washed ashore; many more, likely nearly 7,000 more, had died at sea since 2016. Some had been struck by ships or tangled in fishing line. Others were emaciated. Autopsies found whales with stomachs full of a black dough, signs of a body digesting itself.

Throughout this extreme mortality event, I was speaking about whales and their killers, and my time in Inachpyk, to audiences around the United States. It was not uncommon for someone to ask, horrified, how I could witness a whale death. Wasn't it simply *too much*, one woman asked, *too much to bear?* The implications were old as colonialism. On one side there were the right people, the civilized ones, and on the other – well: anyone eating whales could not be on the right side of history, the side moving ever forward to better things. The plot of progress is indifferent to place; it treats time as a race and rightness is the distance run.

I began warning people about my carnivorous content. It was, I think, the wrong disclaimer. I should have said: look at this strawberry yogurt cup. This is your sustenance, you in my audience, your appetite and mine too. It is also evidence that you are already traveling out among whales, that you are in their home. Through your food, yes, and in that unknown effluvia of industrial life that has so changed the oceans that gray whale breath smells of iodine. And in the container ships that pull into the Port of Seattle or Oakland, weighted down with the things Americans demand of Chinese factories, cutting through the dominion and sometimes the lives of gray whales. The norms that ended industrial cetacean slaughter are all to the good, the norms of watching whales rather than killing them by the millions. But they are not preventing gray whales from eating themselves from the inside out.

I should have said: what we call wealthy society exists in a condition that disarticulates appetite and sustenance from their sources, from the beings who make our bones and our homes. Don't confuse the distance civilization keeps from death with the end of dying. The land where you live, in close focus, might present another way to arrange the fragments of the past into a story.

Before leaving Avan, Nikolai and I climb the hill west of the village. We turn, winded, to look down at the circles of bone, their marks outlasting any left by the tents of Vasilii's generation. To the east is a hulk of heavy artillery, the cause of Vasilii's expulsion. Above us, further up the western hill, a small hut looks out to the sea, an ear of the state constructed decades ago to listen across the Cold War border. On the other side of the ridge is a harbor once frequented by New England whaling ships; behind us, miles to the south, an abandoned Soviet blubber refinery. Just in our view, half a dozen past futures.

I think of all the things I do not know. How gray whales see light. How long they live. Do they keep a sense of kin. Do they have a collective memory of the twentieth century, and if so what is its shape. What language did the builders of the houses in Avan speak. Where did they begin their history. Did they experience it ending, or was the end a series of changes that rebuilt the ship beneath them into some new form, not a race but a slow act of recreation.

Somewhere, over the edge of our sight, a whale. Like a plot, she is a being in and of herself and also one among many, not so much partial as alive in a multiplicity. Swimming south, lifting every few minutes to breathe, pausing in the air and light, as she crosses the fiction of a single Date Line. ■

CARLEEN COULTER
Cordillera Administrative Region, Philippines, January 2020

THE STEEPEST PLACES: IN THE CORDILLERA CENTRAL

Ben Mauk

$$\frac{4}{c} = \frac{e^{-x/c}c^{-x/c}}{2}$$

is the sine curve that describes Mayon, the stratovolcano whose slopes form the most regular cone in the natural world. (Let c = 8.6 millimeters.) It was somewhere to our south, at the tip of the long ribbon of Luzon, glowing at night with a bulb of magma in its mouth. Mayon is the most active volcano in the Philippines. Around its base are densely populated towns whose inhabitants do not frighten easily. The last major eruption, in 1993, killed seventy-nine people and forced nearly a thousand times as many to flee their homes, as lava and mudflows coursed down the mountain's dozens of ravines like puddled steel in a smeltery. It has since erupted in 1999, 2000, 2006, 2009, 2013 (a sudden phreatic explosion that killed four mountain climbers from Europe and their Filipino guide), 2014 and 2018. Mayon smoldered and glowed but did not erupt the season of our arrival in Manila. Taal erupted instead.

We were rooming on a street of flowerpot-lined churches in Poblacion, the old market center of Makati, where one evening the parked jeepneys were discovered coated in silken film. A sign appeared in the hotel lobby: THE ROOF DECK IS CLOSED UNTIL FURTHER NOTICE DUE TO ASHFALL.

Forty miles to the south, fumaroles sent up curtains of white smoke around Taal's caldera that returned to earth as damp, unassuming dust on cafe tables as far north as Quezon City. It was our introduction to a sight that would become routine three months later: a city of masked faces. We went looking for a pair of the recommended N95 face masks. They were sold out everywhere.

The volcanic warning level was raised to four out of a possible five. Carleen looked up the chart on her phone at breakfast. 'Level four means a hazardous eruption is imminent,' she said, using the same tone of voice with which she had earlier pointed out that a museum on our itinerary was closed for the day. The slopes of the caldera were beginning to inflate like earthen lungs as magma pressed up against surface rock. Color photographs around Batangas showed an ash-desaturated landscape, with roads, crops, cars and houses cast fuzzily in monochrome silver. Lapilli – volcanic cinders as large as billiard balls – fell on houses in villages around Taal Lake. The government evacuated 20,000 people, and eventually more than 100,000 were displaced, many of them farmers living off the rich volcanic soil. Left with no caretakers, their livestock began to starve to death.

At least one Luzon resident was not cowed. 'I will eat that ashfall,' President Rodrigo Duterte told the nation. 'I'm even going to pee on Taal, that goddamned volcano.' Duterte is nothing if not quotable. In defense of the drug war that is his administration's signature platform, and in which tens of thousands have died, he has compared himself favorably to Adolf Hitler and his slaughtering of drug addicts to the Nazi persecution of Jews. During his 2016 presidential campaign – unofficial slogan: 'Kill the criminals!' – Duterte boasted that, once he was elected, funeral parlors would be overwhelmed by business and the fish in Manila Bay would grow fat on the flesh of 100,000 Filipino corpses. He has since enjoined citizens to murder their drug-addicted relatives and declared his support for gangs and corrupt officials who target journalists, Indigenous leaders and human rights activists, many of whom are 'red-tagged' by government forces as violent communists ahead of their summary execution.

At particular risk are land and resource defenders, who have become frequent targets of extrajudicial killings by soldiers, paramilitaries and lone gunmen on motorbikes; in 2018, more such killings took place in the Philippines than anywhere else in the world. Duterte has boasted gleefully of having cultivated this atmosphere of impunity, promising to use his powers to pardon any soldier or police officer accused of human rights abuses, and assuring supporters that, if anyone ever attempts to bring him to legal account for his role in all this mass murder, he will pardon himself.

In the mountains, however, Duterte seemed to have met his match. Not even the president could stop a volcanic eruption, or prevent one from opening a dramatic caesura in the churning chaos of consumption and growth that powers the country's airports, dams and offshore drilling. Schools and businesses shut down; all flights at Ninoy Aquino were grounded. Against a darkening rim of sky, Duterte's flamboyant rage felt thin.

A friend in Quezon City sent me a text message: 'You've arrived in disaster season!' There were earthquakes and a polio outbreak in Mindanao, plus a novel virus in China that seemed at risk of spreading to other countries in Asia. Manila's notorious traffic, second only to Moscow in its average commute times and rococo fleurs of gridlock, all but disappeared as many of the city's transplants fled home. Carleen and I left, too. We turned away from Taal and the southern volcanic chain, heading north, toward mountains that for centuries have protected and enclosed.

In the beginning, the sky was low. You could touch it with a spear or long pole. How the sky became high is a story repeated with slight variations across the Philippines, but the story of the origin of mountains can be traced to northern Luzon. According to the corpus of myths told among Ifugao people in the Cordillera, one day, Kabigat of the skyworld descended to the earth to hunt with his dogs. The dogs ran swiftly from one side of the level world to the other in pursuit of their quarry. Because the dogs' barking returned no echo,

Kabigat determined the earth must be completely flat. The silence made him pensive. He returned to the skyworld and came down with a large cloth to stop up the place where the waters entered the sea. Back home, he announced what he'd done. Bongabong ordered him to call on Cloud and Fog to produce rain. Kabigat did as he was told. After the rain, he removed the cloth. The waters, which now covered the earth, receded, and in their rushing carved mountains and valleys out of the land. The mountains rose up as the waters drained into the sea.

It is no longer true that history begins with the scribes of the state. For at least two centuries, history has commenced with the geological survey. When a modern empire sets its eyes on an attractive object of conquest, it sends not priests or poets but surveyors and engineers. Thus was Warren D. Smith, the Chief of Division of Mines in the Bureau of Science of US-governed Manila, tasked to produce the first modern geological report on Luzon, a still-recent American acquisition in 1913, in order to inform prospectors of any bonanzan quantities of coal, iron, oil, copper or gold, and to assure speculators that 'the people who inhabit those sections give very little promise of ever being able to take advantage of the mineral resources.'

Luzon is the largest island in the Philippines. The Cordillera Central is its largest mountainous expanse, a massive block of three ranges shoved indiscernibly together with no intervening lowlands: the Malayan in the north and west, the Polis in the east and the Central between them. The mountains run north to south for 200 miles, a sixth of the island's length and large enough to block cyclones and monsoons; the foothills descend steadily to the outer edges of Metro Manila but with great winding sinuosities in all directions. Like movements in a geological symphony, each range is distinct in structure, composition and tone. Although there are coastal plains north of the Lingayen Gulf, where they have served as narrow purchase for traders from Taiwan and the first colonizers from Spain, elsewhere the young mountains appear to plunge, pine-covered and villageful, directly into the two underwater trenches whose catacombs hold all of Luzon's shipwrecked galleons and coral life. In place of beachheads, rock rises in frozen effigy of eruption. 'The mountains are nearly everywhere close to the sea,' Smith observed.

Until the arrival of American soldiers and the rise of regional bureaucracy, the people living in these mountains called themselves by the names of their villages and towns, not their provinces or tribes; there was certainly no name in local circulation for all of the peoples living in the great Cordilleran universe. It was the Spanish who called them Ygolote, probably from the moment of their arrival. They are Ygolotes in the 1576 report of the first expedition in search of the legendary gold mines of Luzon. One etymology holds that *golot* once meant mountain chain, and so Igorot might be understood to mean people of the mountains or, simply, highlanders. Whatever its origins, Americans adopted and codified the term, often pejoratively. Although he marveled over the natural landscape and over such oddities as Mayon's algebraic perfection, Smith had nothing complimentary to say about his country's new colonial subjects. He complained of the almost total lack of roads throughout the Cordillera, excepting 'a great many Igorot trails which do not take any advantage whatever of the topography'. (Strategically important trails were no doubt deliberately hidden from early Americans, as they had been from the Spanish.) Luckily, Smith went on, the government was in the process of putting in an automobile road, which he claimed was the source of better feeling between the 'primitive' northern tribes and the American-controlled government. 'As soon as the railroad and the school have had a chance to work on these people and mix them up, the tribal characteristics will largely disappear.'

Today, some Cordillerans reject the term Igorot as derivative of colonialist thinking, lumping dozens of societies into a single exonym, but it is still widely used by those to whom it has historically applied, often preceded by the name of a specific ethnolinguistic group, tribe or clan: for example, the Kankana-ey Igorot people. It is part of a large class of names by which lowlanders around the world refer to those recalcitrant and irreducibly different people living in the hills beyond the urban cores of the state. The name recalls the crowded procession of frustrated Spanish gold hunters who visited Luzon's mountain towns, each of whom found their hosts irritatingly unwilling to be converted or colonized. Unlike many of the peoples living in the lowlands of Luzon and the Visayas, Igorots were never made slaves of the Spanish, and while some were converted to Christianity – 'reduced' in the language of the missionaries – as large a number are thought to have escaped in the other direction, into the hills, where they preserved their independence for three centuries in societies of state-thwarting dissimilation. The last Spanish census, recorded during the death throes of the regime, suggests that more than half of the non-Christian population of the Cordilleras was still living beyond the reach of tax collectors. Even those under nominal Spanish control often refused to pay tribute or move into the friars' parishes. The instructions left in 1892 by a departing governor general in Ifugao tell a story of resignation and defeat, reminding the commandant who would replace him 'that he will be exercising his authority over pagans who do not know the benefits of good government and who, even when they do, may in many cases prefer the savage independence in which they have lived and have seen their ancestors live'.

At the start of the twentieth century, US troops arrived to crush the newly sovereign Philippine government. It was the Spanish–American War's most brutal and superfluous front, Spain having already lost its islands squarely to their inhabitants. That Filipino people could not be allowed to govern themselves was widely accepted among the American ruling class. 'They are not capable of self-government,' Senator Albert J. Beveridge said on the floor of the US Senate in January 1900. 'How could they be? They are not of a self-governing race.' As he was the only congressman who had visited the country, Beveridge's comments carried serious weight as the ongoing war and possible colonization were discussed. He had 'cruised more than 2,000 miles through the archipelago', he said, finding every foot of the way a revelation in vegetation and mineral riches, particularly on its largest island. 'No land in America surpasses in fertility the plains and valleys of Luzon. Rice and coffee, sugar and coconuts, hemp and tobacco . . . The wood of the Philippines can supply the furniture of the world for a century to come.' As for the people living among this earthly bounty, it would be better to abandon them to some Pacific kingdom than to permit them to determine their own fates. To colonize them would be better still. It was 'the divine mission of America, and it holds for us all the profit, all the glory, and all the happiness possible to man'.

The bus made stops all along the road to Baguio City and raced between towns to make up for lost time. Above the driver's head was an electronic counter like those found at butcher shops. Instead of ticket numbers, it displayed the bus's speed. When the driver crossed the threshold of 91 kilometers per hour, the counter beeped loudly. In response, he slowed down to a more reasonable 89 or 90 or 90.9. The bus was quiet as we all watched the driver creep up toward the limit, inevitably pass it, triggering the alarm, and slow down again. It was a form of democratic surveillance I couldn't imagine encountering at home in Germany, where no bus company would ever publicize its lawbreaking to customers, and where authority is something simply to be obeyed, never examined or bargained with. Whereas here it seemed normal for any passenger to observe and comment on the speed, as some passengers near the front of the bus did, chastising the driver for going either recklessly fast or, just as often, not fast enough.

At the start of our ascent, we passed worked fields and roadside shacks. There were acres of monocropped corn and rice and distant hills pronged with antennae. The bus parked for fifteen minutes at a rest stop in Sison and passengers fell upon the kiosk selling duck eggs out of a bifurcated glass case, both the soupy unfertilized *penoy* and the crunchy, fertilized *balat*. From Sison, the road narrowed and began to rise into the hills, passing through the walls of white mist that hang over the peaks of the Pangasinan spur and never lift. The hills are the true start of the Cordillera and of what early visitors sometimes called Igorotland. Metro Manila's exurban visions of privation disappeared and were replaced by small, thriving towns. Handsome schools stood behind new iron gates; town squares were set off by blossoming trees and whitewashed apartment buildings. Roadside sari-sari stores were cornucopian with dry goods, each modest stall painted blue and named for its female proprietor: Myrna's Store, Sany's Store, Edith's Store. In Pugo, the Tinungbo festival shut down traffic for twenty minutes. Nobody honked or complained. Cars waited patiently for the drummers and flagbearers to finish marching through town along the only road. We watched from our windows and waved the marchers on.

Baguio City's province, Benguet, is the traditional entrepôt for the Cordillera. A slab of andesitic rock veined with mineral fissures, Benguet is the final plateau before the peaks begin in earnest. Above it rise the mountains Pulog, Tabayoc, Panutoan, Osdung, Paoay, Ugu and, most spectacularly, Data, where the headwaters of four of Luzon's great rivers are found in outcroppings within a few miles of each other. We crawled through winding two-lane roads in heavy afternoon traffic, beneath billboards featuring giant plates of American Spam. Throughout Benguet's history, gold was freely mined in tunnels and pits, and panned along the rivers in the rainy season, concentrated in the so-called Baguio Gold District. The Spanish focused some of their earliest extractive efforts here. Benguet was also the site from which the US Army made incursions to slaughter rebels and their civilian protectors in the mountains, the final stage of a colonial war that, by the most conservative estimates, cost a quarter of a million Filipino lives.

Baguio City is better known today as a center of higher education. In the morning we went to visit the collections of one of the city's many universities, a clean and quiet room of artifacts staffed by a curator and student employee, but otherwise empty. Both were new on the job. The student, Divine, had started only that morning. After a few minutes talking to Carleen, she invited us to stay at her family's guest house in Sagada, four hours further into the mountains. Carleen said we would be delighted. 'Okay, *ate*,' Divine said, using a

Tagalog appellation reserved for a big sister or older woman. She picked up her phone. 'I'll tell them you're coming. Is it all right to call you *ate*?' We left the collection with new travel plans and began climbing a long set of stairs back toward the city center. Baguio is not quite a mile above the coast, but as we climbed, I was suddenly breathless. Altitude sickness had struck, as it always did in my experience, a day or so after rapid ascent, a gentle reminder of our remoteness from the seas that are the country's connective tissue. I sat down on the steps and waited for it to pass, enjoying the mild perturbance of the self in unnatural motion. The staircase was inlaid with terraced gardens – there were plots of lemongrass, ginger, aloe vera and sweetgrass – in miniature, museum-like imitation of the infinitely grand terraces of Ifugao. The sweetgrass quivered in the breeze. In a few minutes, I was feeling better.

Joanna Cariño had friendly eyes and kept tea bags in her purse. She had just come from a meeting with her Ibaloi clan in Burnham Park, an eighty-one-acre bouquet of pink showers and Benguet pines spread out in sharp sunlight many stories beneath us. We were in a sunroom on the twelfth floor of a new high-rise hotel on the southern edge of Baguio. Somewhere downtown a fire was burning and shot a pillar of dark smoke into the sky. As we talked, the fire was slowly extinguished and the dark smoke lightened, until after two hours it was cloud-colored and became a cloud. More or less all the land we could see had once belonged to Joanna's great-grandfather, an Ibaloi plutocrat and heroic router of Spanish forces, until his holdings were appropriated for an American army base. He took his case all the way to the US Supreme Court and won – posthumously. 'A historic decision which he never lived to see,' Joanna said. On the village green beneath us, somewhere between the children's park and the orchidarium, stood a monument to Mateo Cariño.

Joanna was a router, too. Back in Quezon City, I'd asked an activist named Beverly Longid about the legacy of Cordilleran resistance bound up in this woman who never married and had no children of her own. 'We call her The Mother,' Beverly said. Then she laughed.

'The Mother of Us All!' The only surviving founder of the Cordillera Peoples Alliance, an autonomous federation of Indigenous communities, Joanna was radicalized over a decade-long struggle against four massive hydroelectric dams, collectively known as the Chico River Dam, planned for the Cordillera by former kleptocrat president Ferdinand Marcos and his international World Bank funders. She first learned of the dam project as a student activist in the seventies, two years after she was detained, tortured and sent to a military prison during Marcos's martial law regime.

By the second year of her detention, Joanna was used to the drudgery of life at Camp Olivas and awaited only change. One day it arrived. 'The military came into the camp with a large group of people. I remember thinking there must have been a hundred tribes represented. I say tribes because some were wearing nothing but G-strings made out of bark. There were men, women and children, all of them taken into the camp, and there weren't enough facilities to house them all so they were just there in the yard, a large, uncovered, fenced-in area where they lived and slept. I had never seen anything like it before. I realized they were Igorots from deep in the mountains.'

Joanna spoke slowly, her fingers interlaced. 'When we saw them at meals, we asked these people what they were all about. They said there was a struggle against the Chico River Dam. We'd never heard of any dam – we'd been in prison since '74. The tribesmen explained they were resisting the dam project and in fact had torn down some facilities owned by the National Power Corporation, for which the government had gone on a punitive spree, arresting every Igorot they could find. I only learned about it because all these tribespeople were brought to the prison where I was being held. It was winter, and shortly after their arrival, I was released. I came back to Baguio, I went back to school – but everything had changed for me. I had learned about the Chico Dam.'

Had it been completed, the Chico Dam would have been the largest in Asia, displacing tens of thousands of people and demolishing local economies and food supplies to bring a thousand megawatts of power to Metro Manila. The struggle against the dam which

Joanna joined on her release united – for the first time – distant and remote communities up and down the Chico River into a single, unprecedented block of resistance, culminating in a major victory for a philosophy of self-determination and land use that was then becoming known in political discourse as Indigenous rights. Joanna has not stopped fighting since, although her mission sometimes gets her into trouble. Most recently, in 2018, the Duterte administration's Philippine National Police Intelligence Group published a list of the country's known active terrorists. There were 656 names and 'Joanna Cariño' was one of them.

Such lists are intended to vilify organizers and link them, however flimsily, to Islamic extremists or the New People's Army, the militant wing of the Communist Party of the Philippines, understood by the government (and its hulking ally in the war on terror, the United States) to be a terrorist group. It was not Joanna's first or second or even tenth game of red-tag. She does not bother to count the number of times her life has been threatened and she has known many martyrs to the cause of Cordilleran self-determination. In 1987, a fellow tribal leader named Ama Daniel Ngayaan was abducted and killed in Cagaluan Gate, a garrison town at the Cordilleran crossroads of Kalinga known for military murders. Killings have risen again under Duterte; the year the list was published at least thirty defenders of land and resources were murdered.

Joanna may have been saved from the fate visited upon these others thanks to the presence of another name on the list: Victoria Tauli-Corpuz. At the time of its publication, Tauli-Corpuz, a Philippine citizen of Kankana-ey Igorot background, was the Special Rapporteur on the Rights of Indigenous People for the United Nations, making her perhaps the most recognizable Indigenous person in the world. Her presence on a list of terrorists was too ridiculous even for an international press accustomed to normalizing the tactics of dictators. The list became a laughing stock. Before long, it was reduced to eight names. Joanna's was gone.

C arleen and I took an afternoon bus from Baguio and pulled into Sagada at twilight. The town was silent. It took us a while to find the guest house Divine's grandparents owned. We walked a mile or so along a dark corniche. Most shops and restaurants were shuttered for the off season and we passed the large building several times before we realized we'd found it, set back deep in an overgrown yard between two half-constructed homes and behind a shack where some chickens were sleeping. There were no signs of occupancy. A young girl answered the front door and led us into a darkened banquet hall. It emerged that Divine's grandparents had left the inn days ago for a campsite further into the mountains. They had put three relatives in charge, the oldest of whom was fifteen. She was helping her younger siblings finish their homework by the light of a single lamp in the banquet-hall kitchen. She paused to give us a room key and have us sign the guestbook. We were the first visitors of the year.

In the morning, a devout Christian named Patrick said he would take us to see the hanging coffins in the Valley of Echoes. Like most Sagadans, Patrick was of Applai, or northern Kankana-ey, background. We met him outside the town hall and straightaway he began to explain the difference between Kankana-ey and Kankanay, its sister tongue, two languages occupying the same mountain fastnesses. I couldn't grasp the subtle vowel distinctions. Eventually, he gave up. To change the subject, I pointed to the large sign that hung from the town hall:

We strongly denounce all forms of
Violence, Terrorism, and Atrocities
that disrupt Peace and Development
in our Community

Patrick shrugged. The sign was less interesting to him, and the product of long suffering. Even before Duterte's drug war, the stagnant conflict between government-aligned forces and the New People's Army, often taking the form of paramilitary terror campaigns against Igorot communities, had resulted in the deaths of some 40,000 civilians in Luzon and led to bloody scenes in Sagada's past, including a marketplace shootout in 1988 in which two children died. Peace pacts, a social technology used for centuries among several Igorot societies, became important methods of demilitarizing mountain towns in the eighties and nineties. One Sagadan activist described peace pacts to me as a process that requires no special devices beyond a boundless capacity for talking. Debates last late into the night. Finally, an agreement is reached between two or more groups: a zone of self-governance is conjured, one that might include curfews, a ban on alcohol or general disarmament. The town hall's modest pronouncement belied the fact that Sagada is a pioneer peace zone of the Cordillera.

Patrick, Carleen and I waited for a while to see if there would be any other tourists that day. It was always quiet in the off season, Patrick said. In the summer, he took large groups out to the coffins. Not many visitors were around now. Only Fede, an Italian osteopath, asked to join us. Fede was one of those solo travelers undisturbed by memory or knowledge. He spent no more than six hours in any one place and slept entirely on buses, boats and airplanes so as to maximize his intake of sights per hour, or per minute, a furious vacation assemblage. He confessed to knowing little about the Cordillera. He had slept fitfully for an hour or two on the night bus from Manila in order to arrive in Sagada in time to join a morning tour. He would go on to Banaue and the famous rice terraces, then back to Manila on another overnight. Then somewhere south – he hadn't decided exactly where – to beaches, islands, palms. He had seen most of the countries in Southeast Asia in this breakneck manner. He took out his phone and opened Facebook. In the foreground of all of his vacation photos (Varanasi, Angkor Wat, Vientiane) he was performing a perfect handstand.

As the four of us set out from the municipal square, the rising sun began to dispel the mists clinging to the pines. Before long, we were sweating. We passed a basketball court and moved onto a dirt path

that rose onto a hillside of wild flowers and tombstones. Echo Valley
was just beneath the Christian graveyard, down a steep rock face into
which stairs had been cut for hikers longer-limbed than any present.
Halfway down the steps, Patrick gestured to the overlook that gave
the place its name. If you called out in Tagalog, it was said, an echo
would come back in English. Patrick, whose mother tongue was
neither of these, didn't think much of this story, and none of us
shouted out anything. The floor of the valley was cool and green,
filled with Benguet pines and sparse undergrowth. Against a cliffside
of limestone schist, the famous hanging coffins were strung on ropes
and rusted wires.

They seemed both mythic and mundane. The coffins floated
impossibly against the cliff and yet the family names of the dead were
written across their fronts matter-of-factly, as though on crates of fruit:
Lawagan, Bomit-Og, Sumbao. The easiest way to date the coffins
was by their length, since the tradition of interring the dead in a fetal
position was gradually replaced by the Christian habit of laying the
body flat. The newest coffins, adorned with wooden crosses, showed
the extension of the religious syncretism of Sagada, through which
the dead themselves had steadily climbed the hillside to the cemetery
above us. The last coffin was raised decades ago, Patrick said.

We walked on through a second valley toward Sumaguing Cave,
another tourist attraction, passing more grottos of coffins tucked
between vegetable patches. There were no tricycles and barely
any traffic. The cave is high in the mountains and at the same time is
the deepest in the Philippines, descending 500 feet from its mouth.
Its great open maw was filled with ferny undergrowth, foliage which
the cave seemed to be in the process of eating. Patrick climbed down
into the darkness with the fluency of a stone falling down a well.

The first chamber was an abyss of openness where earth should
be; a cathedral would have fit comfortably inside it. The roof was
shrouded in darkness, so high that our flashlights illuminated
almost nothing. Patrick had a propane gas lantern and an industrial
torch, but even the latter was dimmed by the distance, illuminating

just enough to reveal that we were climbing beneath a teeming underworld of bats. As soon as we saw them, collected in several giant oblong hives from one end of the cave to the other, their sounds – a faint squeaky static I'd half imagined were shoes on wet stone echoing from below us – became legible, as did the smell of their droppings on the rocks.

With the lantern, Patrick drew our attention to a sheer limestone wall rendered curtain-like with columnar glyphs. He had been understandably subdued around the hanging coffins, but he was voluble when it came to the time-honored tour guide practice of identifying obscene figures in curvaceous water-worn sandstone. The nicknames for the rock formations – 'King's Curtain', 'The Princess' – referenced a complicated mythology of sexual misadventure, which Patrick explained in a fast, droll monotone. As a good devout Catholic, he took great pleasure in prurience and sin. The rude jokes could not dispel the sublimity of the cave, however, nor its testament to mountains as living things that can melt or shoot fire into the air. Rock may appear solid and perpetual, the cave seemed to say, but it is in a constant state of mostly imperceptible flux. Just as the limestone cliffs above had been plant-covered but dissolute, rich in granulated distinctions to which the dead were battened, so was the sandstone in the cave wet, even glutinous, under the steady drip and rush of buried aquifers, creamy syrups of stone folded and refolded, made supple by an eternity of rain flow. Rock becomes dust, shard, mud, dirt and – under different pressures – rock again.

We came to the shore of an underground ocean. It was the aquifer beyond which the cave was impassable. A wide hole in the floor gave way to a lapping underground lake that disappeared into darkness. Our beachhead was a wedge-shaped room of smooth gray stone. At the waterline, Patrick turned his flashlight on a scattershot of copepods in the flesh-like wall, his personal proof of eternal return. The fossils were lacquered by sunless damp spray. 'One day Sagada will be underwater,' he said. 'Like it was here. How many islands do you think are in the Philippines?'

I couldn't remember. 'Seven thousand?'

'Seven thousand, five hundred and ninety. Many were once underwater. They will be underwater again when the water rises. These fossils, maybe they're from the time of Noah.'

Like the mirror world below us, where everything is reflected darkly, tree to tree and shade to shade, on the underside of Luzon are not rice terraces but marine terraces: late-Holocene shelves of coral, rock and weed. They are finely notched and suggest to archaeoseismologists that western Luzon was inundated by an extreme wave event about a thousand years ago, which may have submerged mountain passes in a meters-high tsunami. The tsunami in Luzon's future is predicted to follow a similar megathrust rupture, one that will steadily inundate the western coast. Perhaps even the hanging coffins of Sagada will find themselves underwater.

It was time to start the hour-long climb out of the cave. But first, Fede found a laminate stretch of flat sandstone on the far side of a pool of water and tucked in his shirt. Patrick raised the camera phone. Carleen and I applauded the perfect handstand.

Saint Vincent's convent was gated, its entrance tucked into a mountain switchback guarded by plump rosettes of aloe. There were no other visitors that evening, although the exhibits resounded with the cries, happy and otherwise, of the children at the Catholic school that shared the convent grounds. The Bontoc Museum, built in the low, long style of an Ifugao house, was founded during the years of American administration by a Belgian nun named Sister Basil Gekiere. Sister Basil adored Santa Teresita, had a girlhood love who was killed in the Great War, and hoped to gather together in her museum some of the instruments of Bontoc culture – rattan fish traps, rain shades, snail-collecting baskets – that might otherwise disappear into the hands of American collectors.

In the outdoor garden behind the museum were several other Bontoc-style houses made of wood and thatched palm. A nun was clearing water out of a sunken firepit with a green plastic bucket.

It was Sister Emie's first year parished in Bontoc. There was one other nun who worked at the library but she had the day off. It got lonely. Emie smoked out the huts each week to fend against wood-eating insects and temper the walls. 'That is why the insides of Igorot houses are always black,' she explained. One by one, we stooped down low to get inside the model *ato*, a longhouse where Bontoc elders would meet to deliberate village matters. The house was warm and wallpapered in soot.

In the museum next door, we'd seen an American administrator's photograph of a Bontoc innocent of brick or concrete. The Chico River ran brightly through the village of thatch and sunlight like a silver thread. Such photographs, however lovely, were often intended to produce anthropological truths outside history, clarifying the difference between 'primitive' peoples and their colonial rulers. The recovery has been slow. Tribal Filipinos from Luzon appeared in the nightmarish human zoos of the early twentieth century, in pens of exotica at Coney Island and in the continent-touring Louisiana Purchase Exposition. In 1913, a group of Igorots was found wandering the streets of Ghent. They complained that the circus master who hired them had starved them and stolen their wages. The American embassy in Belgium arranged to send them back to Luzon. The following year, the US-backed Philippine Assembly finally outlawed, together with many other forms of slavery, the export of tribesmen by the Barnums and Baileys of the world.

We followed Emie to the one-room library. She always had to keep watch for the bats that liked to congregate on the doorsills. 'They make the floor so dirty,' she said. 'I really can't stand it.' She kept a large black headlamp on her desk to help with the work, which took her out of doors late into the night. She liked Bontoc well enough, but the work was hard. She was used to Baguio City, where she had spent her whole life before God's will sent her up into the mountains. 'But this is what we must do,' she said. 'Although at my age, my back, well, it hurts. We must preserve this knowledge and show children what life here was like, the Indigenous culture.'

She began pulling books from the shelves. Although the library was small, it was as well stocked as any I'd seen in Baguio or Manila, with long-out-of-print ethnographies and collections of folklore.

'Scott – you know Scott?' An entire shelf of the library was devoted to the American missionary-turned-historian William Henry Scott.

I said we had visited his grave in the cemetery in Sagada.

'All these foreigners,' Emie said. 'They took such acute interest in our peoples. We must rediscover our heritage from them. We are even at risk of forgetting our recent history – the Chico Dam resistance, the fight against the mines, all our local history.' In apparent contradiction to this lament, she began to enumerate some of the famous and obscure events of the last century, a century that was filled with resistance and refusal by the peoples of the Cordillera in their dealings with European, American and finally US-backed endemic regimes. Many of the stories deal with resource and human extraction, from Indigenous slave raids and Spanish goldlust to the hydroelectric fantasias of modern statecraft. Some are preserved in songs or local histories. A few were indeed recorded by interested scholars from the US and Europe. But it is rare for colonial archives to present culture as an active and conscious project, rather than something eternal and unchanging, to be preserved under glass. None of the events were described in the museum next door.

Emie walked us to the door and down the garden path to the wrought-iron gate. The children were gone and we were alone. 'Well, goodbye,' she said, locking Saint Vincent's behind us. 'I wish you luck in your travels. I don't know when we will meet again.' As we were walking away, she called us back. 'Don't miss this flower.' She pointed through the bars to a two-story fern all over which were battened bright purple dendrobiums. 'Photograph it. I use coffee grounds in its pot and, as you can see, the results speak for themselves.'

In the 1970s, women from Mainit, a village outside Bontoc, climbed a muddy mountainside to bare their breasts before the engineers of Benguet Corporation. The mining company intended to displace a stretch of the Chico River, destroying the area's terraces, which for centuries have relied on elaborate systems of irrigation based on the natural flow of mountain streams. Bared breasts are believed to hex unwanted strangers. In their chants, some of which are still heard at rallies today, the Mainit women dared the men to harm 'the womb where they came from', gesturing to the young men from local villages the firm had hired to dig trenches and pour concrete.

Another chant, in its entirety, went like this:

Uray maid armas mi
armas mi nan ima mi
estawes, esta-gawis
ikmer mi snan fitfitli, fitfitlin na raraki
estawes, esta-gawis!

We may not be armed
but our hands are our weapons
We use our bare hands to squeeze balls
the balls of men!

The local workers were petrified; the engineers fled. Afterward, the Mainit women raided their camp. They took the supplies to the town center and left everything in a pile outside the company office. Nothing was stolen. The workers' food was abandoned to rot. It wasn't any foreign historian I learned the story from, rather Joanna Cariño and other women who have remade the Cordillera in their image. The current president of the Philippines, who has said that all women are weak, has never once showed his face in Bontoc.

We hired a tricycle to drive us to the rice terraces of Maligcong. It was hard going on this motorized rickshaw, and when we came to steep inclines we had to get out and walk while the driver went ahead. After half an hour, we were somewhere high above Bontoc in a court of corrugated metal houses on foundations of stone.

Embarrassed and concerned for his Honda's engine, Carleen paid the driver ten times the cost of a journey in town. He waved and drove off, raising a cloud of dry-season dust. A gravel path led us out to the gallery of terraces.

Maligcong is not a tourist destination like Banaue or Batad – both are famous attractions found in neighboring Ifugao – but it is one of nearly twenty lesser-known terraces in Mountain Province, the approximate center of the Cordillera. Each one is an amphitheatrical marvel of stone engineering, and looking across Maligcong it was hard to believe any terrace system in the world, much less the region, could match it in size, or that its builders had hidden such feats from the Spanish, there being no recorded encounter with these massive stone structures until the nineteenth century. I was glad for our solitude as the town fell away beneath us and we gained altitude, walking along the stone walls through fallow fields and newly planted paddies. As we walked, the ponds, which reflect the hills when you are near them, became glassier, then white with sky. Purple swallows chased mosquitoes above the water.

Rice terraces are humanity's oldest effort to overcome the tyranny of the slope. They are the only wonders of antiquity that still serve their original purpose: to grow rice in paddies suspended in air, in defiance of a mountain's erosional claims. In the Cordillera, they occupy ground so steep it often can't be walked up. Each terrace system was moreover built, as several Filipino writers, including Adrian Cristobal, have noted, by a free people under no central authority. 'No tribal Khufu, or Shih Huang Ti fearful of mortality and foreign invaders, called on the Ifugaos to build this great edifice. We can only surmise that they looked at the hills and decided in common to eke their livelihood step after step, not conscious that at the end of it, they would have built an enduring edifice to their needs, a stately mansion to their collective soil.'

A few women were out in the heat weeding their walls, the highest of which were as mossy and demanding as an old city bastion. Some family plots were abandoned, and there were sections where several contiguous levels of wall were so overgrown with ferns and grasses they looked from a distance like a cascading green waterfall erupting, at the bottom of a terrace, into leafy mist. The weeders worked under parasols, hats and headscarves, and greeted us when we passed. It was too hot to stand around and talk. A few women hummed as they worked but none was singing the famous *hudhud*, or songs of harvest, Ifugao's epic tradition, passed down from woman to woman, harvester to harvester.

Carleen suggested we climb the hill for a photo. We walked along the path between plots grading upward, toward the managed forests that are found above all of Luzon's rice terraces. The signature landscape feature in the central Cordillera, the terraces are often described as a testament of human achievement on a vast and pre-historic scale. Their age, however, is the subject of modern controversy. It now seems likely the terraces are a form of 'escape agriculture' developed in response to colonial incursions, a fact that makes their existence all the more incredible. They were probably built quickly, over decades or centuries rather than millennia, amid the onslaught of attempted Spanish conquest, and were produced either by long-dormant cultural knowledge or by sudden technological innovation. To walk even a 'minor' terrace system like Maligcong's is therefore to be assailed by immensities that may emerge from life on the margins of state capture. By *Britannica*'s count, there are 12,500 miles of terraced wall in the Banaue system alone, enough to wrap halfway around the world.

Nor are the terraces fully described by the inert stones that form them. The larger system, a circuit of self-sufficiency, is not so easy for outsiders to recognize. We do not clearly see the engineered forests mitigating erosion and rain flow, or the partly subterranean irrigation systems, both of which harmonize rice farming with a mountain habitat. I tried to recalibrate my sense of these objects as we climbed. From our high vantage, the terraces looked like a topographical map, muddily contoured and, because the pools were brilliantly reflective of the vault of sky above us, blanketed in stained glass. It was the highest point we would reach in our travels in northern Luzon, and the rose window that now bloomed beneath us, camed in stone and filled with undercloud, seemed an appropriate reward. Sure enough, each curving line of shingle stonework was alive with grasses and wildflowers, and stream water was carried down the hillside by elegant waterfalls and a system of rubber hoses on wooden posts. Although the stone itself is the visual showstopper, the combination of forest management and irrigation – the latter once achieved by bamboo aqueducts – makes Luzon's terracing a true wonder, the world's largest monument to the spontaneous civilizational genius born of refusal.

We made our way back to the center of the hillside's amphitheater of terraces, to Fang-orao and Favarey, the original settlements of Maligcong. The three villages shared one midwife, one cement schoolhouse and one jeepney stop.

The stop was a level clearing where workmen sat on bags of cement, waiting for the afternoon jeepney to town. We sat in the heat and waited, too. The driver was late and, one by one, the men walked home for lunch. We were alone. We could hear kids playing in the schoolyard on a plateau above us. The schoolteacher came down the steps. His name was Matthew. His family had two small terraces, he said, one on each side of Fang-orao. This turned out to be the most common arrangement in the village. One hillside's terraces had already been harvested in December, he said. The other would be planted in March and harvested in October, so that each family had two different, staggered stages of planting or harvest. In this way, families defended themselves against droughts, floods and other seasonal disasters.

When we said we were visiting from Germany, Matthew became exercised. The most famous son of Maligcong was a self-taught karate champion who settled there years ago. Had we ever heard of Julian Chees? He came back to the village every year to donate the money he earned from competitions and from teaching in his dojo. During his most recent visit, he had paid the treatment costs for every kidney patient in the dialysis ward in Bontoc and funded the construction of the kindergarten whose beneficiaries we could hear up on the bluff.

'I'm not sure,' I said. 'When was he champion?'

'In 1991.'

Matthew wasn't insulted we didn't know the name Julian Chees. The distance between us was now clarified and he tried to show us there were no hard feelings. 'Well, you know, he's not as famous as . . . as . . .'

He trailed off as he tried to think of a celebrity an awareness of whom we might share. None came to mind. Half a minute passed in silence. The sun beat down. I began to ask about the terraces on the hill to our north when he came to life again: '– as Adolf Hitler!'

Matthew was one of five teachers working at the school, a post that paid so little he descended into Bontoc to work as a tricycle driver three days a week. He had gone to school in Baguio but found it crowded and dirty. Young people like him do not often come home to live, he said, and more and more of the terraces were going unplanted each year for lack of laborers. Every face in the crowds of Baguio City, he said, came from a village like this one. 'They're looking for work,' he said. 'Here we have only farming.'

It would be good to have some kind of revitalization project, Matthew went on, some support to keep the marvel going for another century. But even the local elections in Maligcong had been delayed for lack of funds. They were waiting, he said with a chuckle, for Duterte to decide if and when they would be deserving of elections, and until then they would carry on leaderless as before. Then he asked how we'd gotten here, since he knew we hadn't come by the morning jeepney. We told him about the Taal eruption, the bus from Baguio to Sagada, the other bus to Bontoc and finally our tricycle ride up the mountainside to Maligcong. He blew air through his nostrils. 'You paid too much,' he said. 'But it is a hard, hard ride.' ∎

MARGAUX NUSSBAUMER
Hamburg, Germany, 2018

THE DAM

Taran N. Khan

From the dimly lit underground, a flutter of white against a cloudless blue sky. All around, the city is as idyllic as a postcard – gleaming with sunshine, its beaches and parks crowded, music on its streets. 'It is not always like this, you know,' people tell me over and over, about this summer that seems to exist outside of time.

Walking up the steps from the U–Bahn station, I see the tent anchored to a strip of pavement. Like an oversized bird bound to the earth, its walls buffeted by the wind. 'No human is illegal,' I read, the words leaping and twisting on the fabric. 'We are here to stay.'

This patch of earth is where Steindamm begins.

*

Steindamm, meaning 'stone dam', is a long thoroughfare in the area called St Georg, which runs close to the main train station in Hamburg. In the blazing summer of 2018, I found myself often wandering its length.

I was in the city writing about Afghan refugees and asylum seekers.

Three years before, in the summer of 2015, close to 1.3 million refugees had arrived in Europe, fleeing war and the complex aftermaths of conflicts. Nearly 890,000 of them were admitted by Germany. In the early days of that summer, they were met by large crowds and solidarity rallies, declaring 'Refugees Welcome'. The heart of activity in Hamburg was the train station, where the new arrivals were guided by volunteers to places to sleep and eat. By the time I arrived in 2018, the flush of this Willkommenskultur had faded, and a rising anti-refugee sentiment was polarising the country. Rallies and demonstrations were organised by both sides.

My own days and evenings were spent with people who inhabited this terrain of tumultuous arrival. Some of them were young men I had known when they were living in Kabul, like the one I will call Masoud. A film-maker, he had grown up in neighbouring Iran, as part of the large community of Afghan refugees in the country. Masoud had first come to Kabul, a city he had never known but considered home, after 2001. When we had met, he was part of a collective of friends and media professionals who held day jobs and made films in their free time. They recorded the city as a way of exploring it – shooting on its streets, working with whatever resources they could rustle up together. I had last spoken to Masoud in 2013, and shortly after that, he had left Afghanistan. Days after I arrived in Hamburg, I found him living in a suburb with his wife and two young children. One of the millions behind the faceless refugee 'crisis'. Several of his friends were also scattered across different parts of Europe, he told me, including some in Hamburg. 'We are all here, but we are different,' he said. 'We are nearby, but our lives are changed.'

*

Like Masoud, most of the Afghans I met had a tenuous relationship with their present setting, one that was mediated by the long, bureaucratic and emotionally taxing process of becoming refugees. They also had a fraught relationship with what they had left behind – parents, family, their own identities as film-makers and artists.

So when we spoke, our conversations were often not of the future but of the past, not so much of where they were but of what they had been. Our days ebbed and flowed with Skype calls and photos flicked through on phones, lists of marriages and deaths and the names of newborns. We traced the journeys of mutual friends across the world, avoiding talk of their routes, dwelling only on destinations. Between us flowed impressions of films and music, anecdotes of screenings and festivals, gossip and reminiscences: 'Do you remember my cousin, he now drives a bus in Sweden.' 'Imagine, that guy in charge of a bus!' Between us stretched the memory of a shared Kabul – dusty, chaotic, winking in the long twilight of Hamburg's evenings.

Sometimes, after these conversations, I would walk with my companions by the harbour on the Elbe River, watching the ships glide by. Other times I went there on my own. Hamburg is an active port and its waterways bring in commerce from around the world. Watching the flow of this channel was like watching a river of people and goods entering the city: a flow that was welcome, visible, legitimate, celebrated.

In between my expeditions around Hamburg, or as a convenient spot for a rendezvous, I would end up in Steindamm – walking around its shops, or waiting in the midst of its crowds. On this 'stone dam' that used to be an elevated paved street, I found a different river: of people who are not entirely wanted, a 'wave' that the city would rather keep out, would rather not see, despite being in plain sight.

Both places were busy.

*

In my notes, Steindamm appears on the margins of the pages; not the focus of my curiosity, but often the location of my observations. Many roads seemed to lead me there.

Around 900 metres long, the street seems to change character every few steps. On its eastern stretch are a series of office buildings, constructed in place of a residential and shopping quarter destroyed during the Second World War, when large parts of Hamburg were targeted by air raids. Towards the west – the part that connects to the train station – is where I spent most of my time. This is the section derisively called the Dirty Mile, and Döner-Allee. On this part of the street, there are restaurants and supermarkets offering so-called 'ethnic' food – Turkish, Afghan, Syrian, Indian, among others. In some places, grocery stores display fresh fruits and vegetables on the pavement. Around them are barber shops and sex shops and hijab shops, casinos and pharmacies, hotels and discount department stores, travel agencies offering cheap international fares.

'Everything that scares us, we put here,' a local journalist told me. 'Sex, mosques, migrants.'

Like in my notes, Steindamm exists at the margins of the city, though it is located near its centre.

Afghans are prominent in the mix of languages and communities visible on the street. Hamburg is home to the largest Afghan diaspora in Europe, a community formed in part over decades of conflict, with each cycle of war forcing more people to seek refuge. In 2015, there were close to 35,000 Afghan people in the city.

One of the nicknames for the unkempt part of Steindamm, I learned, was Klein Kabul. Little Kabul.

*

Walking down Steindamm it is possible to find relics of the past still embedded in the terrain. Often, these are quite different from its present. Like the Hansa-Theater, an iconic venue for vaudeville in Germany, which dates from the 1890s. The building was destroyed in 1943, likely bombed by Allied forces, and later rebuilt on the same spot by the owners. Nearby is the Savoy, a plush single-screen cinema built in the 1950s, which shows movies in their original English versions. Across the road are residential buildings that have survived the war, nestled among gaming parlours, shisha shops, money changers and adult entertainment stores. The structures are beautiful, and sometimes I stop and gaze at their graceful facades, and the afternoon light on their walls, appearing and vanishing from behind the flow of people on the street.

On the steps of a church in south-western Germany in 2018, I had met a woman in her fifties who had driven from her home nearby to attend an anti-war concert. 'My father was in a war, my grandfather was in a war,' she had said. 'I don't think it's a good legacy.'

Borders are familiar to her generation. The Berlin Wall came down just over thirty years ago. The war ended less than eight decades ago. On Steindamm too, the memory of rubble on the street is never too far from the surface.

It is a memory that seems to cling to Masoud, cleaving to the curve of his back as he walks ahead of me in the buzzing crowd, making his way through the shops and the restaurants, through the crush of bodies around him, collecting and dispersing like eddies in a stream.

*

A little off Steindamm is Hansaplatz, a wide square with a now dry fountain at its centre. The monument was built in the late nineteenth century by a consortium of traders and businessmen, when the suburb of St Georg was home to the affluent.

In the 1980s, Hansaplatz was one of the centres for drugs and prostitution activities in Hamburg. Women friends told me that if they went shopping on Steindamm, they would avoid meeting around the square. Now, they said, they are less inclined to keep their heads down. It is less dingy than it used to be. But it is still one of the edgiest parts of the city, and carries a reputation as a criminal hotspot, despite the evident patches of gentrification around it.

Walking from Steindamm to Hansaplatz, I passed drug users and sex workers, homeless people and more police than I had seen in other parts of the city. I passed the figure of Hansa – an embodiment of the city's prosperity – at the top of the fountain. The trash cans were overflowing and the stench of urine and beer hung in the air. On the walls, posters advertised concerts by Turkish and Afghan singers. On the other side of the plaza were chic cafes, with families enjoying lunch in the pleasant afternoon.

In 2015, Masoud told me, when the refugees had arrived in Hamburg, they had been housed in facilities where they were not permitted to cook. Many of them came to Steindamm to spend their food allowance, to find a diet that seemed at least somewhat familiar. He would see them, he said, when he went shopping for groceries with his family. Skimming through newspapers from the time, I read a report where a restaurant owner from the area recalled it being a good time for business.

I also shopped for food each time I came to Steindamm. At an Indian grocery store on the corner of Hansaplatz, I picked out daal and packets of spices, listening to the devotional songs playing on the speakers. A matriarch in a shalwar kameez bagged my purchases at the cash counter. Outside, a scuffle began and I grew uneasy at the sound of voices cursing, rising in aggression, not knowing what they were saying. She didn't bat an eyelid.

*

Emerging from the underground stairway near the pharmacy at the beginning of Steindamm, I see the flutter of white, then the tent, then the name on its entrance. Lampedusa Platz, I read; the name becoming a bridge to an island in a faraway sea.

This white tent had been erected in May 2013 as a marker and resource centre for the 300 or so refugees fleeing the Libyan conflict who had arrived in Hamburg that year. Mostly migrant workers, they had initially landed on the tiny Italian island of Lampedusa, which lies closer to Africa than to mainland Europe. Their arrival in Hamburg that winter had sparked gestures of solidarity by different sections of the city; schools, churches and cultural institutions had opened their doors and offered shelter. Traces of their arrival still marked the city's topography five years later. Across the grungy districts of St Pauli and Schanzenviertel, I had seen walls sprayed with the words 'Lampedusa in Hamburg'.

Erecting the white tent in the middle of the city was how the refugees reminded people of their existence, I had read. It was a way of staking claim to the city, of not vanishing from public memory. That morning, I saw commuters and tourists walking around it, barely glancing at the structure. I approached the tent and saw a few people sitting inside, stacks of paper and posters with slogans on the wall. To me, it seemed like an island in the middle of the city, unseen in plain sight.

*

In Steindamm, I often used a word to describe myself that was understood by Persian, Turkish and Arabic speakers. I am a musafir, I said, a traveller. The term often opened doors to hospitality and invitations, because a musafir has a claim upon the generosity of the host. You are our guest, I was told, you are welcome.

It was a word that led to stories – a path into conversations with workers at the Afghan grocery store, or while having tea and baklava in a cafe. It prompted questions about where I was from, where I would go.

And directions to places that I should see, now that I was in their land. Come back any time, many of my interlocutors said as I took my leave. This is your home.

*

As an Indian woman, the invisibility of Europe's borders often leave me fretful, because borders rarely work to my advantage. I would rather be able to see them coming, be prepared. When I travel, I leave for the airport early, carry masses of paperwork, rehearse answers to many questions. I carried around my passport all the time in Hamburg, though I was never asked to show it.

As an Indian writer, my desire to write about the world frequently collides with the reality of my location. These obstacles often appear to be practical, even impartial, like visa requirements and currency exchange rates. Behind these are more insidious ideas of power and expertise; maps that run from an imagined centre to its perceived margins. Which may be why, in a local newspaper office, and by other writers and journalists I meet, I am asked with different intonations what exactly *I* am doing there, writing about Germany.

Which is another way of saying that when we talk of writing on travel, we are often describing borders.

And when we read narratives of travel, we are usually moving in just one direction.

*

In one of the discount shopping centres at Steindamm, I watched a Somali family buying a set of suitcases, their little girl running through the store in excitement. The sight reminded me of the cheap, soft-shelled baggage my parents bought from a roadside stall on Tottenham Court Road in the years my father was a doctoral student in London. These were capacious enough to be stuffed with odd-shaped gifts for the family, and returned stuffed with home-made treats. On one journey my father carried a jar of mango pickle in his hand baggage.

Soon, its pungent smell filled the entire aircraft. He laughed about it, but I, at age ten, already knew it was no joke to be accused of your food smelling weird.

My father, with his de rigueur shaggy hair and beard, and his suitcases full of books, was often pulled out of line at airports. We would wait for him to return, while other people would come and go, moving smoothly through queues, departing unchecked. I watched their sense of ease with fascination. It seemed so distant, it didn't even seem possible to envy it.

Perhaps this memory is what made me associate travel with vulnerability for so long; part of the reason why I plan for delays and interrogations. Perhaps that's why I carry dozens of papers on every journey I make, make sure my appearance is as acceptable as possible. Waiting for my father to reappear, I had learnt how arbitrary our journeys are, and how little we control the paths we take.

That not all travellers are equal, and that invisible borders are not the same as open borders.

*

Steindamm is sometimes described in German as a 'Bahnhofsviertel', a station district – that is to say, an area shaped by travellers and their needs, not by those who belong to the city. A place of temporariness, with all its associated problems. Another way of seeing this temporariness is through the people who inhabit its spaces, like the sex workers I saw around Hansaplatz. During the 1990s, I was told by a local journalist, many of these sex workers came from Latin American countries. Now, due to stricter border rules, he told me, they are mostly from Eastern European countries like Bulgaria or Romania. Their figures on the street can be read as maps of borders shifting shape.

*

The Afghan asylum seekers I spent my time with also used a term to describe themselves, a word I find frequently in my notes: muhajir, migrant. A term that in their case comes with no return journey, for people who cannot return home.

Like Masoud, who had not seen his parents since 2013, when he had claimed political asylum, and had forfeited the right to return to Afghanistan. On a wall of his home in Hamburg, he had arranged a collage of photos, some taken in Kabul, others in Germany. Many of these, I noticed, were images of roads and bridges. Of train stations and airports. He had arranged them like the pieces of a jigsaw puzzle, with white spaces in between. On the wall of an asylum seeker's home, were these images of travel, or a trajectory of escape? During his journey from Iran to Afghanistan, and then from Afghanistan to Germany, perhaps Masoud had figured out this one thing: that the act of seeking refuge in a distant land also means travelling a great distance from your own self. It means shedding the layers of your past, the complexity of your stories, the music of your life, and donning completely the persona of being a refugee. It means inhabiting the white spaces that lie between the pictures on his wall.

Musafir, muhajir.

In between these two words is the distance between the fine weft of travellers' anecdotes, and the voicelessness that often comes with being a refugee.

*

Why did I return to Steindamm so frequently during my time in Hamburg? Was it for the groceries and spices, for the meals or the exchanges with servers at restaurants who played Bollywood songs and were thrilled to meet someone from Mumbai? Was it the need to seek out what was familiar in a strange land? Or was it simply because I could walk this street, located on the fringes of the city in so many ways, without being asked why I was there?

In the urine-soaked, garbage-strewn spaces of Steindamm, nobody asked me what I was doing there. Why *I* was writing about *Germany*.

*

In 2020, as movement became complicated and travel was halted, even the most privileged saw borders appear in unexpected places. Often for the first time, a large number of people felt the wrench of not being able to see their loved ones, of not being in control of their decisions.

India also entered a strict lockdown for three months. In Mumbai, I was cut off from my family in the north of the country in a way I had never experienced before. I thought of Masoud's family, and the people I had met in Hamburg, and of their intimate knowledge of what so many of us were experiencing then to some small degree. That borders can appear anywhere, and that you can be forced to cross them, or be prevented from crossing them, with little choice in the matter.

*

One afternoon in 2018, I went to an Iranian restaurant in a street behind Steindamm with Masoud and another friend from Kabul, and their families. We had a late lunch, and in a ritual of South Asian etiquette we argued over who got to pay the bill. Then we walked down Steindamm to have ice cream at an Afghan restaurant, where, my friends told me, it was served just like in Kabul. I walked with the two women, Nargis and Sufia, who were pushing their young children in strollers. They were siblings who had grown up as refugees in Iran together, and their banter had the easy shorthand of a shared childhood. Together, we walked past shop windows with mannequins in thongs, past the Aladin Center and World of Sex, to the restaurant. We climbed the stairs to the first floor and sat by tall windows looking out onto the street. The ice cream came frozen in layers, nestled in foil containers, the way it did in Kabul.

Before all that, on our way there, we had crossed two police officers checking the papers of a short, thin man. A woman waited by his side. We had walked past them quietly.

Behind the changing facades of this stone river lies the realisation that temporariness can sometimes last a lifetime.

*

In March 2020, the Lampedusa Platz tent was removed by the city authorities. I saw photos of this clearing online – men in white protective garments dismantling the metal pipes, filling black trash bags with papers. A ring of police officers stood around them. The images reminded me of the protest sites in Delhi from the eventful winter of 2019–20, when large numbers of people took to the streets to oppose a controversial citizenship law. These sites were emptied and bulldozed early in the pandemic. Walls that had been ablaze with poetry and art were painted over. I saw them as a flash of white, from the corner of my eye.

*

In December 2020, as Europe prepared to lock down once again for a second peak of the coronavirus outbreak, deportation flights from Germany to Afghanistan, which had been suspended during the pandemic, were resumed.

*

The images on the shopfronts of travel agencies in Steindamm were of planes taking off.

*

I think of the sun on the paved street that afternoon, like the glimmer of an invisible river.

***

Over the course of writing this essay, Afghanistan changed. As I write these lines, the Taliban are back in power in the country; Afghan refugees are back in the news.

As I write, I listen to the voices of friends in Kabul, looking for a path out of the city. As I write, I listen to Masoud's voice on the phone, looking for a way to get his family to safety.

In their voices I hear the flow of war; across cities, across decades. ∎

ELOGHOSA OSUNDE
Emmanuel Iduma (right) and his father Francis Agbi Iduma, 2016

TRAVELLING SECRETARY

Emmanuel Iduma

1

In a coffee shop in New York City, I sit beside a man with impaired speech. I nod to him, he nods back, and we begin a conversation with arms, fingers and haphazard gesticulations. Between us on the table is the day's *New York Post*. Soon – in what sequence this happened I can't remember – he writes a note to me on the back of the newspaper: 'Have you ever changed into a thing?' After a pause he writes again: 'Me? My heart is small & I have suffered long but I can become many good things when I am in pain.'

A year later, I see a Black father and son in a crowded train. The son sits, the father stands. We get to a stop and there's space beside the son for the father. 'Dad,' son calls out. Dad comes and sits, but both son and dad are too burly to fit as close as that comfortably. They manage to sit, regardless, for a fraction of a minute. Son's head is bent, with his hands held over it. Very soon dad begins to say, 'I am tired, I am tired, I am tired.' He punctuates these declarations with unclear cautionary whispers to son, who is bobbing his head around. Then dad stands, walks towards the door of the train, and keeps saying loudly, 'I am tired, I am tired, I am tired.' Son keeps bobbing his head. And when he looks up, I see him crying.

For years, as a foreigner in America, I gathered scenes based on my brief encounters with the interior lives of others, surveying agony at a remove. I self-published those scenes as blog posts – as dispatches from a world I was growing familiar with. Yet that familiarity could not allay my sense that I had traded being with my family in Nigeria for . . . what? Descending the subway one day in my sixth year, I began to weep, with a quiet intensity that lasted throughout the train ride from Brooklyn into Manhattan. I was unaccompanied, and so my desolation wasn't dramatised, as that of the man and his son, or clearly defined, like that of the man with his self-absorbed scrawl. The remote causes of my weeping were clear to me. All the while, like the faraway trace of an image I couldn't yet discern, I knew I had begun to plan my relocation to Nigeria.

When my father graduated from the University of Ife in 1983, he was advised by one of his professors to enrol in a master's in psychology in nearby Benin, Nigeria's best programme of its kind at the time. Only one other student was favoured with a similar nudge: if the two students were so inclined, said the professor, they could return from Benin with their MSc and get teaching jobs. At that juncture in his life, my father chose a different, uncommon path. He entered into Christian ministry. Psychology, he argued, was the science of interrogating the inner life of others, and catering to it. A minister of the gospel attended to similar needs. As if to examine this intuition, he volunteered with the Scripture Union, an interdenominational Christian organisation, for his first post-university year. The following year, he accepted an offer of employment. His designation was 'travelling secretary'.

Posted to Akure, a town in south-western Nigeria, he was required to travel throughout the surrounding area. He'd visit what was known as 'pilgrim groups', when they met each Sunday or later in the week, exhorting with a sermon and staying back to offer individual counsel. He came to Akure as a single man, but within a year he married my mother. From Akure, four years and two sons later, he was moved to Port Harcourt, 500 kilometres away. Thus, his lifelong dislocation began; the longest he'd ever stay in a place for work was six years, even after he shifted loyalties, in 1997, to the Presbyterian Church of Nigeria.

What notion of belonging might have been possible for my family if he had chosen life as an academic? The preceding condition for any life is found in one that predates it: my life unfolded within the net effect of my father's choices. From his impermanence I grew into mine, remaining in New York after graduate school on the assumption that I could put off the decision of whether to return or settle.

Until the day on the train when I began to sink on shifting ground.

The word 'Presbyterian' – from *presbyter*, 'an elder in a church', from ecclesiastical Greek *presbyteros*, 'one that presides over assemblies or congregations' – reflects the system of a rotating cast of parish ministers in a church governed by laity. Founded by Calvinists in Scotland, it is a church in which a coterie of elders, known as the 'Session', is the highest-ranking body in each parish, moderated by the current minister. The unintended consequence of this structure is that its clergymen might never define belonging in relation to the places where their life's labours unfold. They transfer its meaning elsewhere, to their ancestral homes, or to a period when – finally exhausting their patience for the petty politics of parishes or chapels – they retire to a self-sustaining ministry.

Those early years in Akure were marked by severe immiseration. This is what my father implied when he recalled how he began full-time ministry. Once, he had driven to a midweek evening service in Owo, fifty kilometres away. He went knowing there was no meal at home for the next day, and felt embarrassed by his inability to meet a basic need. When the service ended, a woman waited by his car, with tubers of yam and an envelope of naira notes. He was thrilled by the miraculous turn in events, evidence, as he characterised it while relaying the story to me, of divine providence.

During those years, going about his chosen work with the overhanging ache of want, did he ever lose faith? I do not think so. I see him in my mind's eye as I grew to see him, perhaps as he was then, rising to pray before convening the rest of the family in the living room at 5.30 a.m. After the joint prayers, he spent additional time alone with multiple devotionals. Then he went to his bedroom for a shave and shower. Most days his breakfast was quick, and most days he took great care never to arrive at his first meeting late. On occasions when no one required his immediate attention, he was no less sparing with his schedule, going to his office to outline a sermon. In his last decade, he often returned to his writing after dinner, working on a table on the veranda or in his study.

In 2018, back to my family's duplex in the University of Port Harcourt for the final time, my brother and I entered the room he'd worked in. We gathered his bibles and sermon notebooks in a worn carton. We were now at a stage of grief when it was rare to break into a sudden wail. Yet we didn't dare browse through the stacked books. On our way out, I took a photo, standing at the point where he would have sat as he faced the window. I recorded a dense scattering of shrubs reaching the furthest limit of the frame. The view was unspectacular. Not that I cared. My impulse was to illustrate a sense of the irrecoverable – true as well of a second, better composed photo, showing the length of the university's interdenominational chapel, his terminal outpost.

As soon as my father settled there, he began to make plans for the aftermath of the job, due to end in three years. He hoped to launch a freelance ministry, earning income from preaching gigs and the sale of his books, and settling in Umuahia, where my mother worked full-time as a schoolteacher.

In one sense he achieved the stasis he sought. His ambulatory body is stilled.

During the last twenty years of his life, my father's chief enthusiasm lay in writing. I consider the dedication – the regimen, the prolificacy – with which he self-published eleven Christian books in nineteen years. By grounding himself in literature, I suppose he felt he could rise above the constraints of constant mobility.

In 1998, he used a large table in the church hall as a desk to write *Nakedness: Secrets of Enjoying Marriage*, the book that remains his best selling. At the time my youngest brother had just been born. In search of an apt illustration for the cover, my father thought it best to use a photograph of his naked, toddling son. According to his telling of what happened next, I warned against the idea. When my brother grew older, I argued, he could be so embarrassed by the ubiquitous cover photograph that he could sue my father for displaying him nude without his consent. My immature legal advice seemed reasonable to him. He chose, instead, a cover with an illustration of two bells twined with a ribbon. Afterwards, I wonder if he felt discomfited when he recalled how he considered using his naked offspring for publicity.

When I was fifteen, he launched *Family Values in a Changing World*, his fifth book. In the third chapter, he included a poem I had written for my mother. 'The poem,' he wrote, 'was a gift our second son gave to his mother on the Mothering Sunday of the year 2004. I secured permission from both the boy and his mother to use it to introduce this chapter.' I return to his prefatory note, and all I imagine – since he wrote his books longhand – is his limber fingers copying out what I'd written. *I secured permission*, he noted, as though it were his honour, not mine, for the poem to be reproduced.

By my mid-twenties, either due to my impatience with his refusal to work on a computer or my growing angst about my own writing, I took his work for granted. On one visit home, he handed to me nearly 200 pages of a new manuscript – *Banner of Love*, a couple's devotional – and implored that I type it up for him. A year later I had finished no more than a dozen pages, but when asked, claimed I was almost done. Then he asked for the typewritten document. To compound matters, he made the request a week or two after I moved to New York, and days before he was to arrive in Lagos to gather the rest of my things, including the handwritten manuscript, from the house I'd lived in.

I search my inbox to see with what words I apologised, but what I find is a different email, from January 2014, when I attached a new draft of the manuscript. He got someone else to type the entire manuscript, and then sent it to me to edit. 'Once again I am really sorry for how I dealt with this and I promise to make up for my failure,' I wrote. But still I feel my impropriety skulking in the shadow of my memory, due perhaps to the discrepancy between my actions and his reaction. Only once, after the book was published, did he mention that I delayed the work. He was often so conciliatory he could be mistaken as guileless.

I know he forgave me, or at least understood my failing. One day, after his death, I turned to the acknowledgements in *Banner of Love*. I was one of two people, he wrote, who edited and formatted the book. 'Though outside the country, he still opted to be part of it because of his love for me.' Did I do it because I loved him? Once, during the first of two final visits to Port Harcourt, he came to my room while I was working on my computer. He stood at the entrance, holding the door. I looked at him with an uncomprehending frown. 'Sorry to disturb you,' he said. 'No, daddy, it's fine.' He had come to ask how much progress I had made with editing the manuscript of *Living Above Reproach*, what became his posthumous book. 'Can you finish it before you leave?' 'Yes, daddy,' I replied, and he said, 'Thank you,' then turned away in a gentle, inobtrusive sway.

It is the duty, I thought then, of a son not to say no to his father. But love, I am now inclined to believe, was defined for him as the convergence of small gratitudes, including for any help he got in his life work.

I recall the preceding fall, a year before I wept while on the subway. I was at the peak of my itineracy – travelling for writing residencies, conferences, book festivals – on one occasion with just a single day between transatlantic flights. I was, equally, beginning to shed my greenness: I could state the distances between train stops, speak of the gentrification of the South Bronx, suggest meetings at a coffee shop that had become my favourite, even produce itineraries for visiting friends. Money was easier to come by – although, as I was often waiting to receive cheques from writing or teaching gigs, I repeatedly asked for small loans from friends – and hence I decided that it was the best year to return home for the Christmas break. Once I managed to buy my ticket, I shopped for gifts for each member of my family. I wanted it to be clear that, after four years of sending news of my impoverishment, I had come into some means. Those weeks at home sparkled with happiness, reaching a climax when my father shyly took a photo of me with his phone as I sat with my younger siblings, the unprompted gesture of a man who had never bothered with new technology.

Now I wish to see the rich twilight between that height of contentment and the sadness I'd begin to feel later.

Seven weeks after our Christmas reunion I returned again. First to Lagos, to participate in an arts festival, then to Afikpo, the Igbo town where my father was born. His close friend from adolescence, Auntie Nnenna, was being buried, and all members of our immediate family, save my older and younger brothers, were in attendance. As we began to leave, he asked his driver to stop. Then he returned to the school field where the funeral service was coming to a close. He had to attend a meeting that evening, and so it made no sense that he delayed our departure. Ten minutes passed before he re-entered the car with packs of takeaway food, to be shared on the journey. My mother asked why he had taken so long, and he replied with a snappish grunt. We sat squashed in the back, my two sisters between my father and me, my mother in front.

As we pulled back onto the road, the mood brimmed with irritability. I put it down to the urgency with which we needed to return to the University of Port Harcourt. How could I not have read the signs? I was blinded to the real cause of his prickliness, clear in hindsight. He'd reached a point in his life when each new bereavement – all his brothers were dead, for one – was like a scald on an old wound. Seven months later, when he was diagnosed with a liver inflammation and lay in the hospital, he told my mother it was time for him to go.

I pick at the significance of that day in Afikpo, and the morning that followed in Port Harcourt, the last time I was with my father.

2

Once, while I was a boarding student in Abuja, I sought home with a shameless desperation, prompted by a longing unlike any other I had known. One way I could get an exeat – a card signed by the principal, his vice, or an authorised teacher – was to be certified ill enough to require treatment outside the school. For that to happen, I needed the head nurse in the sickbay to append her signature to my application letter, which, when taken to the administrative block, would almost automatically guarantee my freedom. Yet, of course, the nurse could only sign my letter if I showed symptoms. And so, one afternoon, I spent several minutes hammering my head against the goalpost in the football field. My hope was to get a headache, to exacerbate what was a distant, surely psychosomatic fever, to run a temperature, making it inarguable to all concerned that I had contracted malaria.

There were boys, and I suppose girls, who took a more daring approach, and left the school without seeking permission. We were enclosed in an estate of several hectares in a rural, mountainous region of Nigeria's capital state. There was a fence, but where it ended – if the cluster of streams behind the hostels were enclosed within it – I could never tell. No one, however audacious, could aim for home from the rear of the school. The only route was a track across seven hills, and unless you had the ambition to walk for days through an unmapped forest, it was best to seek out a route closer to the school entrance. Of course, there was an exception to this exception: one day, a group of boys went hiking, and whether by whim or premeditation, decided to follow the trail of the hills. Despite it being an hour by road away, they ended up in Wuse, a commercial hub of Abuja, close to a week later.

I never had the misfortune of being paraded on the assembly ground as a luckless student caught seeking an illegal route – or better to say I feigned illness because I lacked the courage to return home by any other means. Under the steaming heat that Friday, I stood beside the goalpost. After each sequence of striking my head against the scalding metal, I touched my neck and forehead for a rise in symptoms.

The supplementary provisions with which I arrived each term – a staple of cornflakes, biscuits, powdered milk, Bournvita, sugar and garri – ran out within a fortnight. The food served by the school was almost always undercooked or bland, sometimes a plate of beans with sediments of stone in it, or yam porridge as pale as if no palm oil had been used. The bad food was compounded by another distress: there was the matter of beatings. In theory, no senior student was allowed to punish a younger fellow. In practice, there was sufficient opportunity to be brutish without consequence, particularly when we retired to our hostels. During my first year, just a day or two after I was enrolled, a group of us were commanded to kneel, and take turns standing to approach a senior. Then, when we were in front of him, bend over in a pose known as 'touch your toe'. His arm-length stick landed against our lower backs, and on being struck I bawled and fell over, prompting the amused senior to spare me the promised second lash.

But I do not attribute my longing for home that weekend to either the fear of a senior's wallop or the need for a good meal. My desperation was sudden and primal, yet had amassed weight over the previous weeks, when the fact of being away from my parents and younger siblings loomed as a persistent threat to my well-being.

S purred by nostalgia I return to photographs of myself as a boy. This one, taken in front of our house in Nyanya, in the first three years of my time in secondary school: I am smiling without baring my teeth, resting my back on my father's grey Volvo, whose roof is only a few inches above my head. Our bungalow – cream-coloured, burglar-proofed and mud-bricked – stands behind the car. The shadow of a gmelina tree is cast against the trunk of the car, falling past the edge of the frame. I beam with what must be sheer pleasure. Even today I think of the years spent in Nyanya as holding the clue to one version of my happiest self.

More than an hour from Karshi, where the boarding school was, Nyanya was a suburb bordering Abuja and the neighbouring Nasarawa state. Our family was the first to occupy the newly built manse, in the year following my father's ordination as a minister of the Presbyterian Church. The bungalow was one of three structures in a compound of almost a hectare. From a gatehouse at the entrance, a path led to the church hall and curved rightwards towards the manse. The rest of the unoccupied land was a terrain of much uncertainty – the occasional scorpion and cobra, the frequent litigations about ownership – but with its vastness it was equally the source of idyllic consolations. I broadened my vocabulary about farming, learning about ridges, hoes and rakes, as well as the planting seasons for maize, beans, fluted pumpkin and tomatoes. My mother, who taught me all that, kept dogs and a cat, raised chickens, built a kiosk to sell odds and ends, concocted a drink from lemongrass to treat ailments – making do during what, from the stance of twenty-two years, now seems to have been a disorienting season of austerity. Still, it was the only home I knew. Every term in Karshi was an expulsion to a foreign ground. Not once did I imagine the end of term, and the holidays that lasted for six weeks, without the jubilant air of return.

I was deemed sick enough to be allowed home that Friday. I borrowed my transport fare from a friend. The bus was headed to a central terminus in Nyanya, from where I would take a motorcycle taxi to the church compound. We drove past a rush of sparse landscape. Then buildings gathered in density. Only as I alighted in the bustle of the park did it occur to me that I also needed to convince my parents that my trip was necessitated. I scrunched my face and hunched my gait, tottering towards the church compound. My mother began to laugh as soon as I gave my excuse. 'Just say you are tired of school,' she said. 'Look how thin you are!'

How much of the past do I misapprehend? I wonder if my father had sent me off to Karshi – to join my older brother, enrolled two years prior – in part to keep me from conditions in the manse. When we began to live there, right after my father returned from the United States after four years of seminary education – years he spent without his wife or children – there were no amenities befitting a modern house. For the first year or two we pulled water from a well and lived without electricity. It is still impressive, one of the earliest congregants of the church told me years later, that my father agreed for us to live in the house at the time. They received him with mixed feelings, the congregant told me, expecting him to reject the posting. A man used to Western convenience was bound to expect relative luxury. He stunned them by accepting without protest.

Sometime in May or June 1998, armed robbers visited the manse. My mother later alleged they must have observed us for some time. It was an inside job, she claimed. I remember vaguely, but the man guarding the gate was asleep, conveniently, when the robbers slunk in. Hours earlier my parents had returned with a stash of cash for a scheduled surgery. 'It is you we want, Madam,' they told my mother. And asked her to sit, to point out where the money was hidden. No one was hurt except my father. They struck his face when he knelt, perhaps sleep-eyed, to pray, 'Lord forgive them, for they do not know what they do.'

His blood-eyed face was, to our satisfaction, avenged. Days after the robbery my mother was invited by the police to identify the robbers. She recognised one of the men by the size of his feet, but declined to point him out. Who knows, she thought, he might be released, and come back for me. Only he wouldn't. That afternoon, the police killed all the robbers they arrested.

I idealised the house my father was expected to reject. Now, thinking of the daily indignities he knew would come with his choice, I remain in thrall to his self-denial, but also his stoicism, if the incident with the robbers tells something of how he fared in a crisis.

As time passed, daily life in Karshi no longer seemed alienating. We were consoled by Christian ritual: twice daily, at 6 a.m. and 9 p.m., we prayed in front of our hostels, in addition to prayer meetings held right before night prep at 6.30 p.m. After I was appointed an executive member of the Fellowship of Christian Students, I attended nearly every meeting held under its auspices – for prayer or planning or to rehearse songs or a playlet. During the lull of the weekends, our congregating intensified, given the amount of spare, extracurricular time.

Then, months after I successfully faked illness, my father completed his tenure in Nyanya. He was posted to lead an out-of-state parish, in Ketu, Lagos. Our family, by necessity, was to relocate from the north-central capital state to a south-western one, 700 kilometres away.

During the two years my family was based in Ketu, I remained a student in Karshi. When I travelled home during breaks, it was mostly at night, in large buses then known as 'luxurious buses'. I entered Lagos as dawn broke. I felt a somnolent, multisensory chill, watching the new city from a seven-foot height. My lethargy was offset by the uproarious hum of people darting in and out of ramshackle buses. I had the acute feeling of being under a haze of unknowing: a difficulty in ascertaining what version of home Ketu had become.

3

I n the Uber, the radio is dialled to Lagos Talks FM. Three men are bantering, about football, food served by their wives, strip clubs and the gesticulations of their colleagues when they talk dirty. They laugh so hard, interrupting each other to compete for the loudest joke, until it becomes difficult to follow their segues. We are driving past a toll gate, which is out of service due to the fallout of the recent protests, then the moneyed facades of Ikoyi.

The driver has changed the station to Inspiration FM. A jingle comes on. 'When someone says expect the unexpected, slap him on the face and say, "You didn't expect that, did you?"' And unexpectedly, without a follow-up to what must have been intended as a corny wisecrack, a newscaster comes on. '9 a.m. and here are the headlines.' The government has frozen the accounts of up to twenty persons who mobilised to raise money during the protests. The funds, the Central Bank claimed, are suspected to have been collected for terrorist activity. One lawyer interviewed by the radio station decries this as unlawful, unconstitutional and insensitive. Since I heard of it three days ago, I have been stunned by the argument that peaceful protesters are treasonous. As my fury collects, I see a barefoot man by the roadside screaming at the driver of a bus who'd hit his bumper. The traffic slows further, until the aggrieved man, having exhausted his barrage of insults, returns to his car, still waving his hands in the air.

How to make sense of it all? This unkind leap year when, not-withstanding a pandemic, the largest uprising against police brutality and bad governance in a generation had ended one night when soldiers shot at protesters. I live with my wife (whom I got married to six months after I relocated to Lagos) three kilometres from the toll gate where the shooting occurred, and could still hear gunshots after dawn, by which time news of widespread arson and looting across Lagos had begun to circulate. No less than twelve were dead. The city felt unsettling, unsettled – covered in plumes of real and imagined smoke – even if we drew our curtains and kept from peeking at the street.

The newscaster wraps up the news. After a commercial, two men begin to discuss the contents of the day's newspapers. For at least ten minutes, one of them teases out his tedious ideas on the energy of the moment. 'The cosmic is where energies gather,' he says. 'The cosmic is beginning to accumulate the energy the youth is giving off, and one day it will fall like rain.' I am a Christian, he'd said earlier, but even if you belong to the occult you know that two forces govern this world – light and darkness.

Soon I am thinking of my father, and his response to Nigerian politics. 'This country,' he'd say, shaking his head with slow bemusement. 'All I pray for is my daily bread.' Not just that memory. This morning, standing in front of the mirror as I tucked in my singlet, I recalled that he, too, had preferred white undershirts. I see myself these days as what he must have seemed like to himself. I argue with myself, too, as to whether I am close enough in gait to his lithe frame, if my belly remains as flat as his. And I recognise a chief worry of mine is how little I will look like him as I age, whether my face is growing into his.

We turn off a highway leading out of Lagos to Ketu. I do not recall Ketu being this sedate. Then I recognise two signs: an Anglican cathedral, and once we are past a junction, at the entrance to a street, a fast-food joint I'd known. Built in our first or second year in the neighbourhood, Mr Bigg's was shiny and unapproachable to teenagers like me whose parents swore off food cooked outside the home or who considered weekly treats of meat pie and Scotch egg wasteful. Now only the frame of its hoarding remains, as well as broken windows and a dark, empty interior. Hah, I think, then feel a small jolt at my keenness to return here with no clear sense of who or what I hoped to be reunited with. I wonder if I might obscure the past by approaching it slantwise.

The street where my father's old church is located has changed in name, but I know that this is it. An old man sits by a metal barricade, and as we approach he rises to meet the car. 'Yes?' he says. I tell him, 'I'm going to the Presbyterian Church.' We are let in, and once I see the letters spelling the name of the church, I say to the driver it might be best if he made a U-turn closer to the broad entrance to the street. He insists on taking me further. 'I'll have space to turn in front, so you won't have to walk.' I want to walk from there on, but I do not protest. We come to the church, and I am let out. Painted sea-green, it is changed from the one my father knew. Then it was fenced off, but now the bigger building opens into the street, with a cordon marking the entryway. A bus inscribed with the church's insignia is parked outside, as well as the newer model of a saloon car, a Camry, also labelled with the church insignia. I am pleased by these signs of prosperity.

I peek into the church hall, and see a group sitting in a circle. I recognise Arit, one of the women, who does not seem to have aged a day. As soon as someone seems stirred by my presence, I turn to face the direction of the street. Whether or not I'll return to speak with Arit, I need a brief, solitary recess.

I walk back to the road the Uber had driven past. The church is right next to another, a Zion Family Centre, occupying what seems like an old warehouse, the same building where my father had once preached on the invitation of a neighbourly pastor. Past that, a two-storeyed Foursquare Gospel Church, bearing on its entrance the notice of a number to call if interested in the in-house crèche. I can't tell if this has always been here, as I mark the similarity in the paint colour used in both my old church and the Foursquare building. Opposite, approaching the barricade, a Kingdom Hall of Jehovah's Witnesses. The hall towers with the same aggrandising eeriness as when I walked past it as a teenager returning from errands – or maybe I characterise it as such because of the prejudice I've imbibed towards the adherents of that denomination.

In family photographs from our Ketu years, my father, closing in on fifty, looks exactly as what I imagine middle age to be: a man caught between staying on and letting go, like a taut cord just before it starts to fray.

Now I attempt to recreate the walk we would have taken in the year we lived outside the church compound. I'm facing a street named Aladelola, separated from Bello Folawiyo – where the distressed Mr Bigg's stands – by the major Ikosi Road. But we'd lived on Taike Street, not Aladelola, sharing a building with its namesake Chief Taike, an unamiable man who took a liking to my father. What has happened to the old chief's claim to the street? I am not discouraged by the discrepancy of names, or the improbability, as I scan the unrecognisable terrain, that I'll be reunited with our old house – since it is possible that I am on the wrong street. I wish only to be in a general area, to orchestrate a return without fixation on purpose.

The kindly sun alternates in intensity. Once or twice I breeze past the cool shade of foyers. I observe the way people sit in storefronts or stand on balconies. A group of men gather behind the entrance to a timeworn mint-green house, naked from their waists up. They possess the assured lull of those whose presence on the street long predated mine, or if not them, then their fathers. They are waiting, it seems, to be saved from a workaday impulse, to revisit an earlier state. Lying on old mattresses, the arc of their bodies retraces the small history of the day, circling towards respite. ∎

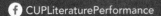

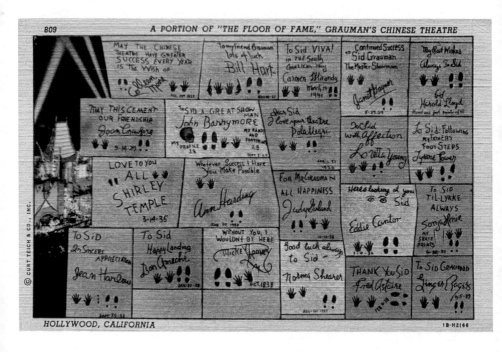

A portion of the Forecourt of the Stars, otherwise known as 'The Floor of Fame', Grauman's Chinese Theatre, California, USA

GRAFFITI MOBILI

Jennifer Croft

From a distance, the map of the forecourt of Hollywood's famous Chinese Theatre looks a lot like a county map of Iowa or Pennsylvania, but when you get closer, you see that instead of Pottawattamie or Lancaster or Osceola, the squares contain the names of movie stars. West of the entrance to the picture palace are the handprints and footprints and signatures of American royalty like Danny Kaye and Irene Dunne (two of my favorites), along with Fred Astaire and Ginger Rogers (among my grandmother's favorites); east are Humphrey Bogart and Meryl Streep. Bookending the box office are Harrison Ford and the cast of *Star Trek*.

I live in Los Angeles now, but I can't say I understand it yet. Sprawling, rising and falling, sweltering in the San Fernando Valley and often chilly on the coast, flaunting palm trees against a backdrop of increasingly fire-prone chaparral, rife with both hardship and privilege, Los Angeles is lived not only in English and Spanish, but also in Armenian, Persian, Russian, Korean, Tagalog, Chinese. The skies of my neighborhood are frequented by hummingbirds patrolling the California fuchsia and deafening LAPD helicopters scanning the streets for the perpetrators of more and more violent crimes. A couple of days ago, a few blocks away, a man was shot and killed outside an Urban Outfitters at noon.

High school, Pasadena, California, USA
'The season's Greetings'
Postmarked 23 December 1906

One thing that helps me to cope is to look down. Not only at the forecourt of the Chinese Theatre, but everywhere. I like to look at all of the inscriptions in the city's sidewalks done by ordinary Angelenos, non-stars whose lives are recorded in streaks underfoot: dates and initials, declarations of neighborhood pride, religious belief, love and political conviction – comments made on wet cement that act as concrete reminders that this and every place is many places, countless individual objects and organisms coming into contact, undergoing transformations, fusing, richly clashing, breaking apart. The graffiti of Los Angeles enable me to grapple with my surroundings much as postcards always have.

Omaha, Nebraska, USA
'*Vi vänta att få höra från Mrs.Wam*', 'We are waiting to hear from Mrs. Wam'
Postmark torn, but dated by the author 17 March 1908

The word 'graffiti' first appeared in English in 1859, in an anonymous piece for the *Edinburgh Review* titled 'The Graffiti of Pompeii'. The article lists examples ranging from humdrum to spectacular. Together, this 'motley' collection creates the kind of day-to-day portraiture that artworks intended to portray specific people at specific times in specific places nonetheless rarely achieve. Here, neither creator nor subject takes the trouble to pose, since graffiti are just 'scribblings', unlikely to last, although of course they have lasted, along with innumerable other examples: epigrams by ancient Roman women poets on the legs of the Colossi of Memnon; in Jordan, Nabataean signatures; in Saudi Arabia, eighth-century pleas for forgiveness; twentieth-century slogans of political protest in Santiago de Chile and Buenos Aires; in Managua, lines by Ernesto Cardenal. Spanning millennia and continents, graffiti are the emphatic traces of our travels in space and time. No matter what they say, they always communicate a particular person's presence in a particular place at a particular moment, the impact they made on their era and location and the effect their circumstances had on them. In a way, graffiti always say: 'I was here.'

Lago de Palermo, Buenos Aires, Argentina
'Signature, 30/11/15'
Postmarked 11 a.m., 29 November 1915

Six years after the *Edinburgh Review* ushered the word 'graffiti' into English, a Prussian postal worker named Heinrich von Stephan advocated for the official introduction of an innovative new communication technology that would come to be known as the postcard. Stephan believed in enabling everyone to communicate with everyone else, no matter the distance, and he would go on to establish the Universal Postal Union, which completely transformed the interactions of citizens of different countries. He also made Germany's first phone call (fittingly, from the post office to the telegraph office in Berlin). In 1865, however, the idea of a cheap postcard that would keep messages short and sweet while also exposing them to anyone's gaze was deemed indecent by the German Post Association, and Stephan's proposal was rejected.

The Wireless Tailophone, Denver, Colorado, USA
'Greetings from Denver. Jean Bonar'
Postmarked 7 a.m., 19 July 1907

Soon after I arrived in California, I met a gentle man named Francisco who told me how he rose to graffiti stardom in the 90s in LA, until the police caught wind of his work and launched a massive manhunt. He spent about three months going from house to house, trying to evade the authorities, until finally, exhausted, he decided to move to Chicago, where he had relatives. He went to his mom's house to spend his last night in LA with her; at 7 a.m. the next morning, his mom's house was surrounded by cops. He told me he tried to run away from them; I asked him if he wasn't afraid of getting shot. He said he just wasn't thinking in the moment, but that they had all had their guns drawn. He was in jail, he said, 'for a while'.

While early postcard publishers may not have faced brushes with death at the hands of law enforcement, the undermining of traditional etiquette did provoke widespread concern and even outrage. Conceived as the first truly democratic form of communication, might not postcards make threadbare the very fabric of society by offering the masses access to the epistolary institutions of the aristocracy? And yet, in 1869, Austrian economist Emanuel Herrmann made a similar suggestion to Stephan's in the *Neue Freie Presse*; his idea was taken up, and from Austria the postcard spread with astonishing rapidity around the world. 'During the first six months of 1898,' write Lynda Klich and Benjamin Weiss, 'Germans mailed over twelve million postcards; not even four years later, they were sending almost that number in a single week.' In 1905, there were over 4,000 postcard shops in Tokyo alone. 'In 1909 the British postal service sold 833 million stamps for postcards, nearly twenty for every man, woman, and child in the United Kingdom.'

The United States was a relatively late adopter of the postcard, but when the event occurred, Americans embraced the modern medium at least as wholeheartedly as their Old World counterparts. 'Sold in virtually every five-and-dime store, news-stand, and hotel from Brooklyn to Bakersfield,' writes Jeff Rosenheim, 'postcards satisfied the country's need for human connection in the age of the railroad and the Model T when, for the first time, many Americans regularly found themselves traveling far from home.'

Woodchopper, Big Tree Grove, Santa Cruz, California, USA
'The grove of big trees fills one with wonder. We have seen so much in two days since we left Pasadena it seems like a dream. Ocean into valleys. Everywhere Ok. This is a grand old state. 300 ft high 125 around. A tram drives through. Some are 4000 years old.'
Postmarked 6.30 a.m., 12 April 1906

Initially, postcards featured an image on one side and space for an address on the other. No other writing was permitted on the address side, meaning that any messages from sender to recipient had to fit within the picture itself, or else the white border that was in widespread use during this period. This changed in Great Britain in 1902 and in the United States in 1907. Following the introduction of the 'divided back', fewer messages were inscribed on the images of the postcards, though there remain those correspondents who prefer to foreground their 'graffiti mobili', even to this day.

'King City, Oregon 97224'
Postmarked 24 June 1998

If graffiti is an accessible way for individuals to make their mark on something larger (the collective imagination, the march of generations), postcards are an accessible way for individuals to reach each other. For me, in my twenties, prior to the rise of digital photography (let alone Instagram), postcards made travel without guilt or separation anxiety possible by enabling me to share my experiences of places with relatives back home. By then I had daydreamed of making it to Paris and Moscow for so long it was almost impossible to accept them as real, but every postcard I addressed to Oklahoma served as a reminder to myself of how far I'd come.

Sunny South, Home of the Mountaineer
'Dear Friend, You can get foreign postal cards down at McCarthy's, two for five, I thought I would tell you so if you want to get some. From your Friend, Lavinia'
Postmarked 10.30 a.m., 29 January 1906

Just as letters of the alphabet aren't merely squiggles on a sidewalk or a page, postcards evoke three-dimensional spaces precisely by being small and one-dimensional – by alluding, like language, to a vast reality that the recipient of the postcard must summon up actively in her own mind – and by having traveled. If graffiti is an ad hoc way to subtly reconfigure the world, postcards may be a way to totally reconfigure the world in someone's head, often the mind of a beloved person, someone who hasn't had the chance to see the world yet or hasn't seen it in some time. Postcards have always been saved, treasured in albums that juxtapose Bath with Bangkok and Caracas with Krakow, unique atlases where biography determines the maps.

Sears Tower, Chicago, Illinois, USA
'Someone decided to chop off the very distinct attenas from the Sears Tower, so I added them.
I hope you agree that was the right thing to do!'
Postmarked 28 January 2021

The picture of a postcard is a geograft, a scion of a place thrust into the life of a resident of somewhere else. Like the message it partly prompts, the geograft is cut from among the stronger sections of the place in question: the Panthéon and not the Starbucks; the black sand beach, not the dilapidated parking lots. Hollywood's Chinese Theatre is itself the result of postcard thinking. Designed in the 1920s by a man from Pennsylvania named Raymond M. Kennedy, its most significant influences were the Piazza San Pietro and the Sant'Andrea al Quirinale in Rome, yet it also incorporates temple bells, pagodas, stone Heaven Dogs and other artifacts from China, the installation of which was supposedly overseen by Chinese film director Moon Kwan.

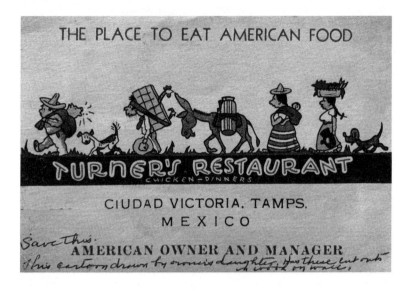

Turner's Restaurant, Ciudad Victoria, Tamaulipas, Mexico
'Save this. This cartoon drawn by owner's daughter. Has these cutouts on wood on wall.'
Not mailed

Postcards make graffiti more transmissible, not through reproduction, though postcards themselves are almost always made in multiples. They also transition graffiti from 'I was here' to 'I wish you were here', uniting writer and reader in a speculative first-person plural: a 'We were here' that could have been but never was. An unusual lack of grammatical specificity in English allows us to also read these sentences in a way that emphasizes the inextricability of person and place, just as image and text are two sides of the same postcard. 'I am here' can be read just like 'I am clumsy' or 'I am competitive', while the past tense of 'I was here' emphasizes the fleetingness of the descriptor 'I was young.'

'Saco, Montana'
Not mailed

In 1907, James Douglas suggested that '[w]hen the archaeologists of the thirtieth century begin to excavate the ruins of London, they will fasten upon the Picture Postcard as the best guide to the spirit of the Edwardian era'. He predicted that postcards would carry into the future 'a candid revelation of our pursuits and pastimes, our customs and costumes, our morals and manners', and indeed they have. 'Postcards help remind us that history is lived and experienced by individuals,' notes eminent deltiologist Leonard A. Lauder. They also remind us that places are only a little less impermanent than the people who set foot there, who build and demolish and plant and burn down – who leave traces, whether they intend to or not. ■

D.R.HARRIS & Co Ltd

~ ESTABLISHED 1790 ~
CHEMISTS AND PERFUMERS

Specialists in soaps, skincare and shaving since 1790

29 St. James's Street, London, SW1A 1HD
www.drharris.co.uk | www.originalpickmeup.co.uk

SHIPPING INTERNATIONALLY

16 SHEETS FROM LOG

Roni Horn

LOG (March 22, 2019 – May 17, 2020) is an installation produced daily over a fourteen-month period – 406 sheets each composed on an 11 x 8.5-inch piece of writing paper. Original texts, photographs and drawings (in graphite, colored pencil, collage).

LOG is a collection of notes, casual observations, facts, quotes, events of weather and private life, news and anything otherwise notable that came to mind or hand each day.

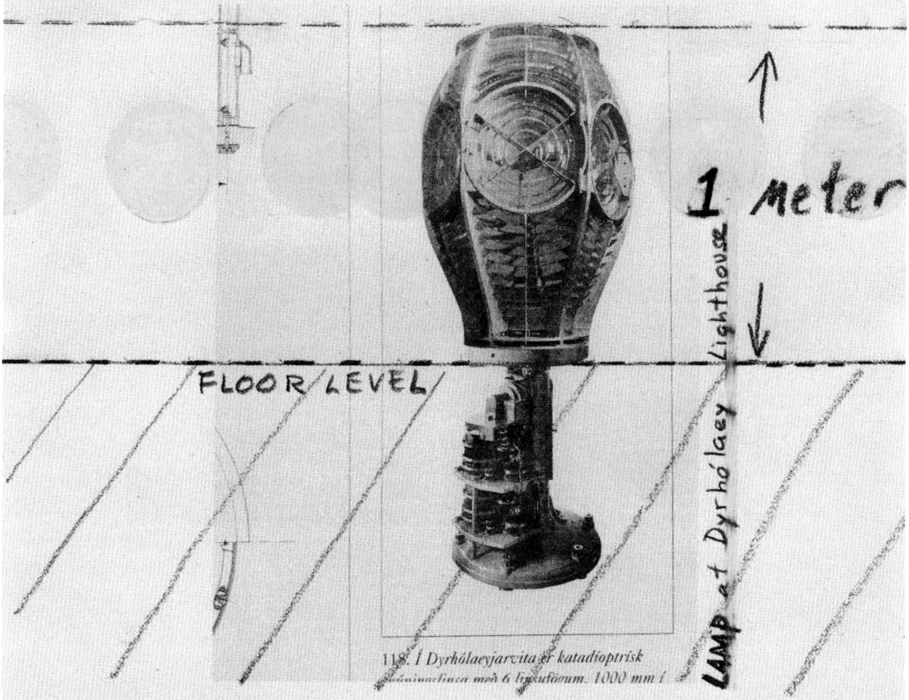

1 meter

FLOOR LEVEL

LAMP at Dyrhólaey Lighthouse

118. Í Dyrhólaeyjarvita er katadíoptrisk
díniuelinea með 6 linsutáosum. 1000 mm í

APRIL 11, 2019

In 1992 I was living in a lighthouse
in ICELAND. This was the light. I
slept one floor below it in the tower.
Its many tons rotating, grinding, vibrating
through the night. But when the sun stopped
going down the light shut off. After that
the building was so quiet and still, it
kept me awake.

April 24, 2019   NYC
Skhaftá River, 1994, Iceland

YOUR HALF   ↓   OTHER HALF

TEAR HERE

May 12, 2019   NYC

Arctic Circle (1994)

Eruption: Askja, Iceland (1961)

August 19, 2019   Austerlity, NY

Big news from Iceland today – radio
and web, "Obituary for a Glacier."

The glacier OK ⬤ is gone.

⬤ See Library of Water: Column No. 9

Library of Water: Column No. 9

Glacial water from OK,

Okjökull, Iceland (April 2, 2007)

August 21, 2019 Austerlitz NY

August 25, 2019

Austerlitz NY

ROADSIDE	No. 3

(May 28, 2017)

Snæfellsnes,
ICELAND

September 2, 2019   New York City
(A fresh piece of volcanic ash from the
eruption of Hekla.)

HEKLA, ICELAND 1991

(ACTUAL SIZE RETRO)

September 3 2019 New York City

HEKLA, ICELAND 1991

'Missing' woman
mystery solved

A group of tourists spent
hours Saturday night looking for
a missing woman near Iceland's
Eldgja canyon, only to find her
among the search party.

The group was travelling
through Iceland on a tour bus
and stopped near a volcanic
canyon. Soon, there was word
of a missing passenger. The
woman, who had changed
clothes, didn't recognize the
description of herself, and
joined in the search.

But the search was called
off at about 3 a.m., when it
became clear the missing
woman was, in fact, accounted
for and searching for herself.
— QMI Agency

September 12, 2014   Paris

OCTOBER 18, 2019 NYC

SACRED ROCK!

October 19, 2019   New York

SAGA CLASS BUSINESS LOUNGE

KEFLAVÍK AIRPORT, ICELAND
(September 10, 2019)

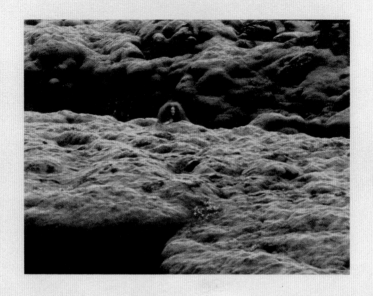

December 1, 2019   New York City

ROADSIDE | No. 9 (June 1975)

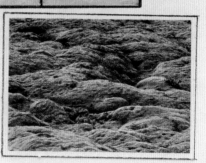

Eldhraun,
ICELAND

My Oz

January 9, 2020   New York

Iceland Chose Me

The island.
The ocean surround.
The going north.
The light.

The emptiness.
The full-up vacancy.

The wholeness.
The absence of parts.

The wholeness of something entire.
The completeness of something whole.

The frequency of white.
The whiteness of white.

The open space.
The nothing of open space.
The accumulation of nothing.

The nothing plus nothing that is still nothing.
The nothing plus nothing that is still transparent.

The horizon.
The horizon that always exaggerates the
  proximity of the horizon.

The possibility of infinity.
The visibility of infinity.

The visibility of the weather.
The visibility of other worlds.
The sense of seeing beyond sight.

The plain circumstance.

The now.
The perpetual now.
The unsuspendable now.
The no-other-than-now.

The treelessness.
The treelessness that provokes no desire for trees.

The views.
The views in the scale of the planet.

The openness.
The continuity.
The fool-me-endlessness.

The being faraway.
The feeling of being surrounded by faraway.

The sense of place.
The palpable sense of place.
The with-my-eyes-closed-sense of place.

The possibility of being present.
The sense of being present.
The being present.

The unsolicited awareness.
The ineluctable awareness.
The sheer awareness.

The solitude.
The solitude of distance.
The solitude of only.
The solitude of no way back.

The cool air.
The cold air.
The nothing but air air.
The air that is spirit not thing.

The wild, wild air.

The largeness of the moon.
The closeness of celestial bodies.
The light from non-terrestrial sources.

The shadows.
The darkness of shade.
The darkness of light withdrawn.

The black earth.
The black sand and the black ash and the
  black rocks.

The pink pumice.

The unnatural looking natural red earth.

The rocks.
The rocks shaped to platonic stardom.
The rocks in their organic ambiguity.

The basalt everywhere.
The basalt with its liquid past.
The basalt: cool and cracked, and whole
  even when in pieces.

The erratics.
The always solitary erratics.

The desert.
The unbroken emptiness of the desert.
The not nothing of the desert.

The absence of threat.

The absence of threat.

The mystery.
The mystery that is chaperone.
The mystery that accompanies the
  light: dark and bright.
The mystery held in simple sight.

The wind.
The many, many forces of the wind.
The indifference of the wind.

The stillness when it is still.
The silence when it is still.

The weather that is wildlife.

The weather.
The weather, sublime and dangerous,
  wild and unknowable.

The simplicity.
The clarity.
The youth.

The chance.
The opportunity.
The desire.

The absence of the hidden.

The absence of secrets?
The feeling of the absence of secrets.

The unused.
The unoccupied.
The uninhabited.

The absence of hierarchy.

The transparence of time and space.
The transparence of place.

The crazy infant geology.
The unworn and the broken and the
  always complete geology.
The self-evident geology.

The water.
The water.

The water.

January 14, 2020 New York City

Icelandic Peacock

March 29, 2020   Austerlitz

THE BETTER HALF

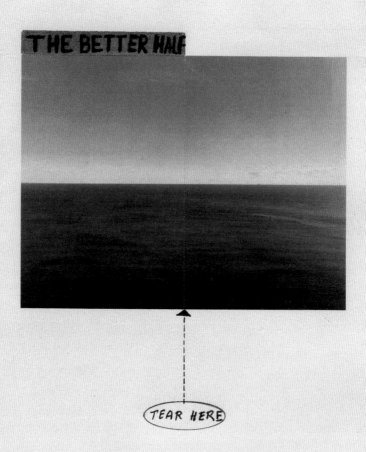

TEAR HERE

May 13, 2020   AVSTERLITZ

EROL HODJOV

THE NINTH SPRING: ONE DAY AT THE KOLIBI

Kapka Kassabova

O n the map, neat little huts are scattered over the two great ranges on each side of the Mesta River – the Rila and the Rhodope. Each hut has a family name attached to it: Pironkovi kolibi, Mangovi kolibi, Panovi kolibi, Leshovi kolibi, Evrovi kolibi, Manovi kolibi, hundreds of kolibi. Koliba is a mountain house for shepherds and other forest dwellers, and the word is used in Greek, Bulgarian and other Slavic languages. It probably goes back to antiquity, just like the way of life it stands for. Near the kolibi are marked-up mandras, or dairy stations, which are also all named. Every settlement, gully, cliff, peak and glade in these highlands is sentient, named after individuals, or ethnic groups like the Turkic pastoralist tribe the Yuruks: Yuruk Peak, Yurukovo. Sometimes they're named after animals too, or plants, trades, or even emotions evoked by long-ago events: Bulls' Huts, the Horses, Nuna's Grave, Birch, Oak Glade, the Fort, Moussa's Ridge, Kara (Black) Mandra, Avramovo, the Oldie, Raichevi Fields, the Water Roller, Cobbler, Potter's Peak, Evil Shadow. Some place names are mysterious, lost like the people who'd have known what they meant: Léevé, Fanos, Nehtenitsa, Ropalitsa. Some of the names in this part of the Rila–Rhodope massif are probably remnants of Thracian, a language now lost. We know that the oldest traceable inhabitants of the massif were the Bessi, a Thracian tribe famed for their resistance to Roman colonisation and for their priestly caste, which contributed to the rise of the philosophical movement of Orphism.

Every square centimetre of this long-inhabited massif is encoded with story, even on the map. This cartographic business absorbed me, and I imagined that the place names still served their purpose, that these highlands bristled with multi-generational communities of cows and sheep, goats and humans, horses and watering stations, cobblers' workshops and storytellers by the fire.

But the mountain was silent at dusk, silent in the dawn that breaks golden over blue-green folds, doubly silent – once with remoteness and twice with abandonment.

I first came here with Erol, only days after arriving in the nearby riverine town of Yakoruda in southern Bulgaria. The Mesta River is smack in the heart of the southern Balkans, equidistant from the Adriatic Sea to the west and the Black Sea to the east, and running into the Aegean Sea to the south. I was still hill-shocked by the forbidding topography along which I had travelled. The two mountains squeeze the river like a birth canal. You travel along the geological fault out of sheer fright and faith, seeing neither the end nor the beginning.

The river itself starts its 230-kilometre journey just south of the Balkans' highest and coldest place – Rila's Musala Peak (2,925 metres). By the time you reach the top, you understand its name: you *are* mus-Allah, 'near God' in Arabic.

Many minor tributaries birth the river, but I came to be near the two major ones, named with poetic symmetry White Mesta and Black Mesta. Locals say that the names are inspired by the white stones in one and the black stones in the other. Erol hadn't been to the source of either, because the further you climb upstream, the less hospitable the ground, the darker the glades, the more frequent the bears and the more sudden the accidents.

'White Mesta originates in Djéenem Déré,' Erol said. 'Which says it all.' Djéenem Déré means Hell's Gully in Turkish.

Yakoruda, Erol's birthplace, is a handsome mountain town with a famed weekend market, a mosque and a church whose bells once sang with human voices. Yakoruda means literally the Great Ore; the mountains to the south had been mined since antiquity. In the 1950s geologists found intact tools inside the sealed tunnels and, astonishingly, woven baskets and wooden ladders from before the Roman colonisation, preserved thanks to the lack of oxygen. Yakoruda straddles the massif, with the Rila to the north and the Rhodope to the south. To get to the town from the riverside road, you crossed one of several bridges. In the reinforced basin, the shallow river glinted at sunset, strewn with rubbish. It was hard to imagine that in the last big flood, the tributaries had merged and swept away roads and houses. But the following winter, during heavy rainfall, I saw the river unfurl like a dragon from its sleep and wipe out bridges.

Yakoruda and the entire Mesta basin is home to a diverse Pomak population, whose syncretic culture preserves centuries of social, spiritual, geographic and ethnographic meaning. Some of the women still wore distinctive, bright shalwar trousers, floral headscarves and hand-knitted cardigans and tunics, while the old men were distinguished by a small knitted skullcap or a beanie.

Erol's family owned a grocer's shop, but his passion was landscape photography. He was a slight man in a down-stuffed jacket, dressed as if suffering from a chronic chill. But the summer evenings were, in fact, like winter. Erol grew up in the shadow of a totalitarian regime, a second-class citizen stripped of human rights, living under a forcibly changed name. This is how the entire Muslim community – both ethnic Turks and the Bulgarian Muslims, known as Pomaks – lived for nearly thirty years (1964–1990).

Erol wanted to show me his favourite area, where he'd come to regain his sanity ever since he was a child. He'd been eleven at the time. They were a prominent Yakoruda family. His parents had refused to have their names changed, and his father was hiding in the hills with others when the army arrived and kicked the door in. A soldier hung a rifle on Erol's shoulder and held him at gunpoint as a shield: 'Boy,' he said, 'let's see if we can find your father.' They forced him to open cupboards, so that if the father was armed, he would kill his own son first. After that, Erol lost his speech. He couldn't speak for a year. It was only after they took him to a traditional healer who performed a bullet-melting ritual with water to 'lift his fright' that he began to recover. And that's when he started coming to 'The Eye'.

The Manure

The place Erol wanted to show me was an area called Guvnishta, roughly meaning 'the Manure' – a name that summed up the history of this place, which had been home to animals for generations. The road we took climbed through a series of meadows and glades, rising and descending like an alpine melody between a switchback road and White Mesta, continuing up to an altitude of 2,000 metres, where it stopped near Nehtenitsa, the southern gateway to the Rila National Park. The Manure was halfway up, at a height of 1,200 metres, and to reach it we abandoned the car and climbed over a wooded mound called Raina Mogila. Mogilas, or mounds, are another recurring feature of this landscape. Many of these mounds, also called by human names, are believed to have tombs or other ancient or medieval remains underneath.

'As children we came to look for buried gold,' Erol said. 'Now the treasure hunters do it.'

Small holes and piles of earth, as if dug by moles, spoke of recent visits from prospectors looking for signs of buried relics. They were one of several destructive forces in the region. Another was the endemic corruption, which had led to a chronic neglect of cultural heritage, laying it open to chancers who were quick to sell any treasure they found to wealthy behind-the-scenes buyers.

'I'm glad we found nothing as kids. That way, I can still believe.'

Where there is ruin, there is hope for a treasure, wrote the Persian poet Rumi in the thirteenth century.

We passed through a forest path like an arboreal tunnel. This is what Erol called 'The Eye' because at certain times of day – like now, before dusk – you seemed to be staring into a giant green iris with a light-tunnel for a pupil.

A large woolly dog came over, wagging. Her left ear was severed. Behind her came a mare with a skinny man astride, wearing a beanie. His sun-leathered face bore the startled expression of one who hasn't seen visitors for a long time. The two recognised each other as fellow Yakorudans, and he invited us for a coffee at their koliba.

This is when I saw them in the flesh: the houses with human names. Some had terraces and porches. Crumbling houses in stone, earth and wood, the size of a large two-storey country cottage, but here the ground floor had been for animals. They were now engulfed by greenery. The novice eye could take in the lie of the land and, distracted by its lushness, miss them altogether.

'In my childhood, it was still busy up here,' Erol said. 'These were cultivated fields.' His grandparents had owned pasture land, now abandoned.

We climbed to the koliba with the smoking chimney. The skinny man's son and mother sat on tree stumps and drank coffee. They all had sharp, eagle-like features. The son's wife was here too, shouting at the sheep while Mehmed, the father, closed the outdoor pen. Four dogs, all with a severed ear, rose to greet us or stop us.

'They're mean,' said the son. His name was Emin. 'They attacked our colt. 'Cause they didn't recognise it as the pack.'

Woolly puppies with intelligent eyes huddled under a Russian UAZ (classic armoured off-road vehicles). Their ears were severed. The females had their left ear cut, the males the right.

'The younger it's done, the better,' Mehmed said. 'So they forget.'

This was tradition – to make the dogs meaner, he explained, and give them better hearing. I'd been told this before and the rationale struck me with its irrationality, on top of its brutality.

''Cause they come face to face with wolves and thieves,' the explainer always added. The puppies looked traumatised under the car. This practice was still widespread. Animal rights counted for little in these remote parts where, within my lifetime, human rights too had suffered multiple and devastating blows.

These dogs were all Karakachanki, a highly prized pedigree breed native to Bulgaria and used throughout the southern Balkans. They are legendary herding dogs of phenomenal intelligence, strength, loyalty and independence.

'How would *you* feel if someone cut off your ear?' I couldn't help myself. Mehmed smiled and shrugged it off.

'Anyway,' he said through his few remaining teeth, though he was only fifty-two. 'Their ears are ugly.'

Seeing the mutilated puppies made me want to turn away from these people. This is what I would have done, but for the pandemic. I had been planning to travel along the length of the Mesta river, but the geography of my journey had been compressed by the closure of the Bulgarian–Greek border. I spent longer in fewer places. Breadth became depth. I climbed mountains, talked to people without taking notes, slept in afternoon meadows and got bitten by poisonous spiders I didn't know existed.

'What's it like, this way of life?' I asked the small family.

'This way of life is over,' said Emin, a fag hanging from his lip. He was twenty-eight, skinny like his father but more intense, his forehead lined. 'Look at these weeds. We're the last ones.'

His grandmother Badé, a stony-faced woman of tiny stature, said nothing, but smiled impishly. Mehmed rolled up a fag, glad of the company. There was a gruffness about the Osmanovi family, a remoteness, and underneath it – something else that felt buried like a secret inheritance. I asked to come and spend a day with them, surprising them and myself. I'd never had an interest in pastoralism. In the Scottish Highlands, where I live, it is a vanished way of life. Farming is a pedestrian, mechanised, lowland business; sheep graze all year round, cows are behind fences, free-range is about as wild as it gets, and the only land-trace of pastoralism is in the forgotten drove roads.

Erol and I passed through 'The Eye' again, this time closed because the forest was ready for sleep, and he said:

'There was a tragedy in this family, from the time of the changing of the names. I don't know the details, but Emin is named after his grandfather.'

The Karakachanka that had greeted us saw us off to the car, and watched us from Raina's Mound as we drove downhill to the lights of Yakoruda.

'She too is lonely,' said Erol of the bitch, or perhaps the river. I wasn't sure whether the 'too' referred to himself or the shepherd family, or me, or some universal condition. Here, in the alpine light where the outlines of things were all that remained and all that was needed of an evening, the land embodied his words.

At seven in the morning, Emin picked me up in town in his UAZ, which he'd bought after he ditched his German jeep, because 'the Western ones conk out'.

The back roads were dug out by a summer of rain, 'the likes of which I don't recall', Emin said. Summers here were normally dry.

Emin had a degree in ecology, and his wife a degree in law. They met at university. But there were no jobs for them in Yakoruda. When he asked for a post in the ecology section of the local authority, the mayor was upfront: you don't vote for me, you're not a member of my party, there's no job for you. Extreme party politics were a symptom of endemic nationwide corruption and had emptied towns and villages of their able-bodied men and women. Emin and his wife were 'a mixed marriage': he from the Pomak community of Bulgarian-speaking Muslims, and she a Christian from another town.

'The other option was to bugger off abroad. But we want to live here.'

So he cut his losses and invested in fifteen sheep. Then he bought more.

'Dad joined me. And Grandma grew up here, so she was happy.'

They had 130 now. The family had always had animals, but even so, it was a bold move to try and survive on small-scale organic farming. All the more given that Emin had previously had a well-paid job as the right-hand man to a wealthy local entrepreneur. Bitter to see Emin quit, his employer had sent him off with, 'You're gonna fail with your pathetic sheep.' Emin's wife worked as an administrator in a Greek-owned sewing factory that made upmarket lingerie for France. Sometimes she came up to help with the sheep. Sewing workshops, often Greek-owned, began to mushroom in the small towns of southern Bulgaria in the late 1990s, making use of captive labour. In these anonymous buildings, women who didn't want to emigrate earned £300 in a good month making clothes for Hugo Boss, ASOS and other well-known labels. In summer, seamstresses decamped en masse to pick fruit in western Europe. This became a Covid-spreading corridor throughout 2020, when seasonal workers returned home in infected groups.

The three-generational family made a living from the sheep. But there was milk only in the warmer months, not in winter when the flock was kept in a lower pen near the town, where they liked to munch on fir branches brought to them in bunches. Ten litres of milk made five kilos of cheese. A kilo sold for ten lev or £4.50. At the height of the season, Emin got forty litres of milk a day. That was 200 lev or £90.

'Come, there's breakfast,' said Badé Osmanova. The Karakachanki wagged with recognition. 'Keep away from them all the same,' said Emin.

I took off my shoes and crossed the threshold of the koliba. It felt different from last night. I was now an invited guest of the heirs of three old Rila highland clans: Osmanovi, Tsarankovi, Pironkovi. Their names were on the map. Their names *were* the map.

'The Osmanovi married within for a while,' Emin said with a smile. 'To keep the fortune in the family. But nobody knows where that fortune went!'

And now I was inside, eating Badé's fluffy doughnuts with home-pasteurised sheep's cheese by the red-hot iron stove. Two rooms of the house were still in use. They were cosy, whitewashed, with beds and rugs, a humble home that stayed warm in winter and cool in summer because of the thick walls.

The day was structured. First, Emin milked the sheep and the few goats into a bucket. One by one, Mehmed guided them through the milking pen. It took about an hour. Emin said he used to get carpal tunnel pain from the repetitive motion, but no longer. It was not a time for conversation, for the animals brought a raw energy when they were herded into his arms and between his knees. I began to distinguish facial expressions and breeds.

'This one's Pramenka, a Romanian breed.' It was curly furred, with horns.

'This one is Assaf, from Israel. A cross between Awassi and East Friesian.'

Words that brought in the Fertile Crescent.

'This one is Marishka.'

A breed from the Maritsa River. Maritsa, also know as Evros and Meriç, is one of three major rivers that spring from Musala Peak, and it crosses Bulgaria, Greece and Turkey.

'Alinka, come on, darling,' he said to another. His favourites had names.

'Come on, you piece of shit,' to one which resisted. 'This one's stubborn. I sweat to get any milk out of her.'

It was true. The sheep had an expression of resistance: I refuse to be a milking machine!

Emin was on the lookout for different breeds. He'd wanted to buy a few dozen highly prized Sharplaninska Pramenka from the highlands of North Macedonia, but because of EU restrictions he couldn't get them across the border.

The few remaining lambs were kept to one side, and the milking was done once they had fed to their heart's content. A few of the mothers didn't have enough milk left, and he let them through unmolested.

'This one is a Vakla [Black] Marishka breed.' He struggled with the last one, which resisted too. 'A bad apple.'

There were five litres in the bucket that morning. It was late summer, and there'd be no evening milking. Badé and Emin sieved the milk through a cloth into a bucket and a sterilised plastic tub. Everything was washed and reused. They couldn't afford waste. The milk was taken straight away to the mandra in town and sold. Up here, there was no electricity and no storage facilities.

Next, Emin and Mehmed took the sheep out to pasture, wanting to get the best hours of the day before the afternoon heat.

'You and I can go for a wander,' said Badé and put on her wellies. 'I'll show you my school and some tasty water. Do you have shoes?'

In the highlands, you don't wear sandals because of the thorns and snakes. Shorts and sandals are for tourists and children. When Emin rolled up his tracksuit I saw how white his leg was, compared to his dark face and arms, like a man of different parts.

Badé

'Here, I saw the adder here.' Badé struck the path with her stick. 'I crushed its head.'

She told me of other reptilian encounters – all her life snakes and lizards had crossed her path, she said, and there had been many freak accidents, like when she stepped on a razor blade as a child and the wound became septic. Up here there was no medical help, so her parents treated the cut with folk remedies – cobwebs, mulched-tobacco poultices and the inside of raw sheep hides, used by shepherds as a blood-stauncher.

Badé found a stick for me too. This was part of the ritual: you go into the hills, and if you don't bring a stick, you look for one on the ground. This has practical and symbolic use. It is the staff of the nomad, the wanderer, the witch of the forest. You use it for fruit felling, river crossings, pointing at things and self-defence.

'I've never trusted doctors,' she said, and rolled up her baggy trousers under the floral dress to reveal a badly swollen knee. 'I put vinegar compresses on it and make do.'

She was in pain. 'But if I stop walking, I'll fall down and die.'

So we pressed on. Her pace was fast.

For an hour or two, we scaled a series of alpine meadows, stopping here and there to pick red oregano, juniper berries on prickly bushes, something that looked like the valuable wild cumin of the Rhodope but couldn't be, because this was Rila, and a camomile-like yellow flower called tansy. 'Once, we picked it for the wholesale herbalists,' she said, 'but it's been forgotten.'

'It wards off dragons,' she added casually, and we moved on, our pockets stuffed with herbs. The tansy is one of those medicinal herbs that has fallen out of favour, despite its broad-spectrum properties.

We left behind the mixed conifer forest and entered the realm of the dwarf mountain pine, found in Rila above 2,000 metres. In some places it has become invasive, like the broom of Scotland, because of soil erosion, forest felling and other climatic changes brought on by human activity in the past seventy years. Until the Communist state began to exploit nature in the late 1940s, Rila–Rhodope had been completely pristine. The massif retains its pre-industrial status today, but there are big environmental threats from quarries and logging. The air thinned as we climbed, leaning on our sticks. We followed some fox prints and saw wolf excrement. Wolves are a pest to shepherds, and always have been – they attack the pen in packs, especially at night or in fog – that's why you can't have 'weak dogs'. Her old Karakachanka was so good, she guarded 300 sheep. She spoke about that dog without emotion, the way she spoke about herself.

'This was all fields,' Badé said. 'Oats, tatties, rye. Wheat doesn't grow here. And look at it now. Look at this forest.'

Rewilding is often seen as a positive thing, but for Badé the triumph of nature over culture was a loss so deep she had no words for it.

We arrived at a high plateau scattered with semi-abandoned houses; each had once been home to two families. Some were still used in summer by relatives who sowed oats and potatoes, and harvested their fruit trees for preserves. She hit a plum tree with her stick and we ate the blue plums from the ground.

'Plums are my favourite,' she said. In summer, she made plum leathers on wooden boards to chew on in winter. A few weeks ago, a massive hailstorm had caught her here, while she was out with the sheep. 'You could scream with terror, but who would hear you? We hid under the plum tree.'

'The sheep love plums. They don't go for thyme or oregano. They're like me – they graze what I graze.'

A gravestone above a house marked the resting place of the family member who had found a pile of gold coins in the river – part of the now-lost family fortune.

'But I bet there's still a string of coins somewhere,' she grinned.

We stopped at a drinking spout attached to an old bathtub. How did they bring a bathtub here in the first place? On horseback.

'Have a drink,' she said. The water was cold and bodiless. The springs of Rila were legion. Rhodope was drier.

'I need water from nine springs,' Badé said. 'I've got six, three more to go.'

The number nine recurs in Bulgarian folk tales, songs and spells. You cross nine mountains to reach the tenth. 'What's the water for?' I asked.

'For fright,' she said, and marched on in her wellies, not one to dwell on things.

'This is the school.'

The teachers had lived in the two-storeyed house. The kids walked in small groups from their kolibi, sometimes in snowstorms, sometimes for hours. Badé went to a ruined shed – the oven. The large round clay dishes were still there: one for bread, another for banitsa, or rolled pastry. A round hand mirror was attached to a nail, the alpine meadow caught inside it.

She adjusted her headscarf for a selfie, our faces cheek to cheek. I had lost my stick.

'Let's go in the shade,' she said. 'Like the sheep, I like shade.'

We sat on the steps of her school before heading back for lunch, the plunging, jaw-dropping panorama of Rila–Rhodope spread out at our feet in all shades of rippling blues and greens.

For centuries, immense herds moved like white duvets over the hills. Wealthier families had up to several thousand head. Here in these Balkan highlands had been the Earth's great animal cities whose clock had been the moon. Animals and humans moved with the seasonal cycle, round and round, from solstice to solstice, winter pasture to summer pasture, climbing and descending, setting up a koliba for the summer, for the night, blowing out last season's ashes to make a new fire.

Pastoralism has a long history in the southern Balkans. Among the highlanders, the most distinctive to this day are the Karakachans, who gave their name to pedigree breeds of horses, donkeys and sheep as well as dogs. The Karakachani (Sarakatsani) of Bulgaria and Greece speak Greek and often Bulgarian too. *Kara-kachan* means 'black fugitive' in Turkish, and indeed, the women wore heavy layers of black wool. But that is an external label. They self-identify as Vlahi (Βλάχοι). In a broader context, Vlahi were simply the transhumant peoples of the southern Balkans, living with their flocks in the major mountain ranges in summer and on the Aegean plains in winter. These last nomads of Europe were not landowners, but traded their superior animal products for other goods as they travelled in seasonal caravans through settled communities. Then there are the Vlachs or Aromanians, a Romanian-speaking, nationless minority with a distinctive shepherding culture, scattered through the southern Balkans. The Vlachs of the Rila–Rhodope are associated with equine knowledge, forestry and log transportation in what remains Europe's most inaccessible terrain. As the place names in this region hint, there are also the mighty once-nomadic Yuruks – *yürük* means 'walker' in Turkish.

The ancestors of Badé are probably a blend of Thracian Bessi and others – in turn Romanised, Christianised, Islamised, Slavicised; on it goes. But the essence remains – they are the original people of the mountain. Kolibi people. The Osmanovi family were at the more settled end of pastoralism. Grazing was done within a certain perimeter of their mountain, while living in a koliba settlement. The early-twentieth-century borders between Bulgaria, Greece, Turkey and Yugoslavia were the beginning of the end of the last great transhumance movements of Europe. Pastoralism survived – but closer to home.

Now, in the shade, I had to ask Badé about her husband Emin.

She had been twenty-five when she was widowed. Mehmed had been five, his sister three.

'We were together for six years, and in the seventh year they killed him.'

Emin had not wanted to change his name during the 1971–3 terror campaign against Bulgaria's Muslims. The campaign aimed to change old Arabic and Turkish names to 'Bulgarian' ones, in order to uncouple them from Islam and to destroy all Pomak cultural traditions, from burials to weddings, from graveyards to the immensely rich textile and decorative tradition whose most visible expression are the flower-patterned shalwars. It was part of a Communist policy of cultural homogenisation through the destruction of the country's Ottoman heritage. Between 1948 and 1989, the state carried out periodic assaults on its different Muslim minorities, resulting in a mass exodus to Turkey and elsewhere. One day, while working up at Nehtenitsa, Emin had been savagely beaten. He died in hospital. Typically, the family received no compensation or apology from the state, even after their real names were restored in 1990.

On the way down, we drank from another spout.

'Two more to go,' Badé said, and handed me my stick. She had found it by the plum tree.

Later, when I was chatting to Mehmed outside the koliba, Badé disappeared. I asked where his mother was. 'To collect water from the ninth spring,' he said. It's what she has done ever since Emin's death. Once she found the nine springs, she started all over again. Rila never ran out of springs.

Mehmed

T he sheep were resting in the shady pen, Emin had gone to town to sell the milk, Badé had vanished after a nap. Mehmed had boiled some potatoes.

'I'll eat them cold tonight, I guess,' he said.

We sat on stumps in the shade of an apple tree and drank oregano tea. Mehmed had a gaunt, unshaven face and most of his teeth were gone, the look of one who had gazed into the abyss more than once but hadn't spoken about it. He was worn out, but the spark that was gone from his body was still in his warm, dark eyes.

For a quarter century, Mehmed worked in a factory for logging machines. Then the regime fell and Russians bought it 'and fucked it up'. After working without pay for too long, penniless and itching for the hills, he became a hired herder. Not just anywhere, but in the upper highlands of Rila, 2,500 metres above sea level. This meant spending entire seasons on his own, with up to 200 cows. These are places only accessible by foot and horseback. He'd always had a horse and a dog with him.

He'd lived for a season in a glacial lake district called Kazan (Cauldron) Lakes.

'All cliffs, cliffs and nothing else. One time there was fog and snow blizzard. I went looking for wood for the fire and thought I was a goner. But the mare found the way back to the koliba. Click-click, step by step.'

His only company there all winter had been two lost German hikers who spent the night in the koliba with him; to his surprise it appeared on their map as a shelter.

'In summer, there are other shepherds, but winters are just you and the wind. One winter, I didn't see a soul for months. One day, I put on my boots and walked two kilometres through the blizzard to the nearest chalet.'

Better die than go insane.

'There was one guy there, all by himself and getting freaked out too.' They had a coffee, then he walked back in the blizzard.

'So many memories. The time when I sat out six months at Ibar . . .'

Ibar is an austere metamorphic peak just east of Musala, 2,666 metres high and famous for the extensive pastures below it. What about the bears and the wolves?

At night, even here at the kolibi, foxes and wolves made the Karakachan dogs howl all night, especially the puppies. 'You can't close your eyes,' Emin had told me. He couldn't sleep here. But Mehmed and Badé were used to the all-night concerts.

'Anyway, the only animal I'm afraid of is man.'

The memories poured out – of waking up in his tent buried in snow and digging out a tunnel, stories of elemental endurance, but these were the highlights of his life. I guessed that he liked it this way.

'It's not that I like it. But I got used to it and now I can't live in town.'

At the foot of Ibar Peak, under a rock, there is a notebook in a plastic bag for the rare hikers to leave a comment. But he had never written his name in it.

In Britain, we speak of bagging Munros, conquering peaks. The people of the mountain don't use such grand words.

''Cause the mountain is not the same thing at all times. It's good when the weather's good. And when the weather turns, it kills you. The mountain has the last word. That's all.'

We went walking along the Manure's erased paths, like through a ruined ancient city, and he narrated each ghost house – who had lived there and when they had left. Some only twenty years ago. There had been a threshing field; the threshing had been done with horses. A mare with a colt grazed in a meadow – the neighbour's. He came up from town to see them once a week.

'Horses are the smartest animals,' he said. 'I'd give up everything I have before I give up my mare.'

'Inside Raina Mogila, there's a horse and a cart,' he said, and his eyes twinkled. 'Roman and made of gold, so they say. But who needs a golden horse? You need your horse alive.'

During the forced changing of the names, the Manure had served as refuge to traumatised families. In the wake of Emin's murder, Badé had packed up her life in town and moved in with her parents here; they had never really left the koliba. They lived in self-sufficiency, with their fields and animals. This is how she had survived – on the generosity of Rila. The koliba had fed her and her children, restored her to herself. Mehmed had no memory of his father.

'I'll eat these potatoes tonight, when they're cold,' he said again and smiled, his way of inviting me to stay. 'Can you smell the end of summer? It's in the breeze.'

I inhaled.

Emin

'Come on, let's do it!' Emin opened the pen.

It was time for evening pasture. Emin and one Karakachanka led the way, Mehmed rounded off the group, and the rest of the Karakachanki kept the flock together from the sides. Among them was a grey puppy with human eyes that seemed more grown up than the rest.

'Cause he had a hard start,' Emin told me. 'He saw his mother pick up his brother and bite through his throat. Then the ear. Then the vaccines. He knows life is hard.'

The taking out to pasture was not a chatty occasion. It was unrelenting like an exodus, and lasted about two hours. We walked with big strides through glades, puddles, not stopping until we reached pasture. Emin lit a cigarette. He wore galoshes – the village rubber slip-on shoe – with thick knitted socks. Two waist-high Karakachanki were on each side of him. Behind him, the sun declined. The momentum of this walk – a taking out to pasture walk – transformed him from a tense youth to a powerful highlander in his element. He had purpose, he knew the way, and he walked the walk. Without his herd, without the Karakachanki, he wouldn't. They gave him strength. His father had had the same walk, but had passed on the shepherd's crook and was now shadowing his son.

With each step, a vast hinterland unfolded: 10,000 years of pastoralism.

Humans and livestock have cohabited, co-evolved and co-depended, and the cord had been cut loose only yesterday. I saw the cities of grazing animals, close to the stars, the men and women who took the flocks higher, ever higher, and who fed and clothed the Balkan peninsula and the whole Ottoman Empire with meat, dairy, hides and wool. I saw the truth of the folk saying that the mountains birth people while the fields birth pumpkins. And the other one, from the Karakachan shepherds – that the one who ploughs the field is bent in submission, but the one who roams with their flock is upright and unchained.

The kolibi were ruined, but there *was* life among the ruins. In Emin's stride, I saw what could not be put into words: he knew that he was doing more than small-scale farming. He was keeping the koliba fires burning. His family were proud and stubborn, hard-working and unemotional, because that's what it took to survive and still be able to smile among the ruins.

A steep climb to the nearest hill, then a descent via juicy meadows to a tributary of the White Mesta. We stopped at each pasture, but not for long. There was a mix of dynamism and leisure about the taking out to pasture. The sheep too had purpose. They pulled at the grass with their large teeth manically, as in a last supper. They knew they had a bit of time left before sunfall.

'Sheep are demented animals,' said Emin, the colour rising in his cheeks, his eyes lighting up from the walk. 'They eat like demented, they run like demented. Sometimes I feel demented too. Buying sheep, selling sheep, milking sheep, herding sheep. Going round and round in a demented cycle. Come back, you piece of shit!' – to a sheep that strayed into a glade. He was foul-mouthed but never hit the sheep, or the dogs.

We stayed the longest by the brook, because it was so lush. We even sat on the grass.

'It's not hard work,' Emin spat into the wild flowers. 'It's just there's no weekends, no holidays, when you live with animals. But I want to prove that it can be done.'

And there were surprises too, he said. They slaughtered a sheep in spring and what did they find inside? A dead lamb she'd carried for months.

'When she didn't give birth, we realised the lamb had died. She wasted away but then unexpectedly got fat and lived on. Inside her, the lamb was calcified and wrapped in fat. That's how she'd survived.'

Mehmed disappeared and appeared in different parts of the valley, with a dog at his side, or his mare. I imagined that one day, when he was gone, he would be glimpsed by rare visitors to the kolibi, his mare click-clicking through the fog. Badé too might be seen on a full moon, drinking from the ninth spring.

Emin gave me a kilo of fresh cheese and a jar of yogurt, the cleanest food I've ever eaten. We drove down at nightfall, leaving Mehmed and Badé in the room with the stove and the three single beds. High above, the Manure became the outline of a buried world, a giant ancient mound. A single ribbon of smoke connected it to the sky. Behind us, the mountains closed like a gate. ∎

SOETKIN VERSLYPE
Forest, 2020

TALA ZONE

Pascale Petit

1

Father, I have made the iron gate to our building spring open, I have slipped through the inner glass door. I have rung the caretaker's bell and explained why I need to see the cellar and he has let me in. It's as if I've climbed over the gate of Tala Zone before dawn and entered the tiger reserve alone, no jeep to protect me. The spotted deer stand watching, their breath rising in the predawn light, their ears pricked for the slightest twig crack, betraying the arrival of predator.

The track is sandy, glows in the moonlight. I bend down, can see fresh pugmarks, large and round: a male. I am going the right way. The forest guard is asleep in his hut. It is here that the ground slopes down, like these spiral steps. I look up, surprised to see a window at the top of the cellar. I've always dreamt there was a window. I am inside my dream.

But this time, you are alive, Father, able to breathe, thanks to the oxygen machine pumping in a corner of your room. Alive enough for me to have asked you for the number of our building in the

Boulevard de Grenelle, where we lived together when I was a child. Even when I travel as far as India, you are with me and I am re-entering our cellar.

Take a deep breath, do that pursed lip breathing you must do. Watch your heart doesn't race. The pump is exhaling, inhaling and I am walking, walking. No one is allowed inside the core of Bandhavgarh National Park after sunset. No one is allowed inside this cellar at the bottom of our building. But the caretaker has heard my story and unlocked the door. He told me not to stay long because there are rats down here and a bad smell from the poison.

I press the light switch at the top of the stairs and the moon comes out from behind a tree. Round and round I go, right down to the bottom, to the earth floor. I must not wake the monkeys: they must not bark a warning. Here is the smell. I recognise it as male tiger spray, and the stench of the remains of a carcass, just behind the lantana bushes. A rat snake slithers past on the path in front of me.

Why is the cellar forked, Father? Why does it grow narrower? My path is flanked by thorny bamboo, by evergreen sal trees. Why is everything coated in dust? How small must I become, to pass under the roof that bulges with electric cables like banyan vines? How do I know which are live? And why do the sal trees and the crocodile bark trees and the dhok trees look like rough doors that I must open? I don't remember these doors from my recurring dream. I don't remember this ticking, like a hundred clocks behind each door labelled with a numbered plaque. I think of other cellars, how going to the toilet in a restaurant always means going downstairs, deep into the musty Parisian underworld with its honeycomb of limestone crypts and shallow drains.

I'm in the cellar's forest and the moon is shining. Between me and the moon there's a man with a cloth over his face. Is it you, Father?

I never thought it was you when I was six, but I'm grown-up now. It must be you, because who else would have sent me to the cellar, told me to count to a hundred but not to go down to the very end because a fire was there with tigers leaping out?

I open the door to the first electricity meter and you are there, Father, your fists held out, asking me to guess which one. I point to the left and you open it, saying, 'Look! Precious gold.' But what I see is an amber eyeball. Then you close your fist again and I can't see you, or where the way back out is, everything is dark, and the moon has dipped behind the trees. Then I realise you're holding the eye of a newborn tiger cub. That its other eye is in your other hand.

You are sitting on a child's mattress, and you're asking me to face you, so you can stitch up my eyelids and lips with bamboo thorns. You say I mustn't cry. I should remember that the caretaker is upstairs, that the forest guard will hear me if I scream. But I don't. There is only the cellar with a forest inside and a series of rough doors that I must open. I can still see through the thorns but everything is red and blurred. My nightdress is pulled up around my neck so I tug it down. I can't open my mouth to scream, so the sound I make is strangled, as if I'm still asleep.

From now on I won't speak to anyone. I will be a mute daughter, just like a newborn cub, or make only muffled squeaks.

I open the second door and find myself in a hide, high up in a mahua tree. I sit watching the Malabar pied hornbill bring figs to his mate. The female has walled herself up in a nest hole in the tree opposite, cemented herself in with a fruit paste, so no snake can eat her eggs. There's a rush of air when the male lands with his huge wingbeats. I watch as he regurgitates his meal and pipes it through the great curved bill with its black-and-yellow casque down into the tip of hers through the slit of her cell. He arrives every hour and each time he feeds her I feel stronger.

I retrace my steps to where the cellar forks. Now I must go down the right fork. The roof is lower as if only made for children. Here too there are doors rough as tree bark and so many electric cables it's like walking under the tails of langurs and leopards in a grandmother banyan. You are calling me, Father, from behind the first door. It opens and you show me your good-luck charm that you've carried since childhood, a leopard's paw. Now the deer watching me from the end of the tunnel have multi-branched antlers, a ghost forest in the dusty predawn light and as I descend they get bigger, towering above me like forest gods. An elephant calf presses himself against me, cuddling me with his trunk. His eyes are brandy topazes. He too is a god.

The next door opens to a night black as bear fur, its muzzle bleeding after eating honey baited with explosives. I want to ask you how my teddy-bear mama's face exploded, Father. Who would plant gunpowder inside honey? But you're telling me to dance. You push a thin cane through my nose and sing and huff, sing and puff, while you jerk the cane, teaching your bear cub the steps. I have to remind myself that it is I who have brought the wonders of my grandmother's jungles into the cellar. My Indian grandmother, who took care of me when I was a baby, whom I will return to soon. As I think of her, I start to dance backwards, out of the meter cupboard and down to the very end of the cellar.

I open the last door on the left of the right fork and there's a peacock inside. I can hear Maman saying how vain you were, how you slept in, then spent every afternoon doing your toilette, before going out to your nightclubs. I've been into the jazz cellar in the rue de la Huchette, next door to the Hôtel Les Argonautes where you lived. But this peacock has a girl's face. She is dressed in a wedding gown with a train made of peacock feathers and no one is here to give her away, there's not even a groom. Her dress is sapphire-emerald as the Earth from space, and her train is erect, rustling like wind through dry grass. Her train surrounds her head in a halo of eyes, all watching me, like atolls in the Indian Ocean held up on waves of plumes. The stars have offered me their eyes, to bear witness. They know what you've done, Father.

I open the last door to the right of the right fork and find a man inside wearing a dust mask. He's whittling a stick. Next to him is a tigress, her paw mangled in a trap. The meters behind her are ticking louder as she weakens. The masked man continues whittling his stick, whistling as he works. He stares through me and looks bored. The tree door is occupied by a jungle owlet, a monitor lizard and a sleepy langur mother with her baby. Spotted deer glance in, alerted by tiger moans.

When the tigress is too weak to hold her head up, the man jabs his stick through her mouth into her throat. She can no longer make tiger-music; the forest guard won't hear her as the man batters her spine. He gets out his skinning knife and slits her down the front. Half an hour it takes him to flay her. Then he wipes his hands and sits on the ground to eat his breakfast on a teak leaf, before digging a hole to bury the flesh and tiger bones to retrieve later. He creeps out of the forest with her pelt.

Father, I have learnt to be quiet as a tree, so quiet even the monkeys come and sleep on me. I am a door no one can open. When I went to live with my grandmother, she told me stories about the jungle. I put all her creatures in the cellar, so I could fall asleep at night. Every time I was locked in, they were there waiting for me. Thirty-four years I survived with her animals' help. Then you reappeared and I realised the animals were wounded, many dead, their skins ripped off, their bones pulled out and sold in the market.

2

By my fortieth birthday I was nothing but boneless meat buried in the ground. No one could piece me together.

Then my grandmother told me the story of meeting a tiger when she was a baby. She had been placed in a tent in the jungle and left alone. She remembered seeing the fiery creature enter the tent and approach her cot, but she hadn't been afraid. She'd held out her hand and touched its fur. It looked down at her, then went back out. That was when I decided to go to India and see tigers for myself, to try to get up close as she had done.

Father, let me tell you what I saw. Come with me, I am at the gate of Tala Zone, the core of Bandhavgarh. You are long dead now. Hundreds of tigers have been poached. I want to understand why anyone would harm them. I want to understand why you harmed me. I go into the park alone, at night, night after night. I watch the poachers at work. I see them set their traps, their snares, and hide their skinning knives under a rock.

But I have also seen Bheem, with his cleft nose and battle eye, his sunrise-striped hulk, as he lies cooling in the stream. I have seen a treepie pick the scraps from between his teeth. I have seen a doe carrying a langur on her back when the monkey was drunk on mahua flowers. I have seen a vine snake steal the eggs from weaver nests – they hung from the tree of life like teardrops. I have seen the Indian roller in flight, the azure skies and lapis seas of his wings! I have seen the tailorbird sewing two leaves into a nest.

I have seen the paradise flycatcher! I have seen his midnight-blue face, his ice-crystal tail streamers trailing through the branches of burning trees, and he did not melt, even though the brainfever bird called, while the temperature soared. I have heard the cicadas singing to fever pitch as the monsoon breaks. And yet the paradise bird flew, trailing his snowflakes like windows in a nursery hung with silver chimes. I have seen him flying like the last winter on Earth.

I have walked in full moonlight, in the tracks of Bhitri as she hunts. I have stood at the rim of her ravine as she emerges in the cool of sunset. I have heard the monkeys bark a warning from the treetops, the chitals' high-pitched calls echoing all around me, the sambars' plosive alerts in the forest-theatre. I have come face to face with the huntress. I have seen her eyes trying to escape their confines, the pupils darting back and forth in their orbits. Then I have followed her home, back to her ravine cave, and heard her cracking the bones of her fawn. I was cunning as Bhitri, whose name means 'innermost jungle'.

Listen! If you are good, you'll see what she sees – the air quivering with scented paths into the perfumed forest. You'll hear the vulture rapture on Rajbhera Meadow, the snuffle of jackals as they gather. Come with me to the feast. Bandhavgarh Fort shimmers in the background, its cliffs laced with griffon nests. And here, halfway up the plateau, lies Vishnu, surrounded by cobras.

I have heard the trees of light and the trees of darkness whispering to each other, their leaves shaking like tiny maracas. I have made friends with every door, every tree in the forest – even the tree of secrets, the one a leopard lies in. She has dragged you up to a lightning fork, where she licks your face as if to wash you. ∎

KARLITO MILLER ESPINOSA (MATA RUDA)
Agave / Noble, 2014

A WIDER PATCH OF SKY

Letters from Javier Zamora
and Francisco Cantú

Javier Zamora and Francisco Cantú met at a literary event devoted to the US–Mexico border in the winter of 2018. The two writers struck up a friendship that was at first tentative and uncertain. They soon discovered that, from 2008 to 2012, Francisco had worked as a Border Patrol agent in the same areas where Javier had crossed and been apprehended in 1999.

In 2019, Javier began writing a memoir about his childhood migration from El Salvador to Tucson, Arizona, where he was finally reunited with his parents after an eight-week journey. From the time he left El Salvador, Javier was accompanied by three men, Chele, Marcelo and Chino, and a woman, Patricia, traveling with her twelve-year-old daughter, Carla. During their first attempt to enter the US, his original group was subsumed by much larger groups of immigrants led by a human guide, known as a coyote. In the desert, Marcelo and Chele went missing. After being detained by the Border Patrol, the remaining members of his group were deported back to Nogales, Mexico. It would take them two more trips through the desert during the brutal June heat before they finally succeeded in reaching Tucson – the first American city Javier, Chino, Patricia and Carla had ever set foot in.

In September 2019, Javier contacted Francisco for help finding the exact locations of his three border crossings. These letters recount their subsequent trips along the Arizona–Sonora border.

*

Javier,

I was trying to remember which album it was that we listened to first as we drove north toward the border – was it *Harvest Moon*, or was it *Graceland*? I remember that it was late in the afternoon, and that we had woken up that morning at the foothills of the Sierra Madre in central Sonora, just after sunrise. We began the day by climbing with Roberto to the top of Rancho Tepúa's highest butte, hunching over to make our way through the overgrown brush, our shoes filling with dirt and sand as we trudged up the steep hillside, loosening the soil behind us. When we finally arrived at the top we looked out across the landscape – west to the river valley and east into the high sierra, a stark topography forced up by tectonic plates and carved away by waterways snaking into the distance. As we surveyed the surroundings, you broke open unfamiliar fruits for us to taste and captured strange beetles, letting them crawl across your hands. Roberto identified far-off landmarks for us and pointed out that we were high enough to look down upon the backs of the vultures and hawks circling below. It was then that you asked me to take your picture, your arms outstretched like you were the king of the mountain, king of that entire landscape, as far as the eye could see.

It was the middle of September and the desert was still green and humid with monsoon rain – so green that it was hard to think of it as a desert at all. We had arrived at Roberto's ranch the day before, late in the afternoon, and spent the last hours of daylight helping him to clear maguey fields and plant dozens of agaves that would eventually, after six years or more, be harvested and roasted deep underground to make bacanora, the Sonoran mezcal that Roberto's forebears had been distilling for five generations on this very same ranch. After handing me a pickaxe, Roberto showed me how to place the young plants in the ground, telling me how far apart to place them, how deep to dig. You volunteered for a more difficult task, picking up a machete and following him to a part of the field overgrown with chaparral and adolescent mesquite. You watched and listened as he demonstrated the best way to hack away at the brush and the weeds, but you soon revealed you didn't need to be shown – this was the same work you had watched your grandfather do year after year in El Salvador. Later that night, after dinner, we sat with Roberto and his father beneath the sky, watching the moon, the stars and the clouds as if seated in a theater, drinking bacanora and speaking of the infinity of living things that made their home in the desert.

Driving north back to Arizona the next day, listening to *Harvest Moon* and *Graceland*, I assured you not to worry about the bacanora we were carrying with us, despite it being far over the legal amount. We rolled the windows down as Neil Young blared out from the speakers, singing along with the whine of the steel guitar. Our bellies were heavy with food and beer we had consumed a few towns back after visiting with a friend of Roberto, a cowboy who ended up selling us three gallons of sotol distilled that very same morning. The man was dressed, you told me later, just like the coyotes who smuggled you north almost two decades ago – the same boots, the same hat, even the same belt buckle. When *Graceland* began to play through the speakers, I recalled all the times I had listened to the album during the years I spent working for the Border Patrol, convincing myself that the lyrics were somehow about the story of migration: lasers in the jungle, sand falling on children and mothers and fathers, cameras following us in slow motion, a constellation dying in a corner of the sky. After learning about the album's recording in apartheid South Africa during the international cultural boycott, it had also become impossible for me to listen to those songs without considering the appropriation and political disregard that marred their creation. Nevertheless, as we listened to the album I remember how you turned to me – maybe it was during the song 'Homeless' as Ladysmith Black Mambazo called forth the image of wind blowing over a countryside marred by destruction, reminding the listener that here, death might come for them, too – and you said, fuck man, these lyrics are good. I remember wondering in that moment if that's what you felt here in this desert, *homeless*.

The problem at the center of *Graceland*, I realize now, is the same problem embedded all across the landscape of the borderlands: there is irreconcilable discord in the way it contains both violence and freedom, a defining tension that must be held on to even as upbeat rhythms propel us across it. We've both been part of that violence, you and I – but there we were, singing together as we drove across the desert, the residue of its cruelty still hanging unequally between us. What might we be able to reclaim here, I wondered as we continued north, what might be undone, what might be remade?

*

Paco,

Since our trip I've been dreaming, recalling and telling stories to anyone who asked about our time on both sides of the border. I showed strangers and friends pictures of us at Rancho Tepúa, Naco and Agua Prieta. Remember meeting that guy who said he knew Mexican citizens building the border wall? Remember learning Pancho Villa's horse chipped the third marble step of that fancy haunted hotel in Douglas, the Gadsden?

I hadn't been back to Sonora since I was nine years old, in 1999, when my coyote used it as our launching point into the United States. The first American city we stopped at after crossing the Sonoran

Desert was Tucson, where I was reunited with my parents on 11 June. Since 1999, I'd only been back to Tucson once, in September 2017, and that was before I had a green card. I had just published my first book of poems and I naively, but sincerely, thought that I was healed or very close to being healed. Of course I wasn't; I'm still not. I don't think I will ever be completely 'healed'. That first visit back was very difficult because everything seemed to retraumatize me. The heat, the landscape, the helicopters flying over the city, the immigration trucks, everything sparked flashbacks and nightmares. I was a Temporary Protected Status holder at that time, but with the Trump presidency, I feared immigration or local police were going to stop me and ask if I was a legal citizen.

You know what I think really retraumatized me? The fucking helicopters. The first night, from my friend's warehouse roof, I saw helicopters in the distance with their searchlights. I kept thinking they were wormholes to a jail cell and that the helicopters were out to get me, like they were in some patch of desert back when I was nine years old.

My body remembered the anguish, my heart beat faster, my legs ached like they did back then, my back felt like I was still carrying that black backpack with water inside it. I could feel my hand being pulled by Chino – one of the individuals with me since El Salvador – through the cacti and the cattle fields. Knowing exactly where that took place, exactly what patch of desert, was my 'excuse' for returning to Tucson a third time in 2019 – by then, as a legal resident, without fear of being deported.

Paco, that 2019 'research trip', our road trip, was the complete opposite of my first return to Tucson in 2017. Maybe what made the difference was the green card, or maybe it was the safety of being inside a car with you, an ex-Border-Patrol agent who knows the border like the back of his hand. I don't know. But those few September days on both sides of the border made me feel 'safe', or safer than I felt the last time I was in the Sonoran Desert.

From the first moment after you picked me up at the airport and asked if I wanted to help make mezcal, the trip took an unexpected turn, one toward joy. I still cherish that bottle we made together in Tucson – reserving it for very special occasions. The next day, we drove an hour north from Tucson to the Eloy Detention Center, where migrants are detained at a privately run center behind three different types of fence: electric, chain-link and concertina wire. You volunteer at the site, helping migrants with their immigration cases, and that week you were helping a Cuban mother, who'd been in detention for months, reach bail. When the security officers refused to let me enter the facility because I didn't have ICE (Immigration and Customs Enforcement) clearance, I returned to your car and drew what I saw in front of me: people wearing bright orange, dark blue or dark brown jumpsuits behind three different fences. After taking the image in, I wrote a poem I've yet to publish and still haven't gotten right. How can anyone get the images right? I was shocked to see how much the immigration machine had changed since I crossed in 1999; now, it's a more violent monster.

I crossed during the last year of the Clinton administration, when a child below the age of sixteen could not legally be detained for more than forty-eight hours. Year after year, policies have changed and by the time of the Obama administration, children were being detained at private centers like the one at Eloy for much longer than two days. I couldn't help but think that if I'd immigrated ten or twenty years later, I could've been one of the adults wearing uniforms, waiting to hear whether I had been granted refugee status or faced deportation back to El Salvador. Both adults and children are detained for weeks, months, sometimes years, waiting to hear something from the ever-slower immigration system. Helpless, in your car, with the AC at full blast, I couldn't stop crying as I watched adults and teenagers line up to walk from building to building in ninety-degree heat, or playing in the yard during the short time that they were allowed outside. That was a heavy day. I don't remember if we left for Sonora right after that, or early the next day, but we drove through rainstorms to Naco to see if that was where I'd crossed. I'd told you that I remembered two lights on each side of a valley. Two towns, you said, and immediately suspected those lights were Douglas/Agua Prieta and Naco. We drove your 4x4 Nissan Pathfinder on both sides of the border, looking for the corridor my coyotes had used. Naco and Agua Prieta seemed so familiar to me. What clicked in my memory was the plaza in Agua Prieta – the gazebo in the middle of it was still painted white like it was twenty years ago.

We slept at the Gadsden that night, a haunted hotel on the American side of Douglas. The next day we woke up at dawn because you said we would be able to see the lights I saw in 1999. I did. We did. Check. There were also fields on either side of the highway. Check. These two things were the confirmation that I, that you, I don't know who, needed. It felt right. It finally felt like my memories, my flashbacks, were based in reality and not my imagination. Then, we headed to Aconchi, to the Rancho Tepúa mezcal ranch, to the better part of the trip, the part I like to tell people about.

I think that's what I needed out of the desert – a new memory. A memory outside of immigration, outside of my time there. Lately, in poetry and in everything literary, I ask the question: where is the joy? Why can't brown and black bodies exist outside of trauma? Bacanora became an alternative answer to my own trauma, and I'm not talking about drinking as a coping mechanism – which I'm far too familiar with. As Roberto Sr and Jr reminded us at their ranch, when we drunk their favorite-ever batch of bacanora, 'Bacanora needs to be respected and not abused.' I already loved mezcal, loved sotol, but I'd never drank bacanora, the special variety of mezcal made only in Sonora, the state I was deported to twice before successfully crossing into the United States. There is something special, almost romantic, about drinking alcohol made from a plant grown in the same landscape that almost took my life as a child. I immediately understood what Roberto Sr and Jr meant when they said respect.

When we drove through a shallow ford on the way back to Tucson, I saw a white egret, and I don't know if I mentioned it, but I consider egrets a good omen. I like that you remember the machete. I'd forgotten the specifics. In El Salvador, some communities call them corvos, which reminds me of my favorite quote by Salvadoran writer Manlio Argueta, from *One Day of Life* translated by Bill Brow: 'Men are accustomed not to part with their corvos.' It's true. Every morning and afternoon, I watched people – mostly men, but also the few women who worked the fields – walk in front of our house with a corvo strapped around their shoulder. People took their corvos to the market, to church, everywhere. That was lesson number one. Grandpa, to this day, still has a corvo he likes to use for everything: cutting coconuts, slicing pipes, trimming leaves, cutting grass. Lesson two came from Dad, a landscaper, who taught me how to clear fields with a weed whacker and a machete, or hoe, or whatever sharp tool he carried in the back of his black Nissan Frontier.

Experiencing Sonora like this, without urgency, reminded me so much of El Salvador, of the timelessness of work, of the world depicted in Argueta's novels. Of waking up, eating, working, taking a break, eating, napping, working and eating again. It was life. A life I knew in El Salvador – or watched the grown-ups perform – and a life that the headlines, research papers, novels and news-clips don't highlight. From Sonora or El Salvador we hear migration, gangs, narcos, violence. But these places are so much more than that. It's work. It's joy. It's drinking under the stars after a big meal. It's drinking bacanora where it was grown and distilled. No TV. No internet. No phone service. Surrounded by mountains, mosquitoes and bats. It was magical. It's perhaps why I'm a pseudo-brand ambassador for Rancho Tepúa bacanora wherever I go.

One night! One night in the Sierras, under the stars with a father and his son, Roberto Sr and Jr, was all it took. I saw so much love, tenderness and care in their relationship. So much dedication to the work, but also a level of communication between them that I think you and I both yearn for from the men in our lives. These men have stayed and worked the land that is theirs instead of migrating. They believe in the land their family has lived on since the 1800s, and believe in the craft their forebears taught them. They believe in it so much that they kept making bacanora when it was illegal to do so in Mexico. They're a model of what life could've looked like had my father, mother, neighbors, friends and I not left our hometown.

From there, you took me to another moonshiner. And he *did* dress like the coyotes in 1999. I'd forgotten what people wore. It was like he was stuck in time. That outfit, the boots, the belt, the hat . . . Even his thick black mustache. You brought the Sonoran cowboy an alcohol-content measuring tool he had asked for the last time you were there. Transporting goods like that reminded me so much of the coyotes who carried packages, food and letters between El Salvador and the US. Which is probably why I was freaking out about the bacanora once we got to the border. I didn't want any little thing to come between my new green card and the government, not even my favorite mezcal.

As for the music choices, I have to admit I'm new to Paul Simon and Neil Young. Weird, funny or just perfect that you happened to have *Graceland* and *Harvest Moon* in your truck. And yes, the lyrics are fucking good. The sounds too. And to answer your question: as I was walking through the desert, the cloudless sky, the heat, the cold at night, the cacti and brush, the occasional tree, I didn't feel 'homeless'. I felt like I did sitting under the clouds at Rancho Tepúa: part of something bigger. I know that this is romantic. But at nine years old, I didn't register the danger in my logical brain; instead I buried it deep in my body. What *was* bigger than myself back then were the forty adults and three children risking their lives, and the desert itself. I walked past giant saguaros, yuccas and agaves that I now know are used to make bacanora and sotol. I didn't understand what 'homeless' was. I knew that I was walking toward my home. Home being my parents, who I had longed for since the moment each left me: Dad at one, Mom at four years old. Thirst, hunger, none of it mattered, until we ran out of water. But even then, I don't know how to explain it, but I knew I wasn't going to die. I guess this is what I now call hope. But maybe it was love for my parents. I was so sure that I was going to see them again. So sure that we were all going to make it across the border. It's scary. Because now I know how close I was to death.

I'm aware of how fast the beauty of the desert can turn on you. Here, I turn to one of my favorite sentences in your letter: 'The problem at the center of *Graceland*, I realize now, is the same problem embedded all across the landscape of the borderlands: there is irreconcilable discord in the way it contains both violence and freedom.' You're absolutely right. I will go farther and say that our friendship has pushed those two things. You as the 'freedom keeper' and me as the 'freedom seeker'. We're so much more than those things. Citizen or undocumented. Border Patrol or immigrant. These are just a few of the uniforms we've put on. But when we're born, or when we die, it doesn't matter what we have on. And now you and I have another uniform, that of friends.

*

Javier,

When the alarm went off that morning in the Gadsden Hotel, the haunted place on the Arizona border where Pancho Villa rode his horse up the staircase, I remember that it was still dark out. We each switched on our tableside lamps and sat up in our separate beds, trying to keep ourselves from falling back to sleep. You asked me if I had dreamed in the night, and I thought for a moment, unable to remember. I became frustrated, because I had wanted to pay attention to my dreams in that place. When I told you I wasn't sure if I had dreamed, you told me that you had been jolted awake at 2 a.m. You dreamed that you were screaming in the night, you said, that a figure was standing beside your bed, and that I had shaken you awake. I hadn't, of course, and you awoke to find yourself alone in the dark hotel room, with me still breathing in a dreamless sleep on the other side of the room. I've often wondered what it might mean when we dream of our own body dreaming. Maybe by hiding our fear, our screams, inside of a dream, our body is seeking to offer us some kind of protection, to place us at a distance from something that might otherwise be too terrifying to behold.

We wanted to get up before sunrise that morning so that we could see the adjacent valley in the dark, so that you might remember the placement of the lights, the orientation of the towns you would have seen as a child walking north from Douglas and Agua Prieta through the night. We drove out along the train tracks as the first glow hovered at the eastern horizon, and you said that you remembered that too – the tracks. Throughout our trip, I remember being struck again and again by the way you had come to see the landscape, by the things you had been made to look for – the situation of mountains and roads, the thickness or sparseness of brush. You remembered cholla and mesquite and paloverde, you remembered the far-off sound of passing cars, you remembered how many times you crossed pavement and fence lines. You had walked for three nights, you told me, and you asked how many miles that would have been, and why the coyotes would have made you travel so far by foot. I tried to explain the effect of highway checkpoints, the staggering growth of enforcement in towns and cities all along the border, where fortifications and patrols ballooned in the 80s and 90s, forcing crossers to make longer and more dangerous treks through the desert to avoid detection. I was describing, in vague terms, the consequences of 'Prevention Through Deterrence', which, of course, you knew far better than I, because you had lived them, suffered them.

Reading your letter reminded me of certain details I had completely forgotten from our trip. Like the Mexican American man at the hotel bar, for example, who knew Mexicanos making their living by building the wall. I remember how casually he talked about it, like it was a simple fact of life, an issue of work, not politics. He had a union job, he told us proudly, helping to build a new water treatment plant right on the border, right next to the wall. Do you remember how he leaned over to show us a video he had taken with his phone at the site? In it, he zoomed in on a man climbing up and over the top of the fence before losing his grip and falling through several rows of coiled razor wire recently installed by the National Guard. I remember recoiling from the screen as the man in the video fell to the ground and then crawled back to his feet to run north, before finally slowing down and falling to his knees, obviously hurt. I can't remember if the man in the bar showed us that video because he found it funny, or sad, or why he might have been compelled to share it with us at all.

Your letter also reminded me of the rainstorms we passed through as we drove to Naco. I remember how the clouds seemed to grow darker as we approached, sprouting legs that reached down to the horizon. I also remember the rainbows. One of them seemed to stretch across the border, lengthening its arms as we drove closer. And then there was the rainbow we saw just after crossing into Mexico. It was only half formed, and it grew up alongside one of those rainstorms that seem to happen only in the desert – the ones that unleash just a small pocket of precipitation, raining here but not there, the kind of storm that can be driven through in a split second.

My mother used to tell me about chasing storms like these with her mom, the grandmother who died just before I was born. They would drive out together along a desert highway toward the monsoon clouds and pull over as soon as they hit the rain, leaping out of the car at the storm's edge to jump in and out of the falling water – wet on this side, dry on the other. Her mom came from the Midwest, from German and Irish stock, and over time she taught my mother to be ashamed of the Mexican-ness she had inherited from her father, but she also taught my mother to love the desert and find profound joy there. In this way, she helped her daughter to develop a deep sense of place even as she irreparably upended her sense of self.

Just last month, you and I saw each other again after the passage of a year that has been almost entirely incomprehensible, and we traveled, once more, to the border. This time we drove in separate vehicles, we stayed outdoors and we wore masks each time we came within six feet of one another. On the first day of our trip, you followed me as I drove west from Tucson and then turned south toward the tiny border town of Sasabe, nestled in between the rolling hills of the Sonoran grasslands. We stopped and got out of the car each time you signaled that you might recognize something, and again I marveled at the details you were able to reconstruct from that long-ago crossing. As we drove toward Sasabe we stopped again and again, and stood at the road's edge looking for clues – the prevalence or scarcity of saguaros, the rise and fall of the terrain and the distance between mountains, the ridge lines dotted with yucca and crowned by shade-giving mesquite.

That night we camped in the Buenos Aires Wildlife Refuge, surrounded, paradoxically, by big game hunters spread out across the desert, camped like us in the dirt pull-offs along the adjacent web of roads. I remembered, without telling you, the first time I camped in this corner of the desert more than a decade ago, during those strange months of limbo after I had decided to apply to the Border Patrol, but before I had yet been accepted into its ranks. I was determinedly hopeful in those days, allowing myself to believe that I might find subtle ways of helping people in this new job, that I might slowly learn to change a system from within. I was filled with a very American kind of naivety then, one flowing from a mythology in which the individual is powerful enough to change long-standing structures through sheer force of will, in which any single one of us is capable of introducing humanity into entirely inhumane systems before we, instead, are left misshapen by them, barely recognizable even to our former selves.

After dark settled over the valley, we stood around a small fire drinking sotol and bacanora from the Río Sonora valley. Your partner, Joey, was with us, and your friend Gerardo, a film-maker from Guatemala, and we all laughed together and drank and sang out loud to music blaring from a portable speaker – music from Mexico, from El Salvador, from the Texas borderlands. The moon was bright that night, and at one point after the fire died down, you told us you wanted to walk out into the desert to look across the landscape in the darkness. We followed you down the dirt road and up a hill, then out across the knee-high grass until you stopped to look at the shadows of the distant trees and bushes. It was impossible to be certain, you told us, but you were almost sure that one of your unsuccessful crossings had happened right here. That was when you mentioned the animal you had seen crossing the road as we arrived at the campsite, a wild coyote whose sighting confirmed to you that this had been the place.

In your letter you mentioned the helicopters you had heard during those first nights you spent in Tucson as an adult. When we woke up around the campsite the next morning, we didn't talk about our dreams, but joked instead about our hangovers as we packed, and then, just after we began to drive back toward the highway, you pulled over and jumped out of your truck, pointing into the distance at a Border Patrol helicopter swooping low to the ground, circling a group of unseen migrants. We could hear the faint whipping of its blades and we watched as a silent cloud rose beneath it, the same color as the desert floor. We each found ourselves dumbfounded in our own particular way, grappling with varying degrees of privilege as we watched the helicopter spreading its violence upon the desert below. There was, I think, a certain kind of helplessness that bubbled up from us in that moment, an insidious kind of resignation to the fact that, despite how far we had each come to arrive here, we now stood at an impossible distance from everything before us. The artificial wind, the blinding dust – it was no longer ours to suffer or to make, but it lingered there nevertheless, a cloud worrying the horizon.

*

Paco,

Watching those migrants get chased just two or three kilometers from the border fence gutted me. We couldn't have been more than four kilometers away from where their lives had just changed. Getting caught can mean months in detention, and for the rest of that day I couldn't stop thinking about whoever got apprehended. The frequency of these violent acts is the reason why I've avoided the borderlands for so long. But I did not live through quite as cruel an incarceration as migrants do in 2020. After my first attempt, I spent one night in a Border Patrol jail, the only child crammed into a six-by-four foot cell with more than fifteen adults. Yet I have not forgotten those hours. Can you imagine the horror, the trauma, created by the weeks, months, sometimes years, kids and adults are spending in private detention cells right now? I can't.

During my second attempt, the group I was with was chased by helicopters our first night in Buenos Aires Wildlife Refuge, just like those migrants were that morning. In 1999, we were disoriented and the group of more than forty migrants dwindled down to groups of four or five. My group, consisting of Patricia and her twelve-year-old daughter, Carla, and a man called Chino, who must've been in his early twenties, spent two full days in the summer heat, finally running out of water. After hours, or days, I don't remember, Chino and Patricia decided to approach a ranch in order to drink water from a hose on the property. As we opened the faucet, an Arizona rancher ran out of his house and pointed his shotgun at us. He had already called Border Patrol and an agent arrived within fifteen minutes. We were immediately deported back to Mexico. And you're right. There's so much privilege in these pages, in the physical distance between us and the helicopter. Between us and our old uniforms. Between my trip in 1999 and my present-day reality as a writer.

I don't think I would've moved to Tucson in 2020 had we not driven around in 2019. You showed me a different Tucson, a different Sonoran Desert, a different Sonora. During the pandemic, I've struggled internally. The first weeks of the lockdown, during which I also came down with Covid for a few days, I had flashbacks of the Mexican coyote, back in 1999, who locked us inside our hiding spot in Guadalajara, a one-bedroom apartment I shared with six adults.

At the same time, I had flashbacks of being incarcerated in a small cell with more than fifteen other adults in the Nogales Border Patrol station. Therapy has helped. After years of people telling me to read *The Body Keeps the Score* by Bessel van der Kolk, my partner, Joey, gifted it to me and it's become a bible of sorts. I read a passage every night before bed. I must read it slowly. 'Sooner or later you need to confront what has happened to you, but only after you feel safe and will not be re-traumatized by it,' writes van der Kolk. None of our trips would've been possible if my physical reactions had been similar to those I experienced the first time I returned to Tucson in 2017. At some level, going back to where I crossed has taken its toll, but it's more manageable. We've added happier memories on top of my trauma. It's a reason why, when I saw you again after I had moved to Tucson, we drank out of the same bottle of mezcal we made together after you picked me up from the airport in 2019. A bookending of sorts, because we drank it in the same warehouse I saw those helicopters that didn't let me sleep in 2017. A celebration of a new phase in my time in this desert landscape.

The first months of living in Tucson were wild. I kept waking up multiple times a night, sometimes in the middle of dreams. I think it's what happened that night at the haunted hotel. Your idea of my dream world protecting me within itself makes a lot of sense. Regarding that shadow, I have an absurd story. One of the very first dreams I had this October was of a man's figure standing next to my bed. Maybe it's my ancestors. Maybe it's the people who died in the desert when we ran out of water. Maybe both. I always feel that figure following me. It's taken me years of therapy to understand that I have survivor's guilt. I've read so many articles, even asked you about the probability of survival for people who run away from a Border Patrol ambush.

I remember waking to five Border Patrol trucks and SUVs surrounding our group of migrants resting in a dried-up stream. By the time we noticed, it was too late. But not all of those people were apprehended. I estimate at least a third ran away. One of them was a migrant who had been with me since San Salvador. Chele is the only name I know him by. I never saw him again. It would've been very difficult for him to make it out of the desert alive. I take that dark figure to be a metaphor for all the people I might have known who might now be dead. They are the reason I want to get the story as close to truth, to the facts, to 'right', as possible. But, as my therapist says, to ever fully recapture the past is an impossibility. Our memories keep changing the details of the story, but not the feelings. Yet, the landscape, and having you explain the markers, have really helped to bring up memories, images, I thought were lost. Those images were always buried deep within my body, my mind, my soul. When they spring up via dreams, flashbacks, body aches, I can begin to acknowledge them, in order to continue on my healing journey.

Similarly, I blocked out the video the Mexican American man showed us in that bar. I now better understand how my brain works. During my crossing, I blocked out any memory that would register as danger. It's why I can't remember my trauma linearly. Sometimes, it erases images, situations, people, in my daily life, even if these things don't pose a danger to me. My brain thinks it's protecting me. I am learning to forgive it because its ability to protect me is probably a huge reason why I survived. I still find it unbelievable that I did not die. Of course I would forget the image of an immigrant falling onto concertina wire. It's perhaps too similar to my memories of sliding under barbwire fences, or being picked up by adults and dropped over ranch fences – memories recovered from our first trip to the desert on that highway between Naco and Douglas. The same highway where we saw the rains that reminded you of your mom and grandma. What a beautiful image of being wet and dry, behind a curtain of rain, one foot wet, one foot dry. I've always wanted to do that. In El Salvador. In the US. But that image, that storm cloud and the rainbow, I took as the desert saying, here, here it was. I smiled. Laughed. I was so happy to see rain in the desert, something I longed for, prayed for, wished for with all my might when we ran out of water. Back then, there was not one cloud in the sky. That cloud was also saying sorry. Twenty years too late, but I know it was apologizing.

The signs. I already believed in them, as you can see from the egrets I mentioned in my first letter. Living in Tucson, I've learned to pay attention to animals: bobcats, mountain lions, coyotes and owls. Freaky things have happened. One night, Joey dreamed of a man who she did not know, but in the morning, when she described him, it was my uncle, Israel Zamora, who was disappeared in 1981 during the civil war. I didn't know him, but I called my dad to confirm the details and they checked out. My dad has always compared me to him. Most of the Zamoras do. Israel wrote poetry, taught himself kung fu from Siemens catalogs and is said to have read every book in our rural library. He loved reading so much that he commuted to the closest library once he knew every book in our town. The next evening, Joey and I walked down the hill and on top of a cottonwood tree we saw two great horned owls. We approached them and they didn't fly away. I started hooting and they hooted back. This went back and forth for forty-five minutes, during which we also saw five shooting stars. The owls didn't stop talking. Eventually it got cold and we left them hooting, with Orion's Belt hanging on top of the cottonwood. It was magical, unbelievable, I still don't think people believe me when I tell them. Israel's partner, Maria de los Ángeles, was killed a few weeks before my uncle was disappeared. Maybe he is the shadow standing next to my bed. I know they protect me and follow me. They must have been watching over me in 1999 during the eight weeks it took me to get to this country.

I've spent four months in Tucson now. Since our trip, I've driven to more places along the border, searching. I feel safe enough to drive there myself. You helped me ease into it. When I first met you, I think I let one of the many stages in your life – that of having worn a Border Patrol uniform – color who you were in the present. I had my guard up. Slowly, I learned to trust you. The first American I encountered in the Sonoran Desert and in the United States was wearing a dark green uniform similar to the one you once wore. That person pointed a gun at Chino, Patricia, Carla and me. You are far, far, far from being that individual to me. I guess I'm saying thank you for leaving the Border Patrol. Thank you for staying in touch, for sharing your passion for agave with me, for taking me to one of the dopest places I've ever been, Rancho Tepúa. You and I grew up as only children. It's absurd how immigration has brought us together. In a way, I look at you as a brother. My father grew up estranged from his brothers; my mother from her sisters. I think siblinghood is something like this. A helping hand, a feeling of safety, knowledge passed down, an unspoken language. ■

RICARDO MIGUEL HERNÁNDEZ
from *When Memory Turns to Dust*, 2018

BOARDING PASS

Carlos Manuel Álvarez

TRANSLATED FROM THE SPANISH BY FRANK WYNNE

The immigration officer took my passport and told me to stand aside and wait. The pandemic era had begun. Inside the face mask my breath condensed, misting my glasses. That was an acceptable metaphor for Cuba: a country in a mask, its breath constrained, its gaze blurred by the breathy fog. Everything that can be simplified stems from an unfair order. The night before, we had gotten a friend out of jail. I stayed up into the early hours, drinking too many beers as we celebrated in a club on 25th Street, while the fingernail of freedom opened a gash of amazement in the mud of our bodies.

A woman appeared and took my passport. They had been waiting for me. A few weeks earlier, they had called my phone to interrogate me. I rejected the call. Later a police officer had been seen prowling around a friend's house. He asked several of the neighbors about me. They were like the shadow of the medieval wolf. They slipped behind walls, slithered under a cart, emitting a hoarse growl. You longed for them to appear, so you could finally stop feeling scared.

Fear had settled into us like an icy prosthesis, like a screw buried in flesh. The social body had no voice, subjected as it was to a medical experiment by the political police. We were accustomed to the dearth of shock, the bureaucratic expression of fear. As a result, a primary way to escape this dictatorship was to embrace it, to go looking for it. When power is forced to show itself, it is invariably weakened.

Some minutes passed. Stretched out by a kind of sadness, the historical sadness of the ultimate absurdity. Why were things as they were? The woman came back with my passport and told me to follow her. An officer in a military uniform, curt, unflustered. She seemed aloof to everything, but I knew that once even she had danced to reggaeton, watched pornography, eaten *frijoles negros*.

We walked past Immigration and Customs. My passport was stamped, they were going to let me leave. Havana was far behind.

Though we had created a future for the city, scrawled on the air with a delirious pencil; though we had moved in lockstep like automata, it was here that the city had finally run aground and been left behind. But behind what? Behind life, perhaps? There was no map of time, no future path, not even in the escape or flight in which Havana once again appeared as it had formerly been: the promise of rescue, of temptation, of personal discovery. Havana had become a city perched precariously between the mists of melancholy and the snare of indifference. Havana still made sense to me only through the salt line of its stifling political situation, one that at any other time would have prompted disgust or contempt. A situation that was contingent, fragile, but now felt like justice deferred.

In an hour and a half, my flight to Mexico City would take off. I desperately wanted to go back. I had spent six months away from that superstition that Lucia Berlin describes as 'fatalistic, suicidal, corrupt. A pestilential swamp. Oh, but there is graciousness. There are flashes of such beauty, of kindness and of color, you catch your breath.'

The woman led me to one of her superiors. He was a tall, athletic man, with green eyes; he was holding a clipboard of some sort. I was interested to note his affability – here was a genuinely personable man thrust into an arbitrary situation. We said little; I appreciated that. He told me it was just a matter of a few questions; they would not take up much of my time. He was lying, of necessity. No man in his official position, who had no opportunity to resign his post, could possibly be my ally when the entire country had made itself my enemy. A good man in a bad situation becomes a bad man who pretends.

I walked past the toilets and the trinket shops of Terminal 3 – a tacky theme park stocked with symbols of the Revolution: the boxes of Cohiba cigars, the bottles of Havana Club, the faces of Che Guevara. A pop-art patchwork of tattered ideology, a tapestry of dreams so often patched with terror that the patches had become the whole tapestry.

I passed another checkpoint and the official left me in a cramped, soulless office. Two men were seated at a desk. I had to sit facing them. Finally. I wanted to see who they were. I stared at them. Their faces were half-hidden by green masks, that sinister dark green of the public hospitals. So, this was who they were. I had seen them so often before, I ran into them on every street, every day of my life in Cuba.

Any Cuban prepared to stare into a crowd, to look along a line of people waiting outside a bodega, to watch the popular national video clips of ragged, boisterous masses would instantly recognize these two men. Any Cuban had only to look in the mirror and, if he did not put his fist through the glass, did not gash his hand, did not take a hammer to the mirror, he would see them there, too.

They were not the classic good cop/bad cop partnership. One, the senior officer, was short, squat and spouted drivel. The other was broad, powerful, almost too big for his chair, and did not seem to have any particular role in this scenario. Perhaps, as Barbara Demick describes in her book *Nothing to Envy: Real Lives in North Korea*, they were assigned in pairs for the same reason that foreign journalists in North Korea are assigned two guides, so that each can monitor the other, thereby ensuring neither strays from the official script. All things considered, as far as these two officers were concerned, I was a foreign journalist, from the specific subspecies of foreigner comprised of Cubans who have renounced the native soil of Castroism.

I suspected the second officer was here in order to observe and learn. A rookie officer supporting a veteran officer, thereby rounding out the inquisitorial process to the totalitarian machine whose cruelty stems not from intelligence, but from stupidity.

I asked their names. They were called something like Carlos or Alejandro or Jorge. Fake names, the same old names, the names of dead kings. They didn't have the names Yasmany or Yasiel, real names, the names of real people who sweated real sweat. I felt sure that they answered to Maikel or Yandro when they stepped out into the street, and people could see them struggling to get by, enduring the same harsh sun as everyone else.

They always used aliases, and nothing betrays a person more than an alias. A number of other journalists who wrote for the magazine I edited were also interrogated during this period, in the midst of the global pandemic. Since the word belonged to history, it was the oppressor who was forced to hide. It was the oppressor who could not reveal his name, who had to move like a phantom through this room of the Last Judgment, an unassuming yet decisive room where we were gambling with the value of that curious creature, freedom.

From whom is the oppressor hiding, since it is he who oppresses? He is hiding from some future moment, from a time that some of us had launched ourselves into, which was precisely why we were being interrogated. Beneath the mask of some present guilt, what the oppressors were really asking was how it would work, this moment of ours, this moment they could not comprehend. It's fragile, we would have told them, it is not a closed time like the one in which you live. But those who ask lots of questions have no wish to listen, only to defeat the other.

In this country I was fleeing, people died at the age of eighty and existed only from Wednesday to Thursday, constantly tiring themselves out over short distances. One day at a time for a whole lifetime, this was all that had been allocated to us. What was devastating about totalitarianism was this oppressive, unchanging, endlessly recurring moment.

The senior officer had a Havana accent, gruff and more prosodic; the other had an accent from somewhere in the east, softer and more cadenced. The junior officer did not say much, but in what little time he was granted succeeded in highlighting his particular gifts. I had met a lot of men like him during military service. Over the years, most of them ended up pickled by booze, smelling of gasoline, desperately waiting for August so they could grab life by the balls, spend a weekend in a ramshackle campsite on the northern coast.

His boss spat words, while he felt uncomfortable in the mask that shifted and stifled him. Every time he tried to say something, the words, like flecks of spittle, caught in this fabric muzzle. There they died, unintelligible, a series of flattened sounds that neither I nor his boss could untangle. Extracting any sense from his babble was like picking up grains of rice. The chief looked on patiently, never reproaching him. The junior officer pushed the mask away and spoke out of the side of his mouth.

When his words finally reached me, the gist and tone of the question was one that his boss had already asked. I've already answered that, I said repeatedly. Maybe he too was being assessed. He had to ask a question and couldn't think of one. He was like a student who joins the last class of a particular course without having had an oral assessment and feels they have to say something just to avoid being failed.

If he didn't have any ideas, his superior had one. An idea that was fixed, absolute and reserved for him alone. It is something we've all seen once. The notion of a boorish man in a position of power who believes he is right. 'How much do you get paid for your Facebook posts?' he asked. 'Who pays you?' 'How do you know the people that you know?' And so on. Ad infinitum. The rhetorical snail of his questions spiraled in on itself. They believed that everyone acted as they did. According to orders, for a meager pittance, governed by obscure hierarchies.

They made my head spin. The official who brought me here suddenly burst into the room and said that the flight would be taking off soon. Then he left, cordially complicit. I could not think of a way to respond to this hilarious outburst with a minimum of honesty, a shred of dignity, or even mild sarcasm, which was how I had somewhat condescendingly imagined I would react when the situation first arose. They had ensnared me in their slug-like logic. We could use a phrase from Robert Walser: 'There are limits in life to any attempt to rise above vulgarity.'

They questioned me about my friends, about my family. They showed me photos of people I didn't know, or had briefly encountered. What kind of connections and conspiracies had they dreamed up in their delusional minds? I thought. If all of this sounds vague, that's because it is. They were looking for something that wasn't there. Something about which I knew nothing and they knew even less, something that existed in the past only inasmuch as they that had put it there. They dredged the memory of the crime in the breadcrumbs of nonsense, smearing everything with sticky logic, making me dirty.

I tried as hard as I could to drive out the thought that they were producing in me the thought of the answers, and every time it happened, I realized what I was actually trying to do was not betray anyone. Not that I could, of course, since there was no one to betray. But my interrogators were not interested in such details because they did not want me to betray people; they wanted me to try *not to* betray anyone. To them, it was proof there existed someone behind the scenes who *could* be betrayed.

But the crime *did* exist; it was Cuba itself. The only way that these two officers could save themselves was by pretending to investigate me. Late totalitarianism, as I experienced it, could not be seen as a metaphor for the total destruction of the individual, but, on the contrary, as a process by which the individual acquired antibodies in order to deceive Big Brother. He did not love Big Brother, he cuckolded him, but he served Big Brother, because not only did he realize that he was being deceived, he wanted to be deceived, thereby eventually creating the sort of dishonest, dissembling individual who was unfaithful to himself, and whose antibodies were just another symptom of the disease.

At the end of the day, in totalitarianism there can be no infidelity that did not already exist within the marriage, but if my interrogators did not stick to this marriage contract, and carried on investigating who had set about destroying Cuba, all that awaited them was exile or civil death, the fate suffered by almost all those before them who had unraveled this simple crime.

In Leonardo Sciascia's novel *The Knight and Death*, the unnamed Vice Chief of Police, known only as *il Vice*, is investigating the death of a famous lawyer, an investigation that leads him to none other than the president of United Industries, another temporary placeholder for power. Meanwhile, newspapers are persuaded to write stories pinning the blame on an anarcho-terrorist group of dissatisfied youths called the 'Children of Eighty-Nine'. The same year I was born. *Il Vice* only pretends to investigate this purported group of anarchists to keep his boss happy, but, despite the plausible new stories, he is not convinced. When he persists, and begins to get close to the truth, he is shot dead, in one of the most beautiful final scenes ever written.

It is not as though the political corruption and general frustration in Sicily described in *The Knight and Death* could not have prompted a group like the 'Children of Eighty-Nine' to rise up. After all, I had risen up, together with many others. It was the fact that power had committed a specific crime, one that they deemed manageable, necessary and unavoidable for other reasons, and then pinned the blame on a predetermined enemy, an enemy seemingly rooted in domestic terrorism. This was one of the greatest historical successes of Castroism. We had to deal with the exhausting task of not becoming a credible enemy, one that fitted the only story they knew how to write, and instead commit our own crime.

On page sixty-four of my edition of *The Knight and Death* is the following bitter exchange:

> 'Have you heard the latest? This country is never boring. Now we've got the Children of Eighty-Nine.'
> 'Yeah, the Children of Eighty-Nine.' Ironically, maliciously.
> 'So what do you make of it?'

'I think it is all so much hot air, pure fantasy. And you?'

'Me too.'

'Glad to hear it. From what I read in the papers, your office is taking the whole thing pretty seriously.'

'Yeah, of course we are. Do you really expect us to miss out on such a juicy fantasy?'

'That's it. The whole thing sounds like something made up over a cup of coffee, as a game, a ruse . . . What else can they do, the poor bastards, the dumb fools who need to carry on believing in something after Khrushchev, after Mao, after Fidel Castro and now Gorbachev? You have to throw them a crumb of cake, something that can be popped into the oven after two hundred years and reheated, something bland and flavoured with revelries, rediscoveries and revaluations: and inside the same hard stone for them to break their teeth on.'

The cake reheated after 200 years is the French Revolution, and one slice of that cake is the notion and the structure of the republic. In a free interpretation of *The Knight and Death* as non-fiction novel, maybe the ominous 'Children of Eighty-Nine' could bite into the cake and avoid the stone.

The officers asked me about Luis Manuel Otero. An artist friend of mine they had arrested on trumped-up charges and been forced to release the night before. They asked how long we had known each other, what had brought us together. This had all been written already. It was they who had brought us together, obviously, though I'm not sure I told them that.

The third officer reappeared. Ten minutes to takeoff. At this point, they adopted a clumsy tactic. They suggested we could have coffee when I came back to Cuba. Just something informal, they didn't want to issue a summons. For an instant, I freaked out, as though I'd already agreed. I remembered that while doing military service, a counter-intelligence officer had called me into his office to ask me to rat out other soldiers if they absconded or slept during sentry duty. Such offers triggered in me a particular kind of revulsion.

I said no. The only way we're going to talk is if you get a summons, I blurted out. They asked what date I was coming back. I didn't know. They told me they would see me when I got back. I told them to do whatever they had to. Then they resorted to a little sophistry. My decision not to come in for interview after they called me on my phone demonstrated a defiance that was unlike me, they said. I told them they had no idea what I was like. In all honesty, I had no idea either, but it was a phrase that, however clichéd, came in useful at that moment – it might slow them down and it sounded good.

They spoke as if it was they who had called my phone. They were right. Although we were in Havana and the call had come from Matanzas, a completely different province, I was dealing with a single creature that, according to time or place, could manifest itself in particular individuals without being fragmented. There was nothing to differentiate between them.

The interrogation had gone on for more than an hour. It is tempting to see such encounters as Kafkaesque. They're not; they are unworthy of the term. There had been too much talk. In Kafka, officers don't ask questions, they have no need to uncover anything. Their actions are brutal, their speech is terse and peremptory and has the dual effect of closing one door only to open up a dizzying network of pathways, and it is in this labyrinth, rather than behind the closed door, that the miserable prisoner is trapped.

By the time the interrogators tried to pressure me, it was already too late, they had run out of time. The third officer reappeared to say that he could no longer hold the flight. Before I left, there was a panicked pause in which they explained that that was why I should report to them as soon as they called my phone, allowing us to have a relaxed conversation and avoiding the need for them to send a patrol car to pick me up. This wasn't a conversation, I said, it was an interrogation. An interrogation, they informed me, was something much worse. They spluttered something else, but by now I was no longer listening, we were all completely numbed.

The whole encounter seemed utterly anachronistic. This was 14 March 2020, a time when Stalinist aesthetics could be seen only as folklore. Outside, the news was all about the pandemic. Before long, tens of thousands would be dying all over the world. Three days earlier, Cuba had identified its first cases of coronavirus.

I rushed onto the plane and looked for my seat. The passengers looked at me disapprovingly. They probably assumed I had left everything until the last minute. In my seat, with my seat belt buckled, with no battery on my phone, I collapsed. It was as though I had sat down twice, or as though I had left a part of me behind. But this was not the only part of me that had lagged behind. Over the following days in Mexico City, various parts that had been lingering in the interrogation came back to me.

It was understandable. There had been a rift in reality, such that you arrived at a place as you were leaving it. The flight took off. I closed my eyes and soared into the lofty darkness of nowhere in particular. What had been was outweighed by what was yet to come. ∎

FROM AN UNTOUCHED LANDSCAPE

James Tylor

Introduction by Dominic Guerrera

T he colony of Australia loves to perpetuate an 'Australian story' – one of hard work in red soil and bushmen on horseback turning the untamed continent into the lucky country. This is white storytelling – storytelling that seeks to falsely build a national identity without taking responsibility for its actions.

The truth is, this continent is home to several hundred Aboriginal and Torres Strait Islander nations and groups, as it has been for thousands of years. Some estimate 65,000 years, but our creation stories tell us that our existence on this land stretches even further back than that. The colony of Australia refuses to acknowledge the invasion and continued occupation of Aboriginal lands, while also actively covering up the genocide endured by Aboriginal peoples.

While the colony of South Australia wasn't established until 1836, Europeans had been invading and trespassing on Ngarrindjeri Ruwi Country and Kaurna Yarta Country since the English navigator Matthew Flinders came here in around 1802. Soon after his arrival, whaling and sealing settlements were established along the harsh coastlines of Karta Pintingka (the Kaurna name for Kangaroo Island, which translates as 'Island of the Dead') and what is known as the Fleurieu Peninsula. These industries were run by early colonists, opportunists who not only established commercial ties with the eastern colonies (New South Wales, Victoria and Tasmania) but also laid the foundation for the colony of South Australia. The arrival of the Europeans also ushered in the commencement of the Frontier Wars between colonisers and the Aboriginal nations within these regions. Horrific acts of violence and genocide were inflicted upon Aboriginal peoples, acts that have evolved and continue to this day.

Most local Aboriginal families have stories of early interactions with whalers and sealers; some of us are even their descendants. A lot of these stories revolve around the enslavement and rape of Aboriginal women. The stories also describe the harsh living conditions endured by these women and their children (who were often born from rape), with some dying in tragic circumstances. The removal of these women was an early act of Aboriginal displacement. Today the colony of South Australia celebrates and memorialises the whalers and sealers, while the Aboriginal stories – particularly those of Aboriginal women – are ignored and denied.

The armed forces of South Australia (the police) were instrumental in fighting and killing Aboriginal men. The presence of police in the lives of Aboriginal peoples continued through the years. Police were actively involved in forcing Aboriginal peoples to live on Christian missions, assisting in the removal of Aboriginal children (the 'Stolen Generations'), the surveillance of Aboriginal communities, the building of the prison-industrial system and deaths in custody. The violence used to build the colony continues to be used to maintain it.

The Fleurieu Peninsula's windy coastline is dotted with small towns that were once whaling ports, now connected by an ever-stretching line of beach houses. Overdeveloped getaways, all reaching for a view of the bays they clutter. It's hard to find a spot where the colony hasn't reached; the landscape is consistently interrupted. Kangaroo Island has some pockets of natural landscape remaining. The presence of industrial farming is inescapable, but the island's disconnection has saved it from being overdeveloped like the mainland. While whaling and sealing are no longer conducted, other exploitative industries prop up the state's economy: mining and fisheries, as well as farming. Meanwhile the urban landscape continues to encroach. All are taking their toll on the environment, while interrupting the relationship between Aboriginal communities and their land.

James Tylor's photographs capture unpopulated and undeveloped landscapes, allowing us to imagine what these spaces once were. The black cut-outs are a reminder of what the colonisers have taken and destroyed, while simultaneously obscuring what they have built. Through his work, I am reminded of not only the harsh realities of our history but also our survival. His images make me, as a Kaurna person, want to learn more, to help the continuation of our culture. As Aboriginal artists, we have an obligation to tell these stories, because if we don't, who will? Certainly not Australia.

Along the coastline, we sit among smooth rocks and watch the grey waves roll in and kiss the white sands. The whales have returned to the bay with their young, seeking the warm waters. Their black figures float across the water's surface and we stare, mesmerised by their graceful beauty, squinting as the sun reflects back off the sea.

Our country remains and it is beautiful. ■

The journey begins now.

Heirs of Deceits
Elizabeth Reinach

Sir Gilbert was rejected by his social class because he first hired his illegitimate children as servants, then recognising them, to the world's horror. Murder and chaos followed.

£13.99 paperback
978-1-9845-8983-5
also available in hardcover & ebook
www.xlibrispublishing.co.uk

Hell Fire Is Real
My Experience
Hope Stewart

This book of repentance provides a biblical perspective on how real hell is. It shares steps to avoid hell, and how to frame your life with faith to enter heaven.

£8.99 paperback
978-1-6641-1270-4
also available in hardcover & ebook
www.xlibrispublishing.co.uk

Weather or Not
Jane Waller

In this novel, a girl comes into possession of a magical book that grants the power to create extreme weather, leading to a war over the weather and climate change.

£10.95 paperback
978-1-7283-9843-3
also available in hardcover & ebook
www.authorhouse.co.uk

The Noble Tigress
E.L. Walker

E.L. Walker hopes to prove that love comes in many forms and families are not just their blood relations in this new fictional romance novel.

£10.95 paperback
978-1-6655-8200-1
also available in ebook
www.authorhouse.co.uk

The Coronavirus and Saving the Planet
Coloured Version
Carol Sutters

In this book, Kate and Tom learn about the coronavirus pandemic. They also discuss what people can take forward for the benefit of society, biodiversity and the planet.

£11.95 paperback
978-1-6655-8623-8
also available in ebook
www.authorhouse.co.uk

Nine Lives of a Scouser
David C. Pickard

Born in Liverpool in 1937, David C. Pickard looks back at his varied career and life experiences.

£9.95 paperback
978-1-6655-8185-1
also available in hardcover, ebook & audiobook
www.authorhouse.co.uk

---

authorHOUSE®   Xlibris

Real Authors, Real Impact   Visit us on Facebook & Twitter

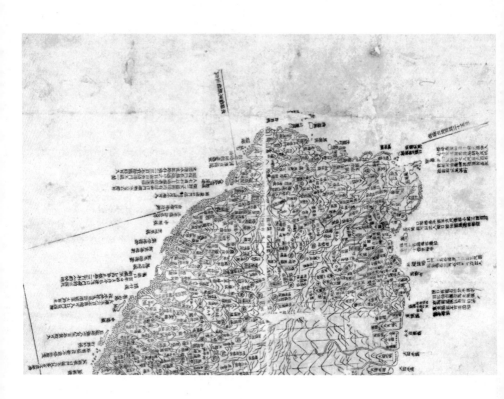

YU CHONG
Quan Tai qian hou shan yu tu (全台前後山與圖 /Map of Taiwan Island), 1878
Courtesy of the Library of Congress, Geography and Map Division

回 | AN ALLEY (RETURN)

Jessica J. Lee

Unnamed Alley, Lane 286, Section 5, Nanjing East Road

When I thought about returning, it was only ever in my mother's language, specifically in the Chinese character I love the most: 回 (huí). It means 'to return', but also: to circle, to turn round or to answer, its ancient root in a spiral. The word was on my mind when I first found myself in Taiwan, trying to wind a way through a city I didn't know at all.

In a jet-lagged haze, I led my mother out of the rental apartment, across the ten lanes of Nanjing East Road, and down a quiet path lined with scooters. Her hand was clammy in mine; even in December, Taipei pulsed with humidity.

'We need to keep moving,' I insisted. 'We stay awake until double-digits.' I glanced down at my phone, tracing our route to the red pin on my map. A Carrefour hypermarket. Quite what that quest would entail – beyond instant coffee, bottled water and snacks – I wasn't yet sure. It was my first time back in twenty-six years. I was twenty-eight years old.

Halfway along the lane, my mother stopped.

'Jess, look!' She pointed up towards two apartment buildings cut through by a narrow alley. It seemed like entire trees hung heavy from the balconies. Dappling the walkway were clay pots planted with shrubs and vines leaning low. There was no one there – no trace of scooters or laundry or other human interruptions – but still the alley had a cadence to it. A swelling of leaf. I had never known an alley to be so green.

Standing in the gap, I smiled and flashed a peace sign with my fingers while my mother snapped a photo for Instagram. Me in a vignette-filtered square, wearing burgundy jeans and a drapey black top. The alley behind me disappears into white.

Later that week my mother would tell me that the boulevards – shaded by trees – were the thing she missed most about Taipei. That they felt, somehow, Parisian to her. She had visited Paris twice in her life and held it as the measure of sophistication. I knew what she meant. Tidy, imposing, with nature in ordered rows.

But it was there in that rainbow-paved passage that I first counted the plants overgrowing: bamboos, dwarf papayas, bougainvilleas, potted magnolias, zamioculcas and orchids all stretching for light between the green awnings.

It seems melodramatic to write this, but I will write it anyway: it was there, in the space between two tenement blocks, that I knew I loved my mother's home town.

The hierarchy of Taiwan streets is fairly straightforward: alleys (弄 lòng) branch from lanes (巷 xiàng), which take root from the larger roads (路 lù) or streets (街 jiē). Of course, I've listed this hierarchy backwards; which road or street you need is certainly most important if you're looking for something specific. But on foot in Taipei, it is the alleyways that mark out the quickest course, darting between buildings or shooting diagonally from a busy road to the metro. Tiny temple altars and roving street vendors find their places between the gridded streets. Foot traffic is given priority. Between the buildings, where signage and sky grow scarce, landmarks become the only reliable means of navigation.

Should you find yourself online, you can walk the lanes, so to speak: hold the yellow stick figure above the map and many of the lines turn blue. Zoom out and most of the country is twined in veins: Street View cameras have documented almost every lane; outside the cities, they've hiked many of the mountain trails. But the narrower paths, forgotten between buildings, do not exist in this mirror world.

And not all of them are so easy to follow. In the western Yonghe District, the alleys spin veinlike from every direction. The tangle of pathways means that this pocket of the city has the second-highest population density in the world. In 2010, when these parts of Taipei county were incorporated as New Taipei City, residents asked officials to streamline the naming and signage of their alleys, as constant building development had until then severed smaller alleys from their main roads, quite literally hiding them from view. Emergency services kept getting lost, and residents found themselves having to go out into the main road to flag police and paramedics down. Fire trucks, of course, stood no chance of squeezing in.

The day we went to Carrefour, I showed my mother how to use Google Maps on her iPhone. She had never really read maps before – as kids we used to joke about the time she'd held a paper map in front of her and said that north lay wherever the top of the map pointed, regardless of which way she was facing. She hadn't tried to navigate since and had resigned herself to getting lost. It felt strange to me – a kind of authority I did not want – having to navigate my mother around her own home town, a place I hardly knew at all. A Chinese-school dropout, I couldn't read half of the street names and felt more reliant than ever on my phone. I toggled between maps and translation apps, finding well-reviewed breakfast stalls and restaurants my mother remembered from the 1980s.

So that day, before we set out into the streets of Songshan District, I showed her the blue pulse that moved with her along the streets, how she only needed to follow the dotted path to the red pin. I wanted her to move as freely as I did. To feel used to travelling alone. I told her she could trust the map.

But a map cannot be faithful to the territory it represents. If you look at maps made in Europe between the sixteenth and seventeenth centuries, Taiwan appears to metamorphose: Abraham Ortelius's 1570 map shows a fragmentary place of many small islands. Given the width of Taiwan's rivers, this misunderstanding seems plausible for a cartographer passing along the coastline by sea. But then, as if caught in an eddy, these smaller islands cluster and re-emerge in Johannes Vingboons's 1625 rendering: Taiwan, tipped on its side, whole at last. The useful ports are marked in ink. The island, by then, had been colonised by the Spanish and the Dutch. Within decades, they were ousted.

Early-eighteenth-century maps by Qing cartographers show Taiwan from the perspective of Chinese colonists, keen to enrol the island in their empire: in a Kangxi-era map from 1704, the humps of the mountains form the horizon – a 'wilderness' beyond which nothing was known – with towns and settlements laid before them, easy at hand, like fruit on a table. Taiwan's original inhabitants – who lived on these lands for many thousands of years before the arrival of the Spanish, or the Dutch, or the Chinese – were relegated to these mountains. The maps show much of the cultural preconceptions that created them, but little of the land itself.

What they do say, if you look long enough, is that Taipei was a rice paddy once. The old maps will tell you that where two busy villages met by a river, Qing colonists planned a walled town. But then, in 1895, the island changed hands (again). Japanese colonists began to measure and map Taiwan at the turn of the twentieth century, and the grammar of the land was once more reimagined: old Qing settlements were divided into prefectures, and city planning acts inspired by those of Britain were enacted. The Japanese opened grand department stores and cut through the old city with French-style boulevards lined with trees. (Mom, I want to say, there is a reason you are reminded of Paris.)

The city walls were demolished to make space for the growing population. But even without them, the old borders would not be forgotten: the Qing gates, ghost-mouths to the city, were left stranded in the middle of traffic roundabouts.

All of which is to say: I couldn't blame my mother for her confusion, for getting lost once in a while. The city and its map had a habit of shapeshifting.

Over the two weeks we spent together that trip, I led my mother between landmarks, searching for the places she knew but could not find. One day, my skills as our navigator were no longer needed.

Auntie Laura and my mother had grown up together, just streets apart. Best friends since childhood, they'd remained close despite my mother's emigration to Canada when they were in college. Laura had stayed, raised her family in Taipei, and though she now lived an hour away in Miaoli, she ventured into the city to see us for an afternoon.

That day, we walked in the shadows cast by rain trees. Their branches scrabbled together, an umbel of shelter, as we followed the path northwards on Dunhua South Road. Auntie Laura walked in front, pointing out landmarks for my mother.

'Here's our school,' she pointed left. My mother paused at the gates while I took a photograph. 'And here is where we would stop to buy snacks.' Laura pointed to a street corner, where a man counted egg waffles. Taxis skidded past, the air whirling with the sound of tyres on tarmac.

Laura was leading us to a lane with no need for a map. My mother, by contrast, had no idea where she was going. She simply pointed to a Häagen-Dazs and asked if I wanted ice cream. 'We didn't come to Taiwan to eat Häagen-Dazs,' I sighed, trying to catch up with Laura. But by now she had crossed Zhongxiao East Road with its billboards and bright lights, and then four lanes farther. She cut right, striding fast ahead of us.

Laura had walked here so many times before; it was a route she had memorised in girlhood. I wanted to walk this way: an arrow slung true. She moved eastwards, into the narrow lane, and stopped in front of a barbecue restaurant and a Korean clothing boutique, waving upwards.

My mother looked up now, knowing finally where she was. 'There. That was my home.'

I craned my neck to see the apartment, tucked at the top of a three-storey concrete tenement. An air conditioner protruded between the windows, and the walls were green with algae. It looked very dark, exactly how I'd always imagined it. I wondered out loud who lived there now. But Laura and my mother, tired of standing in the street, had already ducked into a shop with a French-sounding name. I remained outside, snapping photographs of the apartment. In my mother's stories, the end of her road took her to rice paddies, to open skies. Perhaps that explained why she could never find her way on her own. This lane she once knew now stood in the middle of a shopping district, hedged in by major arteries. Everyone on the street seemed to be just passing through: teenagers snapped photos of takeaway desserts, and shoppers jostled, their bags bumping in the press of people. It all looked expensive – salons and clothing shops and third-wave coffee.

I didn't yet know how quickly the city had outgrown its footprint. Or that if you looked at a map from 1958, all of Da'an District would've still been paddy fields.

In 1945, the Nationalist government claimed a capital that had been envisioned by Japanese urban planners. Taipei by then had shopfronts and arcades (not quite facsimiles of Baudelaire's or Benjamin's in Paris) but a growing need for more housing. These tenements were thrown up in the decades after, city sprawl in the green of Taipei's river basin. Roads were built along irrigation canals, and houses laid out in grids between them. The 'superblocks' demanded new forms of passage. So between every large building, tiny alleys cut a course. Leaks in the hard geometry of concrete.

They re-emerged from the shop, my mother carrying a too-expensive wool scarf. She wrapped it around my neck and tied it in a knot.

'It's winter!' Auntie Laura chided in her quilted jacket. I pulled the wool around my bare arms, already too warm. I didn't know how to object in Mandarin.

Lane 149, Chengfu Road

In Yu Chong's 1878 map of Taiwan's slopes, the land is veined with language: characters pressed into every mountain on the island, labelling each place, such that from a distance the labels appear like roads.

Four years after that visit with my mother, I went to Taiwan alone. During the months I stayed, my only obligation was to write, and I moved across mountains and alleys with a question in mind: could I learn this language better? And by language, in a way, I meant land.

Of course, I wanted to work on my actual Mandarin skills and learn more about my family's past. A normal impulse for the child of immigrants. But there was something more visceral to it. The want to know a place through more than the aperture of others. The knowledge I sought was only distantly familial. It was something I'd seen in Auntie Laura that day, years before. I wanted to walk here and not get lost.

I slept and woke each day in an apartment far east of the city centre, on a lane akin to my mother's memories, where shops and cafes had not yet come. My bedroom was perpetually dark, its walls bumped up close against the back of the neighbours', where a husband and wife argued near constantly. Between the buildings cut an alley without name that I could just about peer down to if I pressed my forehead to the windowpane. Rusted umbrellas and takeaway containers laid splayed on the awning below.

Lane 149 was in many ways a completely ordinary road. The lane was lined with scooters, old traffic cones and potted trees. A 7-Eleven sat on the corner, as well as a restaurant stall whose mercurial opening hours I never quite ascertained in the three months I stayed there. Two doors down from mine, a neighbourhood temple occupied a shopfront. Taoist gods stared from the altar, bright lit beneath fluorescent strip lighting. The neighbours came and went at daybreak and nightfall, wheeling the metal stove into the alley, lighting incense, and playing with the dog who spent his days sleeping at the door.

At the end of the road, the concrete lane twisted into the hillside. The city swelled only as far as the mountains allowed.

My days had a hazy structure to them, well-suited to Taiwan winter. It rained almost constantly, and as December set in I found myself cold in weather I'd otherwise consider warm. I wrapped a coat around myself, bought thermal layers.

When on Wednesdays I heard 'A Maiden's Prayer' piped tinnily through the streets, I knew the neighbours would be meeting outside at the corner, gathering their rubbish and recycling for collection. Aunties in parkas gossiped as they sorted pink bags of plastic. Schoolchildren waited next to their mothers, tugging at their coats. I didn't have to go outside to sort my rubbish – like many serviced buildings, mine had collection – but I liked the ritual of leaving the house at the same time, strolling over to the vegetarian diner when the music called everyone outside. I needed the routine.

Each day I would trace my fingers over the map on my phone, looking for lanes I hadn't walked before. I took care not to get lost. If I had learned anything from my mother, it was that I needed to learn landmarks. The crest of a hillside, the stretch of a long-standing wall. Details. (Is this what she had forgotten?) In the narrower lanes, it was impossible to tell when a path curved, when a corner had been cut for convenience. I walked straight ahead, but changed direction without meaning to.

So I followed the alleys in every direction: across Chengfu Road, into the paths of the neighbouring block, where each shopfront had metal grates in a different pattern. A market appeared near the curve of the lane on weekday mornings – twelve kinds of cabbage leafing into the roadway – and the pavements filled with people. For a time, from one of these lanes, you could see the Taipei 101 skyscraper creep into the sky above the city. (Street View now tells me it is obscured by new construction.)

On Fude Street, beneath the sheltered shopfronts – the closest Taipei comes to the Parisian arcade – I learned to train my gaze to the ground: every shop tiled the walkway at a different height, and I often lost my footing. I hated that walking freely in a city dug up the image of the flâneur – aimless, detached and spectating. Because I wanted more than anything to commit myself to these lanes, and to commit them to my memory. I loved that the pavements here made ease impossible. Tiles turned to concrete and back again – beyond hazardous in the rain – and shopfronts spilled into the streets. One lane was filled with songbirds in cages, who seemed to sing louder for every passer-by.

I darted between the walls of a school and a temple, following a narrow path along the hillside: losing myself between sixteen temples on a southern slope. In front of one, two old men sat at a folding table, sipping tea and playing cards. At another I found only stray dogs, no sign of people or prayer. I never made it to all of the temples, got turned around on unmapped tracks. But I found my way downhill, and at the hill's end I stopped to buy turnip buns, flaky and bursting with salt, from a stallholder who parked at a corner no one ever seemed to pass, unless, like me, they'd gotten lost. I clambered uphill again, made the same wrong turns. I didn't mind because the turnip buns were good.

One route I walked repeatedly. From the end of my lane there was an alley that doesn't appear on the digital map: beneath and between buildings, to a house swallowed entirely with green. Elephant ear and money trees strung through with dwarf umbrella. From here to where the forest loomed, the houses crouched lower, no longer apartments but single homes, fronted with tiled courtyards. There were bicycles and gardening gloves. The scent of laundry and the smell of soil. It was a place I could imagine living.

At the end of this alley, where the online map now resumes coverage, the Street View image glitches: potted plants blur into asphalt, and the lane appears paved with leaf. I said before that a map cannot be faithful; but in some ways, this glitch is more faithful than I can explain.

Alley 11, Lane 147, Section 3, Xinyi Road

A map in hand, I could not feel at home. My attention drifted to my phone, and I missed the details. I don't know why I told my mother to try to use one; she might more easily have learned the route by me saying: soup restaurant, straight ahead, FamilyMart, right, and then alley, alley, alley.

That is how I learned. And how I began to navigate. In walking I asked myself: what is this place to me? Am I anything at all to it?

Now, the lane doubles after the rain. Street lights and neon bounce off wet asphalt, saturating night with bright colour. It is September, two years since I was last in Taiwan, and it is still hot. Not summer hot – not for here, anyway – but humid enough that in the afternoon my T-shirt sticks to my chest. When we arrived and squeezed ourselves into the Da'an apartment we'd rented, my husband – once accustomed to tropical heat – removed every layer he was wearing. I laughed. 'Welcome to Taiwan.'

I lead him past the park, across the traffic of Fuxing South Road, and onto a lane I can just about remember. My phone stays in my pocket; I search for the back-alley temple a friend once showed me, and then follow the lane to the corner where the barley and taro dessert shop shines fluorescent in the dark.

I cannot find the restaurant I am looking for. But it doesn't matter.

In the days after, I lead us from landmark to landmark, no longer ambling in between. I have long since grown used to the lanes, the quickest way through them. I've picked up pace and stopped needing to notice. Is this what I had wanted walking to be?

It feels strange to walk with someone again.

But every so often I turn, and my husband is no longer by my side. He has drifted into a smaller alley, has stopped to take a photograph.

The alley where a woman sells pan-fried buns to office workers, clouding the passage with steam. A laneway where a man sorts cables, twining them into tidy loops. A path empty of people but living still: the same green I've known in so many lanes like this. Potted plants, all clustered together.

He takes an entire series of photos in those weeks, even though I've never talked about my love of these alleys with him: passageways we never walk. Gaps where new things have grown.

I want to stop and say: it is these paths that made me fluent. But I am moving already, fluid. ■

ANDREW JACKSON
from *From a Small Island*

PRIMITIVE CHILD

Jason Allen-Paisant

1

When I was a child, I knew a tree – mango, coconut, guinep, breadfruit, star apple, guava – through climbing. And if, because of their size, they were unclimbable, I looked longingly at them. I stoned them to down their fruit or I would cut bamboo poles or tree limbs to pick something from them.

These were trees that fed us. We gave short shrift to the ones that bore no food.

I had respect for the large trees – the guango, of course, in the savannah-like fields on our way to grung. Grung was where Mama planted yams. The guango was massive and gave me a feeling of smallness, though not a humiliating one. It made me feel that there was something to aspire to, but that I shouldn't aspire too much, like aspire to be like God. There was a sadness that it gave me, like being extracted from the flow of life. It brought me the knowledge of death. It was a dark tree: tall, fat and unclimbable.

As soon as you come off the brow of the hill and enter the vast clearing, there is the guango tree before me on my left. Under it the cows graze with gaulins on their backs. To get to the grung at the end of this track we pass just under the guango then turn off to the right, through someone else's pasture. We go up through this pasture to the common mango tree. The grung is underneath – quarter-acre of land.

There was hardly ever anybody else besides Mama and me. Once a year, in August, men would come to do men's work, like bringing sticks for the yam vines and planting them. They would cook a pot for everybody at midday and I would be with Mama and all the big people. The smoke would go up through the yam vines and into the mango tree. When the time for digging the yams arrived and the harvest was big, Mama would get a man from the village to help her, mainly to transport the yams back to our home. Otherwise, she would borrow someone's donkey.

Apart from that, it was me and Mama. She did all the weeding, the mulching and the tending of the vines. Most times she would also dig.

And I would spend a whole day there. One whole day by myself around the mango tree, never roaming far away into other yam fields or into the woodland. Just there, playing with beetles, rocks and seeds of mangoes, while Mama worked.

I watched and dreamed. Imagined myself going up in a helicopter like the toy one my cousin, Sis Vads, sent from New York. I dreamed of being a preacher and preached to myself and the trees and the grass. I ate common mangoes and grew tired of them. Getting bored became a way of life, then it became enjoyable. It was in this way that I learned to love silence; to listen to the languages of other things, like hoes, like cutlasses. It grew into watching the vines until I could hear them, for if you watch anything long enough you will hear it – the chlorophyll being distilled in the stalks, and moving, the gaulins cry and the cows. The grung music, the grung life.

A different life started in Porus. From bush to small town. From Mama to Mommy. Second trauma. A place of machines, cars, whirring traffic, concrete. In Porus the only happiness was outside in the bushes. I talked to the trees. They were my subjects and my companions. My best friend was called Califf. We roamed the bushes and Mr Bailey's land, the wrap-head revivalist whose property lay behind my mother's rented house. What was perhaps a few acres seemed sprawling at the time, because on it he had all sorts of fruit trees, a coal kiln, a pigpen buried in the thickness of its interior. There were all sorts of avenues among the trees. It was exciting to lay a trail in a place that was wild. This terrain felt then like it belonged to me particularly, because only I knew it in this way – secret paths connecting different trees which Mommy and her friends chatting in our front yard would not even suspect existed. Being in Mr Bailey's bush was to leave another world that lay just outside the canopies, close but far away. We roamed there, playing police and thief. Sometimes others would join us: Mr Bailey's grandson Sheldon, his granddaughter Jamile.

What drew Califf and me together was a similar story of fatherlessness.

His land was bottom-side our house. It was ancestral land; ours was rented property. We would amble down into his back garden, among rows of coffee bush, smelling the sweetness of the berries, breaking open cacao pods and sucking the pulp-covered seeds: 'sweeties'. We would walk with our slingshots, Califf pretending to identify the baldpates, to know a turtle dove from a ground dove. Never shoot a ground dove because a ground dove was possibly an ancestor returned to live on the land. A duppy.

Califf reared pigs. On the way to feed them, we would pick mangoes in mango season. All was a kingdom of magic. The bush was the rhythm of our days.

Then one year, as we came out of summer, I learned about a French woman in our little village of Porus. It seems she had been there for a year, and the boys, my pubescent friends, had slowly awakened to the knowledge of her existence. Her name was Émeline. We learned that she was a French teacher straight from France, real France. And she taught at the all-girls high school in Mandeville, the capital of our parish, the place where the rich, brown-skinned people lived, and where I also went to school.

I can't remember how I ended up at Émeline's yard. Did I introduce myself? How did the first conversation go? What I remember was that Émeline had suddenly become the reason for my days. A new world. A dream.

I had a knack for French. A lot of people could see that, including Mr Alloggia, my French teacher, himself half-French (the other half was Italian), a priest who had somehow ended up at our high school in Jamaica. I had an obsession for the sounds of the language. I can feel that obsession even today, perfectly reproducing the sound of a language the way I heard it. I would never be satisfied with sounding like myself, a Jamaican speaking French; I needed to sound like Mr Alloggia, *exactly*. I dived in, and it was a joy, an exhilaration even. Learning a language is the closest thing to becoming somebody else. Without realising it then, I was fulfilling a need. So at thirteen going on fourteen, I was becoming French. It had started as a kind of hobby. I could already begin to feel myself escaping from my body. I had found something nobody else was good at – speaking French like a Frenchman, without the understanding, without knowing much vocabulary and grammar and meaning, but sounding pitch-perfect.

I was like this when I met Émeline. Home life at the time was not happy. My mother's relationship had turned bitter, and she was left with a child to raise on her own, while the man formed a family with a woman he'd recently got pregnant. We were told how the other woman had worked Obeah on my mother, how this was the source of the acne that had suddenly appeared on her face, and which stubbornly refused to go away. (The most renowned Mandeville dermatologists were left puzzled.) We were told that this was the reason the man was *guzzummed* – no longer himself; the other woman had 'tied' him. And my mother, refusing, on account of her staunch Christian education, to go to the Obeah man to counteract the woman's 'work' and win back her man, settled into a bitter life. I do not blame her for this. Now that I am grown I understand how hurt can turn you into someone you don't want to become, someone you don't even know. But the shouts were on the increase, the lightning eyes.

The looks that say, 'You making me think of your daddy.' The point is that I was trying to come out of my skin. How clear it is to me now, that my whole obsession with language was this.

At twelve years old, I had not met my father. I know now what I couldn't have understood then. That twelve years is really not a long time, not enough to forget the fact that your father has abandoned you, not enough to stop waiting, hoping, thinking that he might show up one day, that he *should* show up one day. And not enough, certainly not enough, to stop feeling angry that he's still not shown up.

So here I am at thirteen years old. I now have a sister, and I am angry, because my mother is angry, and because I am looking for my father, though I don't know it. Recently, I've wondered whether that was an early sign of autism. The internalised traumas and the inability to speak, the absence of someone who could hear me speak, caused me to store up many hurts, and I realise now how I had regressed emotionally, rendered lethargic by the anger and the silence.

I was looking for my father, but nobody ever *really* talked about him, or what he was like, or even that I had a father. The only thing they ever said was how good-for-nothing he was. *Your wutliss puppa.* And my grandmother stressing how she had me since I was one day old. *It was me and you, over that hill, up that hill to Post Office, come rain or shine . . .* And this grandmother, Mama, as I called her, bringing me to my mother's when I was almost five years old, and leaving quietly while I was having a shower. I had lived with her from my birth and thought she was my mother. She'd said nothing to prepare me; she left without saying goodbye. I endured the shock silently. There was no one to tell.

I was all of twelve when my little sister was born and my mother was abandoned again, and the house was a place of terror.

So you'll understand now the need for escape, and language was it. In my mind, there is a close relationship between language and landscape. Both are imaginary, yet physical. Language is place. I can feel its flesh. I can feel the thickness of language as I sink into it. I can feel a cool shadow as it shields me. I can feel the excitement of its foreign sound. I don't know if we've had previous lives and why one person should feel such an affinity with a sound that is supposedly other, but for me it was like coming home after a long exile.

So somehow I ended up at Émeline's, and I came home to a part of myself. It was at Émeline's that I began to spend my Saturdays, evenings after school and some days during the holidays. Initially, she lived in a little lane along the Old Porus Road. The house belonged to her father-in-law who came and went mysteriously, Émeline's husband was there. He worked as a bricklayer, generally in construction. He smoked a lot and so did she – weed. The first thing that struck me about Émeline was that she was bored. Initially a kept woman, she had come to the village from St Martin with Shine, who was at that time her boyfriend. They married at the New Testament Church of God, perhaps so she could get her papers. Whenever she addressed him, it was affectionately, but they didn't speak very much. They never went places, and she must have felt frustrated to have been parked in this little backwater town, where the only thing that happened was people working Obeah on each other, counteractions of Obeah, thieving of land and disputed inheritances. She was bored. She lived for the stage shows, roots reggae and dance artists, local or near local or of larger fame, but she didn't get to see those very much.

I went to her house often. She made a cassette tape for me, it had Jacques Brel; I can't remember the album but I do remember being thrilled to be listening to music in French (at the time, I did also think that Brel was French). It was exciting to sing along to songs by Serge Gainsbourg, which she'd also introduced to me.

Shortly after we met she went back to France for a visit. On her return, she had a bag of gifts for me. The first was a huge Larousse dictionary. The second was a set of mixtapes marked *Variété française* with singers like Édith Piaf and Georges Brassens, and albums by Noir Désir, Renaud and the rapper MC Solaar. On many of my visits, she would allow me to play these cassettes in her tape deck, while helping me understand some of the more difficult bits. The third thing was a copy of *Les Fables de La Fontaine*. I looked at its front and back covers questioningly. 'It's essential, traditional French poetry,' she informed me, 'everybody has to learn it in France, so I thought, *I must bring that for you.*'

I sat in the cool of Émeline's veranda, screened by a wall of crotons, and read the poems over and over, out loud. Émeline listened distractedly while changing cassettes in the living room stereo – Junior Murvin, U-Roy, Half Pint, Gregory Isaacs – and leafing through her books on Rastafari, Black Power and Santeria. As I memorised *Les Fables de La Fontaine*, looking up unknown words and deepening my knowledge of these rhythms, she was also being entertained. For her too, my company was a way of passing the time. As she sat there dreaming, smoking and listening to reggae, I felt the restlessness of her mind, the way it darted here and there, searching. She had left France on an impulse at eighteen years old. A one-way flight to Saint Martin, a place which must have conjured these images of reggae and Rastafari in her mind. We were fulfilling each other's need to be somewhere else. But now, me sitting on her veranda chanting French poetry seems to me like destiny. I was surprised by her patience at the time, that for her it all seemed obvious. I was surprised by the exotic world in which I found myself, by the strange imaginary created by the language, though nothing felt more natural. I was better at it than at football. And as much as I loved being out and about in the woodlands bordering the train line, playing cricket in the street and raiding the fruit trees of neighbours in the backstreets of Porus, I enjoyed this more. I learned these fables by heart, straightened the sounds, navigated their edges.

Then they moved to a property of almost half an acre, just beside the train line. The house was unfinished and there was scaffolding all around. The inside had marl on the ground. In Jamaica, a person might mount the structure of a two- or three-storey house, while they ready two bedrooms on one side of the ground floor for themselves, their partner and children to sleep in. The house might remain in this unfinished state for years, if not decades, because there is something more significant about this state than the act of finishing.

These unfinished mansions with their Corinthian columns symbolise, for their owners, the dream of property, a sort of reclamation of the poor man's right to luxury.

This is where I would go to see Émeline. I do not think I was in love with her, but I had a fascination. She was in her early twenties at the time, perhaps a mere twenty-two or twenty-three, and in the summer of 1996 when this began to happen, I was almost sixteen, a young man filled with blood. My mother made hints about the fact that she was not good company, about how she had corrupted Paul, ward of one of her colleagues, and a neighbour of theirs at the first house. On the school bus, Paul boasted of sexual exploits with Émeline, but the report from my mother's co-worker was that the boy was taken advantage of. But going to Émeline's was a necessity and I would disobey my mother's orders. Eventually, my defiance won out.

The scenery was rustic, primal. The old train line added a certain mystery to the place. The air of something that once was, as if something from the past was still present. A sense of wonder that this isolated corner was a place of transit connecting so many things. By this time, it was only bauxite being transported on the line to Kingston. Time back then was based on activities like going down to the river, which was near Émeline's house, or roaming along the train line, or hanging out somewhere far from home. Time was bush and woodland. The vegetation was thick and dense, nearly uninterrupted green, a nest: a silence so full it was lonely. No neighbours around for about half a kilometre, only the train line and red dirt tracks down which people might make their way to a field; few people at very few times in the day.

Behind the house was an orange grove fenced off with barbed wire. One could hear the birds, see donkeys in the field on the opposite side of the train line. A shower and toilet were outside the scaffolded house. The water was cold; the place had its own microclimate.

For two years I'd continue to visit this house by the train line, sometimes combining it with a trip to the river with Califf. Sometimes both of us would stop off at Émeline's, but more often than not it would be just me.

I started bringing my compositions from school, the assignments from my French teacher. I sat on a concrete block or on the bare concrete wall of the veranda under construction and practised speaking French with her. Émeline would make soup and we would eat together. Hopeton, Shine's cousin, would be around, and he would eat too.

Those days were marked by inactivity, go-easiness. Émeline had by now quit her teaching job at the school in Mandeville, finding the atmosphere too constricting and conservative. All that was left to do now was chill, smoke weed and wait . . . for something. There was a kind of sweet idleness here, of the aimless, languid passing of time.

By early 1998, Shine had gone back to Saint Martin to work for money to finish the house, and Hopeton was always around. In my mind he was just taking care of the house, looking out for Émeline, offering male presence in this isolated place. But he was also offering company. I didn't understand just how much company until the September of that year. I had spent the summer in Madrid on a scholarship to study Spanish. When I came back, I found a letter from Émeline explaining that she'd had to leave town; she'd fallen pregnant by Hopeton. Shine was on his way back. So that was what the company was all about. Émeline sleeping naked on the bed in the middle of the day was not just Émeline being French; there was an activity, a romance, a different life I was unaware of.

Perhaps I had been a nuisance to their romance, coming every weekend, every day during holidays, stopping off on my way to the river. Perhaps he asked her to send me away, but she never did. She recorded more and more cassettes of Brel, Gainsbourg and Édith Piaf; I had those on replay through the summer. Stopping off at the house under construction and scaffolding, I exercised my new tongue on the verses of 'Le plat pays', 'Ne me quitte pas'. It was like magic: the tongues sank into the body, the body sank into the *port d'Amsterdam*. I was another self, right there on the train line and going down to the river, singing and twisting and flying. There was something of me that I could only find far over the waters, I thought. Where my father lived – some indeterminate place. My mysterious father.

All this, then, this search for father had to do with language. Somehow this fascination with language was a search for lineage, for roots. This was beyond some idea of Africa. My roots seemed to be in the ocean; the ocean being symbolic of my absent father. First trauma. Somehow this too is a landscape. Fatherhood too is a womb that brings us into this world.

2

I'm walking through Roundhay Park on my way to the woods and the sun bears down. The burning on my skin is all the atoms of Coffee Grove, childhood village, place of the grung. Time lives in the leaves of these woods; I'm back in that mountain village walking. We walk to the postal agency, my grandmother and I. She has been carrying me to her workplace since I was one week old. She reminds me of it almost every time I see her, and the occasions are rarer the more I grow.

I am eighteen and I am at university, having left hurriedly and eagerly from my mother's home in Porus. I am twenty-one, just earned my first degree, and teaching French at a high school in Kingston. I am twenty-four doing my master's in French at the University of the West Indies. I am twenty-seven, a teacher of English, French and drama in Freeport, Grand Bahama. I am thirty, and have migrated to Montreal, Canada. I am thirty, almost thirty-one, and have just earned a scholarship to go to Oxford to do my doctorate. I have come back from Montreal and I am preparing to go to England. I see my grandmother for what will be the last time.

We are walking, my grandmother and I, she leads me – she has been carrying me since I was one week old. It is a dry road, under scorching heat, but the rains come often enough; nobody complains. It is also a rainy land. Abundant, green. The crops grow, the farmers work. *Percy werk.* Mama told me that that was my first sentence. Brother Percy is working. And I roll the *tonkit*: my word for the shrivelled, dried coconuts that fall along the roadside.

The red ground runs beside us. Potato slips, tomato beds, carrots, cabbages. Long red ground under the sun, backs bent, heat parching skin. This is a farming land. And at three years old, I walk the whole uphill climb to go to Post Office, Mama's work. It must have been two miles, or two and a half. But it was long for my little feet. I must've been heavy for Mama by that time.

Imagine her carrying me every day, in her arms, on her back. A heavy baby. No choice. All love. No questions. Hard life. Joy and love. How did she manage this weight that I was on her ageing body?

The landscape is her life. Hard but also abundant. People work hard, they live off the land and their words are tender to each other.

So the sun makes me go up again, up the hill, over the hill, through the fields, through the cows, over the bumblebees bumbling the dung, and the gaulins flying from cow back to cow back. The daily rhythm of walking and saying good morning to everyone, to the man who works his field, to the woman cooking the pot, to the children going to school. The heat remembers the little boy sweating, complaining *Mama, I can hardly go* . . . The little boy crying inexplicably. Mama not knowing what to do any more. Mama discovering a fattened tick between big toe and long toe in the night. Poor child. What a mama. At sixty-two years old.

The sun helps me to write my story. All the elements carry feeling.

3

In the Roundhay woods, in Leeds, England, the sun splashes on the trees, their exposed skins glisten. The evening glow penetrates me and I move into it. Inside me a living thing is swelling and ripening.

In this month of December when night falls in early afternoon, it is a struggle to get here. And now I see it; I was made to live.

There is a sadness that returns, for the boy I once was, growing up in Porus. What was my poverty? To go far might have been just to enter the woods behind the house. But there was a wall separating me from it.

The pigpen is there, so are the ackee trees, and the mango and guinep. And there, I can walk in peace and take my time. But I never *took my time*. I never knew that time could be taken, that our lives were entitled to time. Even as a child you internalise that. That your life was less deserving of time than the lives of others. That for you, time was never 'to be wasted'. That your life was marked by doing, working. And at a certain point this word begins to hover above you, around you. You hear it on television, you learn it as a concept, you can't remember when you've first heard it. Leisure. Only certain people have it. Do they have it because they can name it, because they decide to christen it, the way Westerners christen ideas and turn them into money?

Our parents also had internalised this lack of time and we learned it from them. They were always hurrying, always had no time to waste. And we, then, had to learn to not play with the security of kids who had 'leisure', the kids entitled to time.

A bird glides slowly and touches down on the green in Roundhay Park, and people ribboned in darkness look up at the light. Ahead, a grackle walks; jet roads criss-cross in the sky. A dog sprinting after a tennis ball forms a circle around me. Time makes holes in the skin. I dream the red sun of Coffee Grove in this pink sky, to see a bird gliding in the milky wave of yam vines, a bird whose name I've never seen or wondered about, gliding slowly to perch on the common mango tree, while I go for the goats in the field, hear the machete scrape of a lazy walker, the bellow of the goats, the prancing of their hooves on the rough asphalt. And I smell the dark burnings of kerosene oil in the evening air, as Home Sweet Home lamps are lit.

The bird is comfort, a conversation going on between me and all I see. This *is* me. And that silence, that light that makes me stop, their walking on the green, the fresh grass giving off burnt scent of honey, the light above, the cold lines from aeroplanes. How can I name it, this me walking through the park in Leeds?

A woman is coming through. I hear the clinking metal of her dog's leash and I slowly start to walk away. I am doing what we have internalised for centuries. Create space for the white lady. I'm anticipating that I will scare her, make her uncomfortable. I know *I* will. I don't know whether anyone would, but I know I will. I'm wearing a large winter coat and it's buttoned up to my nose, almost like a balaclava. I know that will bother her. And who stops and stands looking like this under a tree? *Round here.* Doing nothing. And in fact, I do make her uncomfortable. She shifts course and goes off a different way. It gives me pleasure. I like the power I have.

It's this thing about not being expected round here. It's the anticipation, the way I begin to regulate and police my own body, to create space. In the middle of nowhere, the Black man making space for the white lady. It reminds me that landscape is created; it's what we put there. It's the way we tell stories about the space; it's the way we place our stories within space and say *there, there is our landscape.*

In Yorkshire I've come to meet a landscape I saw all the time as a child, through my education, in the books we were made to study at school: daffodils, squirrels, the heather, the moor. And I feel the sadness coming on again. Sad about having had to live in another person's landscape, sad thinking that their landscape was better than mine, sad about desiring their landscape more than I desired mine.

But I'm also here because of a landscape that I have constructed. It's the story of me and Émeline that allows me to realise that. The bridge between Coffee Grove, with its yam fields and farmlands, and Oxford, with its dreaming spires, between peasant me and current me going for walks in a park in Leeds, runs right through her. This is the future. This is my 'indeterminate place'.

I've a nice job now and time on my hands, so I sometimes go walking in the middle of the day. The green pulls at something inside me.

Trees, barks, plants, mushrooms, leaves, bird calls. Walking among them, I am also reacquainting myself with my childhood landscape. It's all very different, of course. I do not know the names of flowers and have only just learnt to identify a few of these trees. I stroll through the woods with an app on my phone, whipping it out at the site of a curious-looking one whose shape fascinates me – a fern-leaved beech, a blue Atlas cedar, a towering black pine. I'm fascinated by the patterns of the barks, their complex textures. In May, as flowers suddenly appear from a landscape of grey metal, and trees slowly create magical canopies and bowers, I summon my app to tell me who these creatures are.

In the hillside village, I didn't know the riches I had. I did not know that thirty years later, I would hunger for the spunk of chlorophyll in chocho and yam vines. For rain battering zinc roofs, for games of police and thief, and gun war in Mr Bailey's bush. For kung fu in the roots of the cotton tree. I never knew that time could be *taken*, that our lives were entitled to time. But right now I'm here, standing, taking my time, owning space. ■

COPING WITH THE CHAOTIC WORLD OF COMBAT AND FINDING PEACE AFTER A TRAUMATIC PAST

There Was No Music tells the gripping adventure story of a unique mission to Vietnam and its aftermath. The author, Michael Peters, was a naval aviator among the initial cadre of pilots, dubbed the Seawolves. This memoir traces his relationship with Stacey, a young woman who has also led an unconventional life. Their evolving partnership is affected by the post-Vietnam transition: lives tainted by combat experience and the effects of post-traumatic stress disorder. If you believe that we can heal the past by living in the present, then this book is for you. Available via Amazon and other book retailers.

978-1098313739
There Was No Music
Michael Peters

MANU KEGGENHOFF
Sediments in the glacial meltwater reflect the sunlight to appear blue-green in colour, Taku River, Canada, 2020

CONFLUENCES

Kate Harris

C ross the creek at the weir, you can't miss the trail, there's a sign,' explained Shirley. Then she and Steve walked us there just for something to do. Between tree trunks, Kuthai Lake showed in bright, blank glimpses, like a cloud held to the ground. The plywood walls of buildings at the fisheries camp had warped and weathered grey. There were more cabins and sheds and huts than purposes I could imagine for them, given the camp's seasonal population of two. For sixty days the young Tlingit couple had been stationed here, tasked with counting the sockeye returning to the lake to spawn: at first a dozen a day, then hundreds, sliding like bright clots of blood up the Taku River and its tributaries in the region some call British Columbia and Alaska. When the run hit several thousand, Shirley built a smoker out of scrap lumber. Two months of rain, solitude and smoked salmon with pasta or rice had them eager for company and any food that wasn't fish. Only four more days on duty to go.

It was early September, overcast, a cold edge to the air. Rounded mountains spiked with conifers hunched low around the lake. Trembling aspen were still green among the spruce and pine but shrub birches had started reddening along the muddy ATV track my partner and I had followed here, calling out, 'Hey bear, hey bear,' every few minutes. It had taken four hours to hike to Kuthai. We'd finally spotted the fisheries camp of the Taku River Tlingit First Nation by smoke rising through the trees. I was relieved a generator running outside a cabin meant nobody heard us calling to grizzlies as we approached, especially when Shirley mentioned they'd seen just one all summer, chasing a moose and her calf along the shore.

We'd never met, but most people who live in Atlin, British Columbia – home to roughly 500 – know each other by sight, hearsay or the community Facebook group. I recognized Shirley by her long hair and hazel eyes, Steve by the tilt of his ball cap and baggy camouflage – two profile photos come to life. We offered them potato chips and spicy ramen from our rations, and they offered us water refills and tips on walking the trail. It hadn't been cleared in more than a year. It was easy to find in some places, hard in others. Shirley described distance on it in days of travel: most TRT families – shorthand for Taku River Tlingit – took three or four to reach the Nakina River. Her cousin could walk it in a day, just as I knew Jackie Williams used to, even in winter, with half a dozen beaver pelts strapped to his back.

The creek was fringed with tall grass and clear as breath. A wooden weir combed through the current. Sockeye hovered in the knee-deep water, bits of laminar flow condensed to flesh. In the ocean, this species of salmon – one of five that spawn in the Taku watershed – shimmers blue-silver. When they migrate back to freshwater, the orange-red pigments of their flesh are conveyed to their skin, turning the fish crimson. Our bare feet blushed a similar shade from the chill as we walked among them, scanning the far bank for the sign Shirley had mentioned. I wasn't thinking about coming back in six days: crossing the same water, covering the same ground. I've always been impatient for the next page.

You have to hear the stories over and over again to really learn them, Jackie's grandfather had told him, and he told me in turn. *Then you have to tell them back a few times, to make sure you've got them right.* Those stories aren't mine to share but they braid with some that are. As for this story, I probably won't get it right, not this telling or the next, but the first line is a trail and it goes up.

A piece of plywood nailed to a tree announced the NAKINA TRAIL in polka-dotted letters. Painted next to them were a pair of birds, a leafy vine and some human figures made puny by blue mountains cracked with ice.

One version of world history in the Taku watershed goes like this: a glacier marked the limits of the known until suddenly the ice spoke up. The people on the coast could hear it, plain as speech, coming through a cold distance. Glaciers are sentient beings in Tlingit cosmology, but the singing and drumming that day sounded distinctly anthropogenic, according to Tlingit Elder Elizabeth Nyman. As she describes it in her book, *Gágiwduł.àt: Brought Forth to Reconfirm: The Legacy of a Taku River Tlingit Clan,* two groups of Tlingit were separated by the Taku Glacier. They would merge to become a clan of the Taku River Tlingit First Nation, but first they had to dissolve the cold border between them. They did this, the story goes, by decapitating a slave and dragging his head across the ice, trailing blood. 'It was as if hot water had been poured out; just like that it kept collapsing inward, the glacier kept collapsing inward [as if melting away],' Nyman writes. 'It crumbled apart in a straight line, creating a way for them to travel among one another.'

Glaciers are the gates to the Taku watershed, opening and closing over the ages. In 1794, a survey party for the expedition of British navigator George Vancouver reached the inlet and mistook it for a dead end. A wall of ice hid the Taku River. Floating bergs slowed the boats even in August. The expedition found nowhere to land among 'undissolving frost and snow'. They made a hasty retreat and dismissed the Taku Inlet in the logbook for having 'as dreary and inhospitable an aspect as the imagination can possibly suggest'.

A century later, when a young American woman showed up, the Taku Inlet wasn't cause for retreat but rapture. At twenty-six, Eliza Ruhamah Scidmore was already a celebrated journalist when she sailed up the Inside Passage on the mail steamer *Idaho*. She'd read newspaper dispatches by the naturalist John Muir on her country's newest territory and decided to see it for herself. Muir clearly primed her to delight in Alaska's difficulties, for she exulted in how the *Idaho* was forced to dodge ice floes in the Taku Inlet, where ice rose hundreds of feet from the water, 'every foot of it seamed, jagged, and rent with great fissures, in which the palest prismatic hues were flashing'.

The same could be said for her prose. While too lush and high-handed for modern tastes, too pious with the prejudices of her time, Scidmore's writing is redeemed in places by a sense of irony she no doubt honed on her usual beat: reporting on gilded age society in the national capital. Her 'Washington Gossip' column in the *St. Louis Globe-Democrat* was syndicated in several newspapers across America. She published it under her middle name, Ruhamah, possibly in a bid to remain incognito while offering up gently skewering portraits of the moneyed and powerful: 'This prince of pagans occupies a handsome residence on Lafayette Square,' she wrote of a prominent lawyer; 'Senator Logan, never the most jovial of men, has not been in an amiable mood for some time . . .'

This arch and confiding tone carried over to Scidmore's debut book, *Alaska: Its Southern Coast and the Sitkan Archipelago*, published in 1885. Unlike Muir, who tended to leave people out of a scene lest they contaminate its wildness, Scidmore set the grandeur of the Pacific Northwest against the absurdity of those who came to see it. When she and fellow passengers tried to land on the Taku Glacier in small wooden boats, for instance, the moraine's slope was so gradual they grounded thirty metres away. The crew of the *Idaho* duly shouldered the stout, wealthy passengers – men and women both – and struggled to shore with them through sinking mud. Despite the indignity of this arrival, the Taku Glacier seemed 'so far away and out of the everyday world that we might have been walking a new planet'. Only the young Catholic priest among them was unimpressed. He spent his time on the ice hurling boulders into crevasses, then sat down 'to munch soda crackers from a brown-paper bundle – while the wreck of glaciers, the crash of icebergs, the grinding of ice-floes, and world-building were going on about him'.

Scidmore was born in Iowa and raised in Wisconsin, then Washington DC, where her mother ran a boarding house. She never married, never had children, never had money or connections she didn't earn with words. Perhaps her modest background made her particularly attuned, in an era when women lacked the vote, to who called the shots in Indigenous communities along the Inside Passage, where she noticed Tlingit matriarchs 'giving the casting-vote in domestic councils, and overriding the male decisions in the most high-handed manner'. Elsewhere in Alaska, though, Scidmore overlooked the locals entirely. 'There was something, too, in the consciousness that so few had ever gazed upon the scene before us, with neither guides nor guide books to tell us which way to go, and what emotions to feel,' she said of Glacier Bay, ignoring the fact that Tlingit people hunted and fished in the area and had led Muir to it. Scidmore went on to write the definitive Alaskan guidebook of the late nineteenth and early twentieth centuries, telling other tourists exactly which way to go and what emotions to feel, and kick-starting a mania for Alaskan cruises that persists today. Inflatable Zodiacs now substitute for a crew's shoulders on shore excursions.

The contemporary equivalent of steerage class is the Alaska Marine Highway, a ferry service connecting isolated communities along the Inside Passage. I was twenty-two when I pitched my tent on the rear deck of one such boat, secured it with duct tape against the wind and set sail from Bellingham, Washington, for Juneau, Alaska, the modern capital located about twenty-five kilometres northwest of Taku Inlet. In my backpack were a pair of crampons, some topographical maps and Muir's *Travels in Alaska*. I had yet to hear of Scidmore or the Nakina Trail. The stories I learned that first summer in the north, as a student on a glaciology course, concerned the physical mechanisms behind a glacier's accumulation, compression, ablation and flow. The Taku was the only branch of the Juneau ice field still advancing; all the other glaciers were in retreat. After six weeks, we trekked down the Canadian side of the ice field to where it melts into a huge turquoise lake. Áa Tlein, the Tlingit call it, meaning 'big water', but I wasn't aware of this either. All I knew was that Atlin, as my map identified a village on the lake's eastern shore, was the first place I'd ever travelled to that I didn't want to leave.

I met Elizabeth Nyman's oldest son on a menu. 'I'll have the Jackie Williams!' is something you still hear most mornings at Atlin's gas station cafe, meaning one pancake, two eggs and a side of ham or sausage. Jackie chuckled when I asked him about his favourite breakfast, which he ordered so often the cafe named it for him. 'Laugh and have fun with it, that's what I like. That's what the old people used to do. Give nicknames to people.' I joked that he should give me a nickname, which made him laugh even more. Despite working together for several weeks by then, he could barely remember my real name, let alone a clever substitute. Jackie was in his early eighties at the time, but he could detail the play-by-play of Tlingit–Tahltan battles that happened centuries ago. He could locate villages, salmon caches and cliff art across the TRT's traditional territory, a swath of land roughly the size of Switzerland, spanning the temperate rainforests of coastal Alaska, the glaciated Boundary Ranges above them and the coniferous taiga of northern BC and the Yukon. He could name all the mountains and glaciers and stars in the Taku watershed – the last roadless, damless, unlogged, ecologically intact river system on the Pacific coast of the North American continent – but I was a stranger every time I showed up.

I didn't mind. My role was strictly secretarial, certainly at first. Jackie couldn't read or write, but a friend at the TRT government had been jotting down his tales for years: about growing up on the Taku River, learning the old ways from his grandparents, evading residential school (and all the trauma and dispossession that went with it). This friend eventually helped Jackie self-publish a book, *Lingit Kusteeyi: What My Grandfather Taught Me*. A few years later, the Tlingit Elder hoped to publish a sequel, but everyone working for the TRT government was overtaxed: it isn't easy running a modern nation with a few dozen staff. So I was brought in to read Jackie's stories back to him, verify their details to his satisfaction and compile them for self-publication. When he blanked on my name, he simply called me 'the writer'.

Despite commuting with a cane, Jackie usually beat me to the TRT government office in town, where we met every few days to go over his stories. Most days he wore a flannel shirt, a windbreaker and a brown corduroy ball cap with a cartoon bearded white man on it, fishing for lake trout next to the words ATLIN, BC. Under the cap his hair was silver and cropped neatly level. When he spoke, in a voice high and wavery with age, he had a habit of scratching the zipper on his jacket. Sometimes a young woman named Shauna helped read stories when she wasn't busy with her TRT Land Guardian duties, serving as the 'eyes and ears on the ground' of the nation's traditional territory. We often worried Jackie couldn't hear us; a mining accident had left him partially deaf, and he tended to nod agreeably by default. But we knew for sure he was listening when he laughed in the right places: at the time he seared off his eyebrows playing with gunpowder as a child, prompting his grandmother to paint on replacements with charcoal and pitch; at the way the church bell in Atlin seemed to ring out the name of his friend: JOHN BONE, JOHN BONE! Once he'd stopped chuckling, he'd clarify certain details or tighten the timing of the jokes.

Even when he spoke English, Jackie's words were faintly accented with hissing fricatives, glottalized glides, aspirated stops and other noises from the back of the throat I couldn't reproduce. The Tlingit language has more than two dozen sounds not found in English, beginning and ending in different parts of the mouth. When I tried to pronounce Tlingit names, or phrases that had been transcribed phonetically, Jackie had no clue what I was saying. Shauna knew some of the language but even she struggled. We had to repeat ourselves until Jackie could guess his own meaning, mostly from context. He was the last fluent Tlingit speaker in town. His loneliness as we earnestly bungled his mother tongue must have been acute. After our sessions, I drove him to a local grocery store to pick up the scratch-

and-win lottery tickets his daughter left for him behind the counter. Whenever he won a few bucks, he'd buy more lottery tickets, or use the spoils for an eponymous breakfast at the gas station cafe.

Jackie had many other names, none of which, to my knowledge, featured on menus. As a child he was known as Xóots, Tlingit for grizzly bear. As a young man he was called Jigé ('It means, "you hold lots of things in your hand",' Jackie explained. 'Like me, I know all the history.') And when his grandfather died, Jackie inherited his name, Yáx Góos', meaning 'the cloud on the face of the mountain'. As for me, it was a relief to be anonymous, to wrangle with someone else's words. At night I edited his book in the cabin where I'd recently finished one of my own, a travelogue as remote and skidding as Jackie's tales were intimate and deep. Wanderlust was the narrative theme I knew best. 'It must have been born in me like original sin,' as Scidmore described the compulsion to roam. I'd moved to Atlin a few years earlier in hopes of resolving the paradox of my life: feeling chronically restless yet wanting, at the same time, to put down roots. I didn't aspire to be a foreigner here, though it was my inevitable fate: I'd always be a stranger, a recent arrival, compared to the families who have called the area home since time immemorial – or, in the case of settlers, since the 1896 Klondike Gold Rush.

Jackie's stories hinted at how to arrive more completely. Metaphors were not poetic to him, but the most accurate map possible. 'The Taku is everyone's grandfather,' he always said. History is written on the watershed and so is the future. Proof is in the avalanche scar that anticipated the Alaska–BC border, Jackie explained, and also in the confluence of the Nakina and Sloko rivers. The Nakina is wide and deep, the colour and transparency of steeped tea; the Sloko is narrower, its depth impossible to fathom, clouded as it is with glacial silt from the Juneau ice field. Jackie's grandfather taught him that these dark and light tributaries of the Taku River show how Indigenous and settler cultures should come together. The rivers merge just downstream of the southern terminus of the Nakina Trail.

Jackie passed away before his second book, *Yáx Góos': The Cloud on the Face of the Mountain: Storytelling and Tlingit History*, was ready to print. As the pandemic hit, the First Nation still hadn't found someone able or available to correct phonetic spelling in the manuscript into proper written Tlingit, stalling publication further. Around that same time, Shauna and the other Land Guardians set up an information stop on the only road into Atlin, notifying visitors that the area was closed for travel to anyone not living within a 200-kilometre radius. This public health precaution provoked a troubling community debate on social media over who gets to make and enforce the rules in Atlin. In response, the local board of trade posted a statement asserting that TRT authority only applied on Indian Reserve Lands. Accompanying it was a map of the nine small, scattered plots the Canadian government had pretended, in 1916, it had the right to grant those who have always lived here.

Any sort of confluence between worlds seemed, at that moment, a long way off. But I'd heard Jackie's stories. I knew about the trail. The least I could do was try to get there myself.

We climbed steeply away from Kuthai Lake next to a creek we couldn't see through the trees. I sensed a lot of sky around us, with huge slabs of rock in it, but mostly the walk urged a close focus. Mushrooms torqued up from the trail in a dazzling variety. Some were capped with dirt or moss from their hydraulic surge through the earth. Layers of sod furled back around them like blankets. Each fungus seemed to mimic something else: cauliflower, golf balls, cracked plates, rose-orange coral reefs, children's drawings of domes on stalks with fine red gills. I thought about Jackie growing up on the land, learning the shapes of things from it, so that in seeing coral reefs on television or playing golf later in life he probably thought: mushrooms.

Within a day we were lost. First a bog swallowed the trail, but we found it on the far side. Then the path vanished in a large meadow. John Ward had warned about this. The TRT spokesperson, or elected leader, said the trail was deliberately left vague in places. He'd talked me through tough spots with the help of a topographic map: here a gully with shoulder-high vegetation would make us 'feel like grasshoppers'; here a rockslide offered a view to a mountain 'like a dove flying up'. But I couldn't relate my notes on the meadow to what I was seeing. Or rather, they seemed to apply to everything. John had told me to find the firepit and look for a big pine tree at eleven o'clock; behind it would be rising ground covered in willows, and the trail would be to the left of that. But a clock bearing at the firepit with respect to what noon, exactly? I hadn't thought to ask.

Big pine trees dotted the meadow in several directions. Rising ground covered in willows edged much of its perimeter. The distant mountains we needed to head toward were a blur of green, as if moving away at tremendous speed. We could have been anywhere, Russia or Alaska: the Taku watershed was nearly both. Jackie had shown me a photo of himself posing with the remains of a Russian fort on the Nakina–Inklin confluence. His ancestors had booted the Russians out when they tried to establish a trading post. Which meant that in 1867, when the United States bought a swath of land the size of Mongolia from a distant empire that purported to own it, Taku Inlet and Taku Glacier were part of the deal, but the upper watershed wasn't. Unknown to the TRT, the land was already claimed by what would become Canada, though the border between BC and Alaska wouldn't be settled for decades.

Among the names mockingly proposed for America's newest territory, purchased for two cents an acre, were Walrussia, American Siberia, Polaria and Seward's Folly, the latter after the Secretary of State who pushed for the deal. The government settled on Alaska, an Aleut word for 'mainland'. Few Americans had set foot on it by the time Congress passed the appropriation bill, but they were somehow convinced of the region's worth by William Seward's boosterism and a thin report on its resources by George Davidson, a US Coast Survey geographer who had skirted the coast of southeast Alaska by ship. The interior was pure conjecture, as Davidson himself later admitted: 'The whole area of Alaska and the Northwest Territory of Canada was unknown except along the river courses: and even these were very imperfectly laid down.' Perhaps hoping to redeem America's impulse buy with science, Seward asked Davidson to return to southeast Alaska to observe a rare solar eclipse. The path of totality on 7 August 1869 included two possible observing points: up the Taku or the Chilkat rivers.

These major salmon-bearing rivers feed into the Inside Passage 150 kilometres apart. This is roughly the same distance that separates Atlin and the Taku Inlet, and Atlin and the Chilkat Inlet: the three spots draw a nearly equilateral triangle on a map. Because the Taku is further south than the Chilkat, closer to the Russian-turned-American headquarters of Sitka, it was the most expedient choice for an eclipse-viewing expedition. Yet Davidson opted for the Chilkat, despite having to spend more days on rough water in an open canoe to get there. He reckoned the Tlingit village of Klukwan would make an ideal astronomical station – if its leader, Kohklux (Kaalaxch' in Tlingit), decided to cooperate.

Scidmore later recognized this renowned warrior and diplomat by the bullet hole in his cheek. When another Tlingit held a pistol to his head over some grievance, Kohklux turned to look scornfully at his assailant just as the trigger was pulled. Weak powder meant the bullet merely dislodged a few teeth. Kohklux swallowed them, according to Scidmore, spat out the bullet and handed it back. She thought him 'a chief of advanced and liberal notions, a high-strung, imperious old fellow'. As a boy, he had accompanied his father on the 1852 Chilkat raid that destroyed the Hudson's Bay Company outpost of Fort Selkirk on the Yukon River, securing the Tlingit monopoly on the fur trade for another few decades. When the Chilkats found themselves residents of America overnight, without consultation or compensation, they became 'excessively saucy and turbulent', as a government official described them. Kohklux was imprisoned for some petty offense at the time Davidson arrived in Sitka. 'He was certainly not in a friendly mood,' the geographer observed. And for good reason: some Chilkat

Tlingit had been shot while attempting to escape government custody. Kohklux only agreed to host the scientific expedition in exchange for the release of himself and his people from jail.

A temperate rainforest is a chancy place for astronomy. It poured in the days leading up to the eclipse, but to Davidson's relief, the clouds parted on 7 August. As the moon covered the sun and the world went dark, he and his men let out 'bursts of admiration at this magnificent glory in the heavens'. The Tlingit only cheered when the light returned. Kohklux was impressed by the American geographer's apparent sway over the heavens. He asked Davidson to explain how he sent the sun away and brought it back.

I can just picture Davidson adjusting his tiny spectacles, hastening to clarify his lack of complicity in celestial matters. Judging from what I've seen of his diary, he was more interested in documenting Tlingit art and architecture than the rare astronomical phenomenon he was officially deployed to observe. At least his elaborate drawings of the 'Grand Council House of Kohklux, Chief of the Chilkats', a building now better known as 'Whale House', fill several pages of his personal notebook. The frogs, birds and human faces carved into the roof pillars are copied down in meticulous detail and colour. The eclipse diagram looks bland and slapdash by comparison: pencil sketches of wheels bisected by lines, with wiggles and red blobs on their perimeters. Davidson drew a similar diagram on the back of a Chilkat blanket pattern board to show Kohklux how the moon had slid in front of the sun. In ceremonial exchange for this knowledge, the Chilkat leader gifted Davidson something in turn: a map of the Indigenous trade routes used in the raid on Fort Selkirk seventeen years earlier.

Kohklux had never used a pencil before. For paper, Davidson offered the blank side of a coastal chart. Over three days, the Tlingit chief and his two wives – the sisters Tu-eek and Ḵaatchxixchhe – drew their 800-kilometre return journey on a map that spiraled clockwise. They represented rivers and creeks on it as lines, lakes as ovals and mountain ranges as darkened ridges between valleys. They drew

landmark peaks three-dimensionally, as they would appear to someone travelling past on foot or in a boat. They rendered distances not in degrees of latitude and longitude but in days of travel, and orientation not by compass points but directions of water flow, upstream or down. The sisters gave Davidson more than a hundred place names to mark on the map, in at least three Indigenous languages. Apparently Kohklux and his wives were impressed by the technology of the alphabet, the way Tlingit words could announce themselves in a stranger's mouth thanks to some scribbles (I have my doubts, given Jackie's reaction to me reading phonetic Tlingit). What is certain is that Davidson was so impressed by their geographic knowledge, so convinced of its rigour and accuracy, that he incorporated much of it into the US Coast Survey's official map of Alaska.

Other forms of Indigenous knowledge have not typically been taken on such trust. As we searched for the trail, still lost, I thought about a story I'd reviewed with Jackie that was set in this meadow. It was winter at the time. He was travelling the Nakina Trail with his father and sled dogs. The aurora was spectacular one night: blue-white curtains in the sky that every so often swooped toward Earth with a crackling, hissing sound. Whenever this happened, the dogs would duck and cower, as if to avoid being hit. Jackie saw the Northern Lights on countless occasions, but this was the only time he *heard* them. When I finished reading the story back, he was silent for a long time. I worried his hearing aid was acting up. 'I stopped telling that one,' Jackie finally said. 'People thought I was lying.'

We finally found the trail exactly as described, at a bearing that was obvious in retrospect. Each day we lost the way forward, often for hours, only to pick it up again thanks to John's directions and the faintest clues: a shred of faded pink flagging tape, a sawed-off branch, a spruce toppled by a chainsaw. Clean angles made by human tools. I have never felt such a fondness for stumps.

Cairns of grizzly scat grew more frequent the closer we got to the coast. In some places the bears had stepped neatly in each other's tracks over time, scoring permanent paw prints into the dirt and moss. Usually the prints led to rub trees, identifiable by their smooth, branchless trunks and the blond hairs snagged in their bark, often in places higher than my head. Jackie had told stories about bears keeping paths open for the Tlingit in their absence. Unlike a road paved in gravel or concrete, a trail requires less maintenance the more creatures that use it, at least up to a point. Few had used this one recently, judging by the spiderwebs strung across it. I got into the habit of hiking with a hand in front of my face.

Beyond wildlife, the Taku watershed sees little traffic except for the occasional aircraft overhead and commercial fishing boats near the inlet – but only because the Nakina Trail helped prevent a road from being punched through it. For many years Jackie worked at the Tulsequah Chief Mine in the lower Taku watershed, near the Alaska border, where he operated a digger on rich deposits of gold, zinc, lead, copper and silver. The mine was abandoned in the 1950s when its remoteness, coupled with low metal prices, rendered it uneconomical. Half a century later, a junior mining company proposed to revive Tulsequah Chief by building a 162-kilometre access road to it from Atlin. The route they proposed closely followed and frequently crossed the Nakina Trail, a fact that gave the TRT considerable leverage when they sued the company and the BC government for not sufficiently consulting them on actions that would disrupt their traditional territory. The mining company eventually went into receivership. Losses to investors and creditors amounted to hundreds of millions of dollars, but this didn't stop its CEO from starting fresh: he promptly co-founded another junior mining company and acquired the Tulsequah Chief assets. The alternate access route this second company proposed was shorter and tactfully avoided the Nakina Trail, but it still angered many settlers: they were unhappy about the quiet, dead-end road they lived on being upgraded and extended for industrial traffic. Eventually the second company backed down on building any kind of road, at least for the time being, and proposed to ship ore out by air-cushioned barge on the Taku River.

When this second plan was in its early stages, the company held separate meetings in Atlin for settlers and the TRT and said different things at each; a scheduling complication meant I was able to attend both. What I remember most vividly, besides the doublespeak intended to deepen community divides, were the posters the mining company put up featuring Tlingit art. 'Those are my carvings,' the renowned artist Wayne Carlick quietly announced when he came into the room. 'Nobody asked my permission to use them.' The mine was advertised on the posters in bold letters. Wayne wasn't credited anywhere. A company representative apologized and hastily tore the posters down. The company went bankrupt before the mine could be restarted.

Davidson was among the first to recognize the vast mineral wealth of the northern interior. 'The gold is there,' he asserted with typical understatement in an 1888 US Coast and Geodetic Survey report, but he left open the question of how to reach it. Of course he knew the answer: the Tlingit trade routes that Kohklux and his wives had plotted for Davidson offered the easiest access from coastal Alaska to the gold-studded interior. Yet Davidson left them off the 1869 US Coast Survey map that otherwise revealed, in vivid new detail, the panhandle of Alaska. He didn't divulge the trade routes until decades later, when he wrote an article about the 'Indian map' drawn by Kohklux and his wives, and published it in an obscure climbing journal. On the hand-drawn map that accompanies Davidson's text, featuring geographic data he'd compiled from both Tlingit and Western sources, 'Aht-leen' marks the spot where the Juneau ice field melts back to earth.

Maybe Davidson's delay in revealing the Tlingit trade routes was a courtesy, a small act of resistance against the stampede he suspected was coming. In any case, by the time he published the article, he wasn't giving away any secrets. The Klondike Gold Rush had started a few years earlier. Prospectors crowded the Chilkat trade route to the Yukon interior, and also the Chilkoot trade route a little further east and north. Although the Nakina Trail offered technically easier access to the Yukon River watershed, with a reduced risk of avalanches, few came that way even after gold was found near Atlin Lake. This was thanks in part to vigilance by the TRT, but also to luck: the Taku Inlet, with its crumbling glaciers and shallow braided channels, didn't enable massive shipping transport on the scale that delivered prospectors to the head of the Inside Passage. Today, the Chilkat trade route is a paved, two-lane highway that passes through Klukwan on the way to the town of Haines. The Chilkoot is a popular trail hiked by 10,000 or so tourists each year, many on cruise-ship stopovers in Skagway. The Nakina Trail is still the sort of route you need permission and stories to navigate.

Also recommended is thick clothing, preferably armour. Devil's club, or *Oplopanax horridus* – its Latin roots suggestive of weapons, healing and horror – has what looks like maple leaves, only the size of umbrellas and arrayed with thorns. Like the barbed wire it resembles, this shrub marked a border crossing, in this case from the interior boreal forest to coastal temperate rainforest. It thrived alongside ferns in the lush understory of suddenly enormous trees, firs and cottonwoods as wide as my reach, with bark so deeply rucked I could hide my hands in it. The dense canopy turned direct sunlight into a mist of photons. Devil's club lunged to catch them from any available opening, such as a trail. Hiking along it was like wading through wasps. When the devil's club finally gave way to an airy pine ridge, it was hard to know what to be happier about: the end of the gauntlet, or our first view into the upper Taku Valley.

The Nakina River came in on the left, the milky glaze of the Sloko joined it on the right, and together they flowed through rumpled green peaks toward the coast. Their confluence was tucked out of sight behind a grove of trembling aspen. I had the sense, standing on a ridge where countless others had stood before, over thousands of years, that here the world could bear weight, that it wouldn't give way. I thought about Scidmore in Glacier Bay, revelling in the false idea that she was among the first to gaze on the place, with that peculiarly Euro-American glee for precedent. I grew up steeped in such thinking myself. But wasn't it just as powerful to look out over a wilderness and see it as a neighbourhood?

The bumper sockeye run at Kuthai that summer was no fluke. In previous years, Shirley had told us, barely a dozen salmon made it back to the lake to spawn. An empire of beaver dams on the creek draining from Kuthai Lake, and on the Silver Salmon River it eventually joined, had restricted water flow to a lower canyon. Without deep pools to launch from, sockeye struggled to hurl themselves up a vertical kilometre of falls and rapids. So the TRT Fisheries Department evicted some beaver and chiseled back sections of the canyon, easing the salmon's way upstream. The nation has been making similar interventions on behalf of fish, bears, moose, caribou, rivers and forests ever since the gate to the watershed opened. But such stewardship can only do so much when the biggest threats facing the territory now are beyond local control. However undamaged the watershed itself might be, salmon leaving it, as they must in order to return, face toxic mine tailings, commercial fishing nets, warming oceans. The Taku Glacier is in another state of retreat now, dissolving away this time from a more dispersed, subtle and unceremonious violence. The technical term for what is happening to the Juneau ice field is 'unabated wastage'.

The sun slid out of the valley. Mountains and rivers that remember everything, even what hasn't happened yet, went dark. We pitched the tent in the pines and piled dead branches around it for advance warning if a bear came by. When I crawled inside and pulled off my hiking pants, my legs were covered in red welts and scratches, as if the trail had been blazing me.

A raven overhead, dark wings wet with light. Bear prints enormous along the bank. The Nakina was an opening light followed through the trees. Once in a while the current overturned a rock with a dull clap. We made an offering to the river the way Jackie had taught, then turned back up the trail. We didn't go to the confluence itself, a few hundred metres downstream. Next time, we told ourselves. Or maybe the time after that. It seemed the sort of arrival we needed to earn over and over.

After travelling up the Taku Inlet, Scidmore crossed the Pacific to Japan, where her brother worked for a US consulate. She never stopped wandering – to Java, China, India, the Philippines, The Hague, even back to Alaska twice more – but there is a qualitative difference, in terms of respect and affection, in her books about these places and her books on Japan. In Alaska and beyond, she described local cultures with at worst disdain and at best a kind of shipboard remove, as if she couldn't quite make out whole people on shore. In *Jinrikisha Days in Japan*, her 400-page opus, 'the reader does not feel that he is peeping surreptitiously through a lattice inadvertently left open' – as a contemporaneous reviewer put it – 'but living among them, an honoured guest and personal friend'.

Scidmore wrote about Japan, that is, as if she intended to stay. In some ways she did: she spent more time in that country than anywhere else she travelled, with repeat journeys lasting years, and continuing until the end of her life. Between trips, she campaigned to have Japanese flowering cherry trees planted along the Potomac River in Washington. She spoke out in Congress against anti-Japanese sentiment. She wrote a novel, her only foray into fiction, on the sympathetic treatment of Russian prisoners by the Japanese, told from the perspective of a prisoner's wife. And she railed against the 'unjust treaties' imposed on Japan when Commander Perry, on behalf of the American government in 1853, forced its ports open to trade, ending the country's 220-year-old policy of isolation. 'If the people are to lose their art, the fine finish of their manners, the simplicity of living, all the exquisite charm of their homes,' Scidmore wrote, 'Commander Perry should be rated as their worst enemy.'

Yet somehow another people losing their art, their customs, their homes and their way of life along a Pacific coast didn't perturb her, certainly not to the same extent. She never questioned the moral authority of America to rule over Alaska and its inhabitants. She never spoke out against her fellow citizens prying whatever they could from the Tlingit: gold, salmon, trade routes, art. Particularly coveted by nineteenth-century tourists were copper knives, arrow tips, reed baskets, carved spoons and Chilkat blankets woven from the long white fleece of mountain goats, which Scidmore deemed 'fine trophies for wall decorations'. She paid for these so-called souvenirs, but many didn't. Sightseers and settlers looted heirlooms from Tlingit gravehouses and seasonally empty villages. John Muir himself witnessed an 'archaeological doctor' chop down a totem pole in order to 'enrich some museum or other'. By the warped logic of ethnographic salvage, many outsiders in Scidmore's era didn't see themselves as stealing priceless treasures from the Tlingit; they were saving them from a culture they were convinced would sadly, but rather conveniently, disappear.

Nine years after her inaugural cruise to Alaska, Scidmore became the first woman elected to the board of the National Geographic Society. She was also the first woman to write and edit for the society's prestigious magazine, and later to publish photographs in it (of young Japanese girls in kimonos, their faces cradled by cherry blossoms). Unlike many of her contemporaries in travel and exploration, Scidmore denounced the practice of overwriting Indigenous geographic nomenclature with 'the name of some inconsequent and now forgotten statesman whom it seemed officially desirable to flatter at the time'. Was she appalled, then, to learn that a small mountain in Alaska was called Ruhamah in her honour? She was still alive when it happened; I couldn't find record of her reaction. Later a glacier and bay were also named for Scidmore in the area now enclosed in Glacier Bay National Park, where local Tlingit are banned from hunting on their traditional territory.

When Scidmore died in 1928, her ashes were buried in a Yokohama cemetery. The Japanese installed a plaque beside her grave marker that says: 'A lady who loved cherry blossoms rests here in peace.' Although Ruhamah Mountain and Scidmore Bay are still plainly visible on maps and on the land, Scidmore Glacier has mostly disappeared. All that remains is a patch of snow far up the valley the ice once carved.

S ome stories have all the speed and violence of a straight road. As we hiked away from the Nakina, bear scat looked just as fresh as it had the day before. I wondered what blind spots in my own thinking, my own writing, would make future generations wince. Whatever they are, let this be a partial penance: climbing over fallen trees, wedging between pile-ups of trees, crawling through the thorns – devil's club, wild roses – somehow flourishing under deadfall. It seemed statistically improbable that so many trees had landed on the tightrope of space the trail defined. There were far more than I remembered on the way out, but maybe I was just tired. When I spotted yet another tree blocking the way, I wanted to weep. Instead I got down on hands and knees, shimmied underneath it, stood up on the far side, and gasped.

There was a face. On a tree next to the trail. The eyes peered out from the bark at a human's height. The grain of the exposed wood gathered into contours: cheekbones, a nose, lips slightly apart. Sap beaded on the pale skin like ice sweating. The brow shone with what appeared to be concentration. Scattered on the ground below the carving were still-fragrant curls of pine shavings. Wayne didn't sign his name anywhere, but I recognized his work. He never imposes a vision on materials; instead, it's as if trees have faces and he finds them.

For the next few hours I floated several inches above the trail. What was this transfer of energy, this voltage, granted by some careful gouges in wood? Art is a force acting at a distance that science can't explain. The drawings in Davidson's eclipse expedition diary suddenly made more sense to me. It was as if the geographer understood even then that seeing the Whale House was the greater event, that a shadow was creeping over those carvings as he sketched them, that he was its leading edge. A few years later, another Coast Survey expedition took photographs in Klukwan that confirmed what Davidson's sketches hinted at: Whale House, with its elaborate posts and rainscreen and feast dish, was as stunning and intricate as the temples of Angkor Wat, the Buddhas of Bamiyan.

For decades museum and art collectors tried to acquire the building and its contents. Astronomical sums were offered and refused. 'There wasn't thirty-five bucks in the whole of Klukwan at the time,' one thwarted purchaser said, 'and they turned it down – that's style.' The more unobtainable the Whale House carvings seemed, the more valuable they became, until a family member couldn't resist cashing in.

In 1984, the pillars and rainscreen travelled as far as a warehouse in Seattle before a lawsuit halted their exodus to a New York art dealer. A decade of litigation ensued. When the Tlingit of Klukwan successfully argued in court that Whale House was not individual or even family property, but clan-owned, the carvings were finally repatriated to the Chilkat Valley.

Blueberries had burst into form in the meadow. We couldn't walk anywhere without crushing them. The afternoon was sunny and windless, a prelude to the sort of atmospheric conditions in which it might be possible, in winter on a calm night, for us to hear the Northern Lights. In the end, Jackie agreed to include the story in his second book along with a sidebar that validated his experience in scientific terms. A Finnish acoustics researcher had recently recorded audio of the aurora. With empirical proof of the phenomenon in hand, he set about theorizing how it might happen. He proposed that a temperature inversion could trap positive and negative charges across warmer and cooler layers of sky. When strong geomagnetic storms reach low enough through the atmosphere, the layers discharge, generating the static-like noises that spooked Jackie's dogs nearly a century ago, when his story was dismissed as folklore, even a fib.

The way back to Kuthai looked slimed. All the mushrooms had deflated and gone dark. The air was fragrant with pine needles, moss, rotting leaves and a certain herb that smelled tropical when crushed underfoot, just briefly, as if we'd stepped on a wedge of pineapple. There was more space between everything in the boreal: the trees, the clouds, the roots on the trail, stitching it neatly to the earth like something mended. It was hard to see sockeye in the creek because the dusk light filled the water with trees, but the fish were still around. Shirley and Steve weren't, having left camp a couple of days earlier. Next to a building a dog bed was still out, dented as if just vacated, warm to the touch in the sun.

We limped to the dock and made dinner while dangling our sore feet in the lake. A delicious numbness spread through mine. When I wiggled my toes, broadcasting ripples across the surface, three crimson sockeye swam over to investigate. I tried to photograph them but caught only the lake's glare. Then I clicked through photos from earlier that day: the carving, the tree fallen before it. That's when I realized, with a jolt, that the branches on the deadfall were neatly trimmed. I zoomed in: someone had stood on the trail and sawed the limbs off, but for whatever reason hadn't cut the trunk down or cleared it away. Positioned ahead of the carving, the fallen tree looked haphazard, a random obstacle or barrier, but now I saw it as curatorial. This trail was supposed to bring us to our knees. So that in standing up again, it would be impossible not to see what was there.

The next morning it rained for the first time in a week. We ate breakfast under the shelter of a porch, reluctant to leave, the weather an excuse to linger. I sipped coffee and tried to imagine how it might feel to belong here. To learn a place so well it would never fail to surprise, like a good story. Scidmore's middle name, Ruhamah, I remembered, derived from an Old Testament verse on forgiveness: 'And I will have mercy upon her that had not obtained mercy.' Mist smoked off the water and into the air. Clouds hung motionless in the folds of mountains. I stared at the lake through the trees for a long time before noticing, in a spruce not ten feet away, and straight ahead of me, another face. ∎

Icebergs seen through the porthole of Greenpeace ship *Esperanza*, Antarctica, 2020

FROM THE CENTER OF THE WORLD TO THE END OF THE WORLD

Eliane Brum

TRANSLATED FROM THE PORTUGUESE BY
DIANE GROSKLAUS WHITTY

I had my hand stuck in a toilet in one of the nine bathrooms on the ship *Arctic Sunrise* when Tim Lewis pushed his tousled head through the door to tell me they would be showing a movie that evening about a virus that was devastating the whole world – except the Antarctic. Tim, a freelance marine biologist, was a member of a scientific expedition organized by Greenpeace and it was part of his mission to listen to whales, a task he threw himself into as if listening to a symphony from another world. I was concentrating on scrubbing out a dirty spot of unpleasantly explicit origin, and so I absorbed his information absentmindedly. At that moment, in January 2020, I had no way of knowing that Tim was not simply describing yet another disaster movie.

After two weeks in the Antarctic, the only information we had received was that the Chinese journalists who were to accompany the next stage of the expedition had canceled their trip because a novel virus had surfaced in Wuhan. I didn't watch the film that evening. We were in Paradise Bay, 400 kilometers south of King George Island, the base where we had deplaned and boarded the ship. It was the first time I had ever seen this very clichéd name adorn a landscape with such due justice. The ice wasn't white, but blue. Paradise Bay and its 50,000 hues of blue were too fascinating to glue myself to a screen.

If I had known the film was also a prophecy of coming pandemic times, I might have watched it.

To reach the Greenpeace ship, which had spent nearly a year on a pole-to-pole voyage researching the effects of the climate catastrophe, I had undertaken my own journey, smaller on the map yet much bigger in terms of my own inner geography. Three years earlier, I had quit being a writer who looked at the world from São Paulo, Brazil's largest, wealthiest city, to move to the epicenter of the destruction of the Amazon, to a city called Altamira. I was defending the idea that if the planet's biggest tropical forest is essential to the control of global heating, it is imperative that we shift our understanding of what the center is and what the periphery is. When the climate crisis becomes the greatest challenge along the human path, the Amazon becomes one of the centers of the world. And since defending an idea is not enough – it must be lived – I migrated to the forest and began writing from the Amazon.

Living in a city in the Amazon means living among ruins. Not between blocks of concrete left by an earthquake, but on naked land, calcined by the sun, the wreckage of what once was forest. Attacked on all flanks, Altamira is also a front line in the climate battle. Ranked number one among Brazil's most violent cities, it brings two sides of this war together, with one side (public land thieves, loggers, gunmen) killing the other side (those who place their bodies to defend the forest). I saw friends lose brothers, sisters, mothers and fathers to bullets delivered to the right address. I learned to go to sleep and wake up in fear. I acceded to living with my senses in a permanent state of exhaustion.

Everything about the Amazon is in excess. The colors, the sun, the storms, the mosquitoes flaying your skin, the sounds and smells of the planet's greatest biodiversity. The forest is never silent. Or neutral. Your body is constantly assailed by stimuli that come by sky, land and water, and it reacts. In the Amazon, we can only be in relation to all the others who also are. There is no way you can take an absence from your body in a tropical forest where life bursts ferociously forth every second.

My friends from Brazil's large southern cities or European countries who have come to visit me usually get sick before their fascination has had a chance to set in. They blame it on the food, the climate, jet lag, on all the obvious things. I'm convinced that has nothing to do with it; rather, their reactions are about their own bodies, usually subjected to artificially climatized environments and abruptly exposed to the uncontrollability of nature. It is also the shock that occurs when an existence lived without a body, in front of computer screens or amid jungles of bytes, is suddenly forced to corporify. When these people who have been trying to live solely in their minds step into the forest, they are immediately forced to become flesh, and they no longer know how. The libidinous fame of the tropics derives from this phenomenon: a body that is relentlessly assaulted by its senses and goes back to desiring.

When Greenpeace invited me along on the scientific expedition to the Antarctic, I was grappling with these excesses. I was in Altamira. It was almost Christmas Eve and some of the people whose lives I follow as a journalist needed to find a place to hide. This happens every year. During the holidays institutions are on recess, environmental and human rights organizations have their annual shutdowns, and the forest leaders who are facing death threats have less protection and need to flee. For them, Christmas may bring an early crucifixion. It is a particularly tense time in the Amazon, where everyone seeks refuge and tries not to move. The only New Year's resolution is to stay alive.

I travel a lot, both inside the forest and to different countries around the world, since the struggle for the Amazon has no chance unless it is global. But I only see myself as whole amid the ruins of Altamira. Everywhere else, I feel I'm at some theme park, like Disney World. Especially in the wealthy, organized metropolises of Europe or the United States, where most people consume as if the planet were a department store with an inexhaustible stock. Altamira makes me real. Only reality is absurd; people's illusions are always neat and clean. Feeling real inside what's real is my kind of truth.

I accepted Greenpeace's invitation to Antarctica because Antonio Nobre, my favorite Earth scientist, convinced me how important it would be to be able to draw links between these two front lines in the climate war, the center and the end of the Earth. Nobre is a leading voice in disseminating the idea of 'flying rivers', one of the masterpieces of tropical forests. Every day, Amazonia releases a river bigger than the Amazon over our heads. Through the transpiration of trees alone, 20 trillion liters of water fly into the atmosphere every twenty-four hours. As a great climate regulator, the forest is not the planet's lungs but its heart, and these flying rivers are the veins of a complex circulatory system pushed ever closer to collapse by human destruction.

The thirty-three crew members and guests whom I met on the ship were of thirteen different nationalities, but they shared the awareness that we are living at a defining moment in which humans have become a destructive force capable of altering the planet's climate and body. Some of those aboard studied scientific reports and some produced them, but everyone on that ship knew that pandemics would grow more serious and more frequent due to the reality defined by Greta Thunberg with these words: 'Our house is on fire.'

But knowing and living are different levels of experience. When the virus brought humans to their knees, I remembered the great shaman of the Amazon's Yanomami people, Davi Kopenawa. Many years ago he warned us of the risk of *xawara*:

When the white people tear dangerous minerals out of the depths of the earth, our breath becomes too short and we die very quickly. We do not simply get sick like long ago when we were alone in the forest. This time, all our flesh and even our ghosts are soiled by the *xawara* epidemic smoke that burns us . . . If the breath of life of all our people dies out, the forest will become empty and silent. Our ghosts will then go to join all those who live on the sky's back, already in very large numbers. The sky, which is as sick from the white people's fumes as we are, will start moaning and begin to break apart . . . [The sky] will collapse from end to end. For this time there won't be a single shaman left to hold it up.

In the Amazon I learned that shamans do science in poetic prose. Incapable of listening, our world of white Western tradition does not understand this.

We were in the Antarctic to listen. But nothing I've ever listened to, seen or lived before prepared me for this world in which I did not fit. In a small dinghy, in silence, we launched ourselves into the sea, traveling past ice-blue sculptures. I identified them as blue, but their hues didn't exist in any palette I knew. It was as if we were traveling along a path of giant, silent cathedrals, in shapes more sophisticated than our species had ever dared create. Around our boat, penguins performed synchronized swimming while leopard seals sailed aboard floating ice statues, sleeping away as if no humans were around. We were aliens without having left the planet. But the effect of our massive presence was there. Every few minutes, a series of rumbles pierced the landscape. The Antarctic was melting.

If Altamira had tossed me into the brutal reality of ruins, of a world destroyed by humans, the Antarctic and its nonhuman peoples were still ignorant of all our destructive power, even though the climate crisis was corroding it from the inside. The animals dwelling there could sense something transforming, but they didn't decipher us as a threat. They limited themselves to ignoring us. There, I learned what a world once was, and could be, without us.

The first sign that I was entering an entirely new universe was the stamp. Or rather, the non-stamp. We left Chile from Punta Arenas airport, boarding a small plane for King George Island, where a number of nations have scientific bases. There was no barrier where some government agent asked for my passport and, based on his country's biases, and on his own, decided whether or not I was worthy of crossing the border. The only thing that happened was someone asked, 'Chile or Russia?' This question is just so they know which base to dispatch your luggage to. In that geography, Chile and Russia are side by side and might get together to have a beer or vodka after work. Instead of landing on the beach, my group's luggage was mistakenly sent to Russia. It returned safe and sound.

This doesn't mean there is no control in the Antarctic. You have to request authorization to visit each country's base and also to conduct research or take a tourist trip. But there are no walls, no police, no stamps. When I reached the Antarctic with my body, I understood it as a utopia that realizes itself, the utopia of a world without borders. Antarctica, I discovered there, is the name of everything I fight for. This insight hit me so hard I cried when I disembarked – for the beauty of a living idea and because I was stepping where I shouldn't. The Antarctic was a utopia realizing itself, but my species – me – doesn't fit there. I am not alone in being out of place. There are more tourists, more fishing boats and more mineral exploration vessels. Worse, this utopia is melting.

Almost every day we left the ship and jumped into a dinghy wearing five kilos of clothes reminiscent of astronauts' outfits, and duly disinfected so no microorganism would migrate from the ship to the Antarctic continent, triggering a biological catastrophe. Tim took his hydrophone – basically a waterproof microphone hanging from a long cable – and tossed it deep into the ocean. This time, we would listen not to the whales but to the bottom of the Antarctic sea.

The hydrophone was twenty meters underwater. Tim took off his wool cap, slipped on his headphones and closed his eyes. The six of us – a polar guide, two Greenpeace activists, two journalists and one cameraman – observed every change on his face in silent expectation. First, his look contorted into a scowl. Next his expression transformed into one of surprise. And then came a wry smile. At last Tim said:

'I have never heard anything like it. Not what I expected at all.' I think he was enjoying the suspense, but we just wanted to shake him. After twenty more meters of silence, Tim added: 'It sounds like dripping, like the inside of a gorge.'

One by one, my companions stuck the headphones on for themselves and listened. They described what they were hearing in quite different ways, some like a plumber might describe a leak, others like a monk might describe nirvana. I rifled through the dictionaries in all the languages I knew and could not find a single word. Ever since disembarking in the Antarctic, I had searched for but not found the vowels and consonants that could convey what had never existed in my repertoire. The words I had available to me described situations, objects and creatures similar to those from other worlds, but they did not seem exact enough for that completely different universe. The Antarctic was beyond language, and our languages – whether the English shared by everyone there or my native Portuguese – failed in this new world.

Words missing or falling short – this was not a new experience for me. I face a similar challenge in the Amazon. The words I know do not encompass these wholly diverse territories. I had realized I would have to initiate myself in Indigenous languages to fill in the gaps, or else learn to live with voids. Traveling became a journey not just between concrete territories – rock, oceans, mountains, rivers and gorges – but through the worlds of languages and of language. The Amazon has condemned me to live in the between-worlds, at different steps (or missteps) along the trail between the languages I know and the many Indigenous languages that have lived there for millennia.

There is no human tongue native to the Antarctic, which makes it a territory not outside of languages but outside of language. The explorers – British mostly, the ones worshipped as heroes – basically described what they saw through their own beliefs. Despite the enormous obstacles and incredible doses of despair they confronted to reach the 'frozen continent' – at times forced to eat their own boots or even their dead companions so they wouldn't starve to death submerged in snow and ice – they failed to step away from themselves.

For 4.5 billion years, not a single human whisper was heard in the Antarctic. The first men reached this territory just 200 years ago, when steam engines and electric lighting were already a regular part of life for citizens of the north. New research suggests an older human presence, as well as the possibility that Polynesians reached the continent centuries before the first European 'pioneers'. They were men (literally, men) of their times, and their mission was to dominate. Language, as history has proven, is a prime weapon for those who intend to take possession of lands and build empires. It is fascinating to reread James Clark Ross, the British navy officer who 'discovered' the sea now baptized in his honor. In 1841, he wrote in his diary about what would happen to the seals and penguins after their encounter with the explorers: 'Hitherto beyond the reach of their persecutors, they have enjoyed a life of tranquillity and security, but will now, no doubt, be made to contribute to the wealth of our country.' And so it was: up to 2,000 penguins a day were boiled to produce oil. And when compassion for these birds led to their legal protection, it was the whales' turn to near extinction.

This was the allure of the mission for scientists like Tim, deciphering the language of the nonhumans who have inhabited the Antarctic for thousands of years, and decolonizing themselves in the process. Among the most-studied aquatic animals, dolphins, for example, have their own vocabulary. Each individual can display its own signature whistle or identity. And whales can be recognized by their clans. When clans travel together, they learn. One clan can absorb sentences from another. Whales are themselves and are also others, once they have lived the experience of connection. Listening to, registering and then recognizing their sentences across the decades can tell the story of these whale clans, as well as the impact of the climate crisis on their lives.

At that moment, however, Tim wasn't hearing whales. For the scientists on the expedition, he was listening to something tremendously terrifying and unprecedented. Like us, Tim was listening to the sound of the Antarctic melting. What resembled the notes of a magnificent symphony was in fact a requiem. When snow falls, air bubbles are trapped and compressed inside of glaciers for years, centuries, or even millennia. The rumbling we heard on the surface was water escaping into air. What reached us from the depths of the ocean was the opposite: the sound of air escaping into water.

Shortly before our arrival, on Christmas 2019, the Antarctic had suffered its worst recorded ice melt. Less than two months later, in February 2020, an Argentine base registered a record high of 18.3 degrees Celsius. These records will almost certainly be broken again in the coming years.

As the planet overheats, the sound of thawing grows louder and louder. Almost 70 percent of the world's fresh water is locked up in the Antarctic's snow and ice. If the whole Antarctic ice sheet melts, sea levels will rise at least fifty meters. Well before this, the world we know and built will be radically disrupted. When I understood what I was listening to, what came to my mind – even in the middle of the snow and ice – were the shamans of the tropics, who call white people 'the commodities people'. The accusation echoed in my head: 'You, the commodities people, are eating the entire planet and bringing the sky down on all our heads.' The sound we were listening to in that bay bearing the name of paradise was the sound of the climate catastrophe. If humans do not stop eating the planet, one day this sound will stifle all others. And there will be nothing but silence.

On that night without night (since light is perpetual in the Antarctic summer), I went up on deck. I was looking for some icy calmness so I could process within me the sounds I could not name. Then came a shock – I was jolted by decibels that my brain interpreted as noise because my synapses could not decode them. What I heard was the sound of 'That's the Way (I Like It)'.

A cruise ship had dropped anchor near us, and the passengers were dancing as if there were a tomorrow in an immense hall converted into a disco. Suddenly, this was the sound of the end of the world. And it too had to be listened to, to understand what it had to say.

'People think Antarctica is isolated. That is a myth,' the scientist Marcelo Leppe, director of the Chilean Antarctic Institute, warned us before we boarded. 'The changes are so great it is hard to put them in words. I have seen glaciers retreat by one hundred meters, and parts of the land become so green that it almost looks like a golf course.' In that summer of 2020, 73,000 tourists visited Antarctica.

I still hadn't recovered from KC and the Sunshine Band when the tourists cornered us again. We were about to get off the *Arctic Sunrise* and board a dinghy that would drop us at Hannah Point, 145 kilometers southwest of King George Island. It was early morning, and the plan was to accompany the penguin scientists while they studied the island. Ignácio Soaje, known as Nacho, the Argentinian second-in-command of the ship, came to notify us it wouldn't be possible. We would have to wait until early afternoon. The reason was not some approaching storm, or even a fold in space–time or the Abominable Snowman. The (un)reason was the one-hundred-plus cruise-ship tourists who wanted to be alone on the island. The sight of scientists researching the impact of the climate crisis on penguin colonies would destroy their illusion of an isolated Antarctic, of an adventure in a place nobody reaches unless they have a lot of money, of their fantasy of being twenty-first-century Shackletons or Scotts.

There had been a tense radio discussion between the Greenpeace vessel and the cruise ship since 6.30 that morning. Business interests won the tug of war. Cruise liners have an arrangement: when one stops at an island, all others vanish from sight. Tourists pay dear for the promise of feeling unique – about 1,000 US dollars a day, sometimes much more, depending on itinerary and cabin type. Some travel advertisements refer to potential customers not as 'tourists' but 'explorers'. Their commodities are the Antarctic, unattainable but to a few. 'I'm the only one here, my name is Amundsen,' the selfie caption might read. A small problem, however: around the corner, a line of ships wait their turn to be 'isolated on the last frontier'.

For tourists to have this 'experience', six scientists were obliged to interrupt their research and wait until that afternoon, when the weather turned and time in the field shrank. The change meant the scientists ran the risk of coming ashore on rocks to reach the heart of the island, because weather conditions kept our light boat from landing where access was better. 'How strange,' said a perplexed Noah Strycker, scientist, writer and self-proclaimed 'bird nerd'. 'Tourists used to like talking with us. They thought it was another story to tell when they got home.' I pointed out, sadly, that at a time when truth has become a matter of personal choice, science and scientists are becoming pariahs – although merchants of illusions and buyers of illusions alike have to rely on state-of-the-art science in their efforts to affirm the Earth is flat or pretend they are isolated.

One of the great ethical questions of our time is precisely this: just because we can, should we? Even before I stepped onto the Antarctic, this question haunted me. On no previous trip, in none of the many other geographies I have set foot in, had I so profoundly felt the weight of stepping, literally. Ever since we came to understand that we need to decrease our footprint on the planet (enormously), I've been very conscious of my movements, eating less meat, or none at all, and flying less. But I had never felt this as profoundly as when I first sank my sterilized boot onto King George Island, the gateway to the Antarctic.

In the Amazon, I can only enter Indigenous land or the land of other forest peoples if I ask for their authorization and am duly vaccinated. It is very clear I am in someone else's home, and I try to be as minimally invasive as possible, even though this home is being attacked on all sides by invaders intent on razing it with chainsaws, fire or dynamite. Despite a heat index of forty degrees Celsius, I cover up in the forest. I wear stocky boots and leggings to avoid being bitten by snakes, scorpions or centipedes, or cut or poisoned by a plant. I wear long pants and long-sleeved tops to protect myself from the sun and from the mosquitoes that transmit tropical diseases. I wear a hat so I won't get sunstroke and I slather myself in sunscreen with maximum UVB and UVA protection. In the Amazon I dress to protect myself from a nature unknown to a body fabricated in the city. The peoples of the forest do not. They guide me barefoot and nearly naked, as if the forest and all its excesses were their own body. And they are.

Indigenous peoples were already familiar with the destructive power of viruses and bacteria well before the current pandemic. Researchers estimate that during the sixteenth and seventeenth centuries, about 90 percent of the original population was decimated by invisible creatures that crossed the ocean aboard the bodies of European invaders. When I reached Antarctica, I knew I had to protect the continent from my presence. The difference being that there were no Indigenous humans to question my entrance there. All the peoples of the Antarctic are nonhuman, which puts them in a position of absolute fragility when facing an overdominant, aggressive species like ours.

From the very first minute, I felt I was entering someone else's home without asking permission. Anyone who invades another's home is violating a boundary – a rather universal consensus among the various human cultures spread around the planet. But what could the nonhumans do? Even if we kept our distance and never touched them, it was evident the inhabitants would rather we weren't there. If we forgot to look at the ground, our boots might step on the Antarctic's sparse vegetation, which could take decades to recover. Every time I saw my footprint in the snow, in the penguins' living room, I asked myself if I should be there, and what gave me the right to be there. Marcelo Leppe told me we must be able to tell the world what is happening. But the delicacy required to step foot on the Antarctic imbues us with the enormous responsibility of transmitting what we see, widely and well.

Later, the French actress Marion Cotillard told me she also wondered about her right to be there. She and the Swedish actor Gustaf Skarsgård, who played Floki in the series *Vikings*, joined the expedition as Greenpeace ocean ambassadors. Marion had been about to photograph a penguin but had interrupted herself: 'Why am I doing this?' If it were only to take pictures, she continued, the internet had plenty of much better penguin pictures. If she posted on social media, she would basically be showing off: 'Look how cool I am!' So Marion had thought it might be a way to share an image of beauty. Nowadays, when a celebrity shares beauty, it can help awaken consciousness. But Marion still wasn't entirely convinced. 'Humans think everywhere is their house,' she muttered.

Troubled by dilemmas never envisioned by past explorers, we camped on Low Island, 165 kilometers southwest of King George. The island was wrapped in fog, swept by wind from end to end and beset by frequent storms. The absence of any records suggested we might be the first humans to sleep on this ill-tempered piece of the planet. I had nothing to say along the lines of 'That's one small step for a man, one giant leap for mankind', like Neil Armstrong when he became the first man to step on the moon. Or like the Russian Yuri Gagarin, when he beheld the planet from outside: 'The Earth is blue.' As a typical human living through the sixth mass extinction, the only thing I worried about was disturbing the penguins. Even though no humans had ever camped on that small island, chinstrap penguins are still profoundly affected by human action. These waddling little beings have repeated their marvelous survival routine for thousands of years, but now it's not working anymore. All signs are that climate collapse has cut this species' numbers in half.

Scientists use drones and artificial intelligence to count nests. Then, armed with portable devices, they count them again, three times in a row, to make sure meandering penguins do not dodge the census. I've done many strange things in my life, but I think counting penguins on an Antarctic island ranks top on my personal list. Before that, the strangest thing I had ever done was collect sputum from Indigenous Yanomami in the Amazon to investigate the rate at which gold miners had infected them with tuberculosis. I found it moving to help count penguins in that transfigured world. The act was so tremendously small, but still, those scientists were there to try to correct something very wrong.

Noah, the nerd-bird scientist, was awed. Not because we were the first to camp on the island, but by the idea that the chinstraps were seeing humans for the first time. Other scientists had passed through quickly, but that had been generations of penguins ago. We were the aliens who appeared on their planet aboard craft that came by sea. We were wearing big orange outfits and pitching red tents. Everything on us was covered up, except for a small part of our faces. And from time to time, one by one, we walked over to a trench we had dug in the snow, tore open part of that clothing, exposed our butts (for a penguin, quite an odd region of the human anatomy, I imagine) and pooped. Even our stool is toxic, and so we emptied our bowels into a box that would be carried back to the ship. We had to go to the beach to urinate so our pee would be diluted in the ocean without causing any damage. It wasn't exactly fun at that temperature.

Penguins are much more powerful – their poo can be seen from space. The huge pink patches on Earth muddle up Yuri Gagarin's famed sentence. The color is key to understanding life in the Antarctic. The pink in the poop comes from krill. And krill are everything. But the thing is, krill aren't cute. At least not in any conventional sense. They look like weird shrimp, and that's the only reason krill haven't starred in some animated Disney or Pixar film. The krill reached the height of its show business career with a bit part, as comic relief, in *Happy Feet*, produced at the Animal Logic studio. But the krill deserves a movie where it stars. This outlandish creature not only saves the Antarctic, but the world, every day.

Krill is the favorite dish of almost everyone in the Antarctic. For many species, like the chinstrap, it's also the only one. But of course, krill have to eat too. And what do they eat? Phytoplankton, an organism that does something wondrously important: photosynthesis.

Phytoplankton captures carbon dioxide from the atmosphere and releases oxygen. Krill rise to the surface and eat it. Now the carbon dioxide is inside the krill. Next, whales, penguins, seals – almost all vertebrate species in the Antarctic – eat a portion of the krill. Now the carbon dioxide is inside these much larger beings. And when they die, they take that carbon into deep water rather than releasing it into the atmosphere. More phytoplankton, more photosynthesis, more oxygen for the atmosphere, more food for the krill, more krill for the whale, penguin, seal and all the rest.

This cycle not only sustains all life inside a territory of extremes, it also sustains *our* life. The oceans and forests are responsible for what scientists call carbon sinks, which capture more than 50 percent of the carbon dioxide produced by humans. Or, put another way, were it not for the oceans and forests, there would be 50 percent more carbon dioxide in the atmosphere and humans simply could not live on this planet.

While the main protagonists in the ocean are krill and phytoplankton, a being the size of a hair strand, in the Amazon – the largest terrestrial carbon sink – the stars of the show are gigantic trees such as the kapok, queen of tropical forests. Considered holy by some Amazon peoples, this tree can reach a height of seventy meters, with a trunk diameter of up to three meters. For the Mayans, the kapok supported the universe, its long roots connecting with the world of the dead, its powerful trunk with the middle world, or Earth, and its treetop holding aloft the world of the gods. If the towering kapok ties the depths of the earth to the sky, it also conjures up biodiverse worlds all around it, sending its roots as far as 300 meters into the woodland to ensure equilibrium for its gigantic size. The kapok seeks water to irrigate not just itself but also other species that live in the vastness of its shade. But today, both small beings like krill and phytoplankton and giant ones like the kapok are approaching the point of no return because of the predatory exploitation practiced by big corporations and the governments at their service.

Nostalgia for a world we know will soon be otherwise is called 'solastalgia'. I wasn't familiar with this neologism, one that describes the melancholy I've felt for so long in the Amazon and that deepened in the Antarctic. I learned the term, coined by the Australian philosopher Glenn Albrecht, from Carola Rackete, the German ship captain who became a legend in 2019 when she defied the far right Matteo Salvini and landed on the Italian island of Lampedusa with forty refugees rescued from the Libyan conflict aboard. Carola has spent more time in the Antarctic than anywhere else in the world and she was on the *Arctic Sunrise*'s crew. Solastalgia is the homesickness we feel not because we are far from home but because we are in our home and know this home will soon no longer exist. This was our dread as each rumble announced the melting of the Antarctic; this was my shiver at forty degrees Celsius every time smoke announced the burning of another piece of the forest. At that moment, I didn't yet know that a creature millions of times smaller than a whale would soon lock me up inside four walls for over a year. When your home is converted into a prison, there is no going back.

Solastalgia was the name I gave the whale we met. When we first saw it, it was still some way off. Our dinghy approached cautiously. The whale was at least twelve meters long, a humpback, the one that seems to have wings. It circled the small boat, which was stationary in the water. And then, suddenly, the whale surfaced and opened its huge mouth, so close we could smell krill and fish on its breath. Just one movement and we, like Jonah, would be inside Solastalgia's mouth.

'There is something about whales,' Gustaf Skarsgård told me. There is. Whales cast us into another time. If we tried to convert a whale's leap into a musical score, we wouldn't have the notes. Or we would, but there would be no way to reproduce the tempo at which the notes are played. It comes from another language and another culture. And we feel this in our guts, even though we can't explain it. The humpback whale rises up, lifts its back, opens its fins and leaps. It is hunting. First this is almost a slow-motion flight, but then the whale shifts tempo as it dives. Moving through the oceans, this giant, a world in itself, fertilizes the waters. The whale is the Antarctic's kapok. The kapok is the Amazon's whale.

When we came back from that place from which we would never return, I sat at the ship's kitchen table, teacup in my hands. I had hypothermia of my soul, and there it stayed until late that night. It required all the heat stored inside me to take in this experience. I feel I will always hold within me a space where nothing will be born, but everything will be alive and blue. It is the space of the whale's mouth. I am condemned to live in profound gratitude that I harbor within me beings that do not fit. ■

View from the *Arctic Sunrise* as it transits towards Drake Passage from the Antarctic Peninsula, Antarctica, 2020

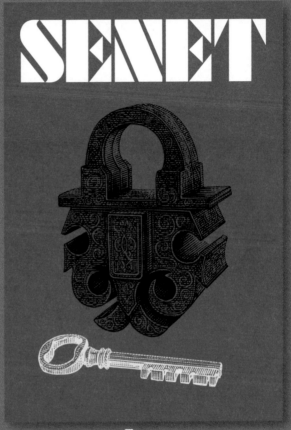

CLARICE LISPECTOR
Hope, 1975

I KNOW WHAT SPRING IS LIKE: CLARICE, CRÔNICAS AND CORCOVADO

Sinéad Gleeson

Introduction

Clarice Lispector (1920–1977) was an acclaimed Brazilian writer of short stories, novels and *crônicas*. In *Discovering the World*, a collection of *crônicas*, her translator Giovanni Pontiero calls the work 'a miscellaneous collection of aphorisms, diary entries, reminiscences, travel notes, essays, loosely defined as "chronicles": a genre peculiar to Brazil which allows poets and writers to address a wider readership on a vast range of topics and themes'. The form is short and concise. Each section is usually titled, and ranges from a handful of lines to three and a half pages.

The following essay takes the form of a collection of *crônicas*.

Changing Narratives

If the recent past has shown us anything, it is that plans are not the concrete things they once were. Travel has changed now, maybe forever. I'm certain that I am not the only writer in this collection whose chosen destination-as-subject had to be revised. Covid-19 rose up; a tsunami of cancellations, grief and fear. Travel bans seem insignificant when people are having their lungs artificially inflated by machines. When the numbers – *the numbers* – kept climbing, and every day new records were set with no sense of triumph. I was asked to write about Lourdes: a sort of sequel to one of the first essays I ever published (coincidentally, in *Granta*). To return and walk its streets through an adult's eyes, not as a girl on crutches bewitched by religion and the idea of a miracle in the ice-cold baths beneath the grotto. Returning to that hallowed, tiny town up in the Pyrenees seemed cyclical, magical, a gift of closure and exploration. But it was not to be. The flights I searched for were never booked. The hotel – the one with the nice view and decent pool – remained unvisited. No drinks were had on its fine-looking terrace. There would be no negotiating the hills I'd called 'vertiginous' in that first essay, walking the looping processional track of the basilica; no immersion in the waters I once felt might be curative.

The journey could now only be taken in the mind, comprised of existing memories. And yet, the symmetry is clear: the destination I decided on is also mired in Catholicism and statues. Warm, non-European and a vast ocean away from Lourdes and Ireland. I couldn't have known it then, but there were many connections – other statues, a different kind of mysticism – waiting for me below the equator.

Cruzando o Atlântico

In 2018, on a brisk Sunday in November, I take the first of three consecutive flights that lead me to Brazil. On the second leg, from London to São Paulo, I settle in to read Clarice Lispector's short stories and *crônicas*. The plane moves through the night, propulsive. Hot, and oblivious to the sleepers around me, I am already moving into her world; a maelstrom of language, a kind of disorientation that suits the sluggish night journey.

From São Paulo, we fly down the coast, frills of waves on the sandbanks beneath. A lone island appears, like a stone on a blanket. Ilha do Bom Abrigo, where African slaves were secretly shipped before being transferred to the mainland. The island is home to the *jararacuçu*, one of the most feared snakes in South America, which grows to over two metres long. In a single bite it can inject enough venom to kill sixteen people. I later discover they are native to Florianópolis, where we land twenty-four hours after leaving Dublin. Our host suggests we eat lunch at the airport. Everyone is feeling that green-at-the-gills trippiness that long plane journeys induce, while our host explains various dishes and orders for us. Listening to her conversation with the waiter, I'm not sure why I had assumed Portuguese would sound like Spanish (both are West Iberian Romance languages). There are echoes and intonations, certainly, even similar words – *agua/água* – but there is something vaguely Slavic about the sound. I think immediately of Lispector, who was born in western Ukraine in 1920. Her family arrived in Brazil when she was still a baby. In his introduction to *Água Viva*, Lispector's final novel, biographer Benjamin Moser wrote: 'Paradoxically, the better one's Portuguese, the more difficult it is to read Clarice Lispector.'

Écriture féminine

I had been invited to Brazil to give two talks, one at a university in Florianópolis, ninety minutes by air to the south of Rio de Janeiro, the other at a cultural centre in Rio itself. The former was to students studying Irish literature, specifically an anthology I'd edited of short stories by Irish women. I wondered what the students of UFSC would make of our literature; if they'd find connections between their country and mine. I planned to discuss the work of several of the women in the collection, women who were writing in a Catholic, patriarchal world, into – and against – religion, gender and what feminist theorist

Hélène Cixous called the 'masculine libidinal economy'. Many of them negotiated with Cixous's concept of *écriture féminine* – writing outside of the masculine sphere, writing of otherness and of a distinctly female (often experimental) experience, rooted in the body. Cixous has also written substantially about Lispector, describing her as 'a woman who says things as closely as possible to a feminine economy, that is to say, one of the greatest generosity possible, of the greatest virtue, of the greatest spending'. Cixous is one of the reasons Lispector's work is becoming more widely translated from Portuguese.

'Freedom is not enough'

Florianópolis is an island connected to the mainland of Santa Catarina state by three bridges, including the Hercílio Luz Bridge, which is older than San Francisco's Golden Gate Bridge. Until the late nineteenth century, the city was called Nossa Senhora do Desterro – Our Lady of Banishment. Now locals refer to it as Floripa. The hotel path is lined with palm trees, tall against the insistent blue of the sky. Behind the hotel lies a hill patchworked with houses in no discernible pattern. It is *primavera* – spring – and the pool is empty, and it feels disorienting to have left winter behind in Dublin. Everything back home is dead or sleeping, each bud and bee, but here, in the distance, summer is readying, stitching itself into an ostentatious costume of colours and textures.

Everyone is tired and retires to their rooms and we are told that the location of tonight's dinner will be worth the trip. Alone, I tune in to the surroundings, something sweet-smelling on the air, the sound of a bird's intermittent song, a kind of welcome. Whenever I arrive somewhere this far from home, or where I don't speak the language, a jolt of placelessness moves through me. A kind of suspension of time and mood. I *feel* and *don't feel*. The urge is usually to walk, to orient myself and figure out where I am on the map, how far I am from the sea or the hills. There's a surfeit of both here. A tiny balcony abuts the room, dropping down to a grass gully. I lie down on the cool sheets but cannot sleep.

Contamination

Clarice Lispector feared that writing so frequently and publicly (the *crônicas* appeared weekly in the *Jornal do Brasil*) would affect her work. 'I am apprehensive. Writing too much and too often can contaminate the word.'

Flor das cinco chagas

As the sun sets on the first night, we drive for what seems like a long time, but is only a few kilometres. Time feels different, expanded. Up hills and round slivers of roads, looking out over the island. The sun fades, the light shifts incrementally. The restaurant is at Ponta das Almas beside Lagoa da Conceição in the northern part of the island. As if being surrounded by water is not enough, there is also a large subtropical lagoon, connected to the ocean by a narrow channel. At the end of a wooden jetty is the clean white line of a sailboat. Insects swarm, so we move inside and sample Brazil's national drink, a caipirinha, made with cachaça, sugar and lime. It is a delicious jolt, tart and refreshing, lime stinging the roof of my mouth. Salads of unfamiliar fruit arrive: carambola, açai, pitanga, the dark flesh glistening. Brazil accounts for over half the world's production of *maracujá* – passion fruit. When missionaries first arrived here in the sixteenth century, they were determined to convert the Indigenous peoples to Christianity. As part of their teaching (and possibly to bridge a language barrier), they used the five-petalled passion-fruit flower. In Portuguese, the name is *'flor das cinco chagas'*, or 'flower of the five wounds', which represent Christ's wounds received during the Crucifixion. Like Ireland, Brazil is a predominantly Catholic country. Its influence seeps into buildings, place names, fruit. At the end of the night, I hover by a large fish tank, watching two jellyfish, all albumen, gyrating in the neon blue. In Portuguese, the word for jellyfish is *água-viva*, an echo of Lispector's many-tentacled novel of the same name, translucent and mysterious.

'Fuck the System'

After an early breakfast of *pasta de guayaba* (guava-paste pastries), we leave for the university. The campus is large and bustles with students. Toilet doors are full of political graffiti, anti-fascist declarations, the evergreen 'fuck the system', and of course Jair Bolsonaro. The conference theme is (Con)Figurations of Families in Irish Literature with a panel focused on the anthology of Irish women. The concept of a national literature is a complex one: what are the parameters of a nation when conveyed in writing? The shorthand, the signifiers of what that nationality is. Examine the literary output of any country and its borders, and social mores are embedded within. The stories we discussed were, on one hand, intrinsically Irish, but they contained themes that seemed resonant with Brazil: social change, the dominance of the Church, emigration, the ghosts of colonialism. The students are attentive and interested and the day goes quickly.

Afterwards, a young man wants to talk about the Anglo-Irish writer Elizabeth Bowen, whose story 'The Demon Lover' has made a huge impression on him. Set in post-war London, it's an atmospheric, sinister piece of work. There are multiple (and conflicting) interpretations: is it a ghost story? About a woman having a breakdown? Do the hallucinatory events in decimated, smoggy London occur at all? The student is considering further research on Bowen and wants to read more of her work. I encourage him to look at her novels, and to keep up his studies, though I know that many of these students have economic obligations to their families.

A persistent topic with everyone I encounter is President Bolsonaro. This student is gay and his parents are afraid for him; they have encouraged him to go back into the closet and not amplify his sexuality. Bowen herself was queer, and closeted in religious Ireland, and this fear of chastisement echoes across the Atlantic. Another female student was kicked out of her parents' home when they realised she was queer. Several students speak of the toxic impact of the presidency on their generation: the increase in hate crimes, homophobes emboldened. Worse, their parents are increasingly attuned to Bolsonaro's rhetoric. A proud homophobe, the president once declared he'd rather have a dead son than a gay son. And like another recent leader in a continent just to the north, a lot of people believe and support his views. Over lunch our host talks about a fear of censorship in the arts. It's a frank, if disheartening, round of conversations.

In 1964, there was a military coup in Rio. While most of the middle classes celebrated, Lispector was 'crestfallen'. In a column that year, she wrote about what she called 'the social thing': how to represent inequality as a writer. 'In Recife the slums were the first truth for me. Long before I felt "art", I felt the terrible deep beauty of the struggle. But the problem is that I have a dumb way of approaching the social fact: I wanted to "do" something to fight social injustice (as if writing weren't doing). What I can't figure out is how to use writing for that, as much as this incapacity wounds and humiliates me.'

Sea wrapped, star draped

The next day, we visit Santo Antônio de Lisboa, named for St Anthony of Padua, who was born in 1195 in Lisbon – then part of Spain – but died aged thirty-five in Italy.

He has many patronages, locating lost things is one, and another is Brazil. He is celebrated here on 12 June, known as Dia dos Namorados – the Day of the Lovers – which is marked by couples in a similar way to Valentine's Day. Near the beach is the Church of Our Lady of Needs, built in the mid-eighteenth century. Behind the belfry is a well-tended cemetery and a mortuary chapel, Nossa Senhora de Lourdes – Our Lady of Lourdes – who has been usurped as the subject of this essay. Inside is a raised pulpit in pale blue wood and a Black Madonna. I'm not looking for guidance or signs, because I am no longer religious, but I have always associated churches as a place to offer an intention, or light a candle. My thoughts drift to my first book: my advance copies are due any day and I am nervous. And then I see it: a statue of the Virgin Mary, an echo of Lourdes. That same sonorous, holy blue, the upturned face of sorrow in both statues. This one sheltering in the shade of a tiny church, far from her weather-beaten sister, outside year round. Whenever she shows up – at Irish roadside grottos, or here under the Brazilian sun – I still, oddly, find comfort in her. A writer friend diligently photographs 'Marys', so I take a photo for her of this Mary in her dark blue cloak covered in gold stars. Sea wrapped and star draped. Stella Maris, Star of the Sea. A week later, back in Dublin, an advance copy of my book arrives in the same blue shade, with a gold star and foil rays. Prophetic, allegorical.

Estátuas sagradas

Statues always remind me of my grandmother, diligently praying, or ''ating the statues', as it was described in her working-class area. She and Lispector were both born in 1920. One grew up in a Dublin tenement, the other in Recife. For my grandmother, statues were a tangible connection to God; a physical manifestation of her faith. Lispector prescribed the idea that God existed nowhere and everywhere; in her deepest thoughts and outside in the green expanse of the earth.

Nossa Senhora

While working on this essay, a translator of Lispector who has heard I'm writing about her sends me an email. The subject line reads 'Nossa Senhora'.

The Hour of the Star

While Ireland and Brazil are both predominantly Catholic, both have become more secularist in recent years. Lispector was brought up in Judaism but abandoned it, yet God and the divine permeate her writing. The protagonist in *A Breath of Life* asks, 'Is God a word?' Rodrigo in *The Hour of the Star* declares, 'God is the world.' In his biography of Lispector, Moser describes her collective work as 'the greatest spiritual autobiography of the twentieth century'. She was interested in the works of the Dutch philosopher Baruch Spinoza, particularly *Ethics*, which she included a section of in *Near to the Wild Heart*. Spinoza believed in the idea of '*Deus sive natura*', or that God and nature are interchangeable. This pantheistic element of nature and God lingers in Lispector's work. Lispector owned *Annunciation*, a painting of a pregnant Virgin Mary and an archangel by the Italian artist Angelo Savelli. In a *crónica* from December 1968, she writes: 'All human beings experience an annunciation . . . That mission is by no means impossible: each of us is responsible for the entire world.' There is an ecological, environmental echo in these words, one that crosses the mind of any long-haul traveller. While Lispector may have resisted organised religion as she made her enquiries into the divine, she also went to fortune tellers and consulted astrologers. In 1975, she was invited to speak at the First World Congress of Sorcery in Colombia, and read her story 'The Egg and the Chicken' for an audience of witches and warlocks (Lispector was often referred to as 'the great witch of Brazilian literature'). Once, in an interview, she told a journalist: 'I am a mystic. I have no religion.'

The nameless mountain

K and J, two sisters who are both researching Irish literature and film at UFSC, accompany us to Santo Antônio. They are funny and patient with my fast-talking English. K is an enthusiastic guide, keen to know more about Ireland and any connections between our homelands. Their father once worked as a policeman in Santo Antônio, and was based in a station near Praça Roldão da Rocha Pires. This was the first street to be paved in the state of Santa Catarina, in anticipation of a visit to the town by Emperor Dom Pedro II in 1845. They tell me that when they were children, people said that the emperor's daughter Princess Isabel also visited Roldão Square. She was an important figure in Brazilian colonial history, abolishing slavery in 1888 by signing the Lei Áurea, or the Golden Law.

Despite the bridges, the island feels isolated from the mainland. A mountain range runs along the opposite bay, and when I ask the name no one knows. 'It doesn't have a name,' says J, and I like the idea of this nameless mountain, looming over the land. We drive to the district Jurerê Internacional, favoured by some of Brazil's most famous footballers. Ronaldinho and Ronaldo (nicknamed O Fenômeno in Brazil) have homes here, and Liverpool's Roberto Firmino started his career in Figueirense in Florianópolis. The pristine houses and affluent location reek of luxury, far from the favelas of Rio. On the narrow path down to the beach, a massive four-foot Teju lizard emerges from the bushes. I jump, and yield to let him pass. He plods slowly into the greenery. On the strand, the sea is pale blue above a floor of sand, cooling our feet. The Teju brings to mind Lispector's many fictionalised animals: chickens, cockroaches, dogs. In a *crônica* from March 1971,she writes: 'Not to have been born an animal seems to be one of my secret regrets. Their call comes to me from some remote past and I can only respond with profound disquiet. Their call summons me.'

Avenida das Rendeiras

In the *crônicas*, Lispector returned several times to angels and the Annunciation. Not as a means of biblical scholarship, but as an exploration of grace. In 'State of Grace' in 1968, she describes the inspiration that comes from making art as a 'special grace', with an 'almost mathematical light'. Its source is not religion, but the light of other people, places and things. A state of grace, Lispector writes, should be short-lived, episodic. I have a sense of this on my final night in Florianópolis; the grateful feeling of being in a place I know I may never return to, already receding into memory. On the last night we are in a restaurant on Avenida das Rendeiras that only serves red wine. Surrounded by others, eating *camarão na moranga*, a creamy local stew of shrimp and cheese served inside a hollowed-out pumpkin, I feel that sense of grace, of the short-lived and ephemeral.

'Anything was possible; people of every sort . . .'

On the advice of the Irish Consul, we fly to the domestic airport in Rio de Janeiro. The road from the international airport is considered dangerous for tourists. There have been kidnappings and hijackings. Florianópolis is not a realistic introduction to Brazil, and is no preparation for the poverty in Rio. The road in from the airport is clustered with tiny buildings roofed only with corrugated metal. We pass people living under the bridges and young men straddle the roadsides selling wares in large packs shrouded in plastic to keep them dry. The favelas are all over the city: Pavão up behind the Copacabana, Babilônia above Leme; Providência is considered to be the oldest favela, and Rocinha the most populous, with 100,000 inhabitants. Whenever I arrive somewhere new my first instinct has always been to get out and train my inner compass to the city, to wander, but I'm advised to stick to the seafront and avoid the backstreets. The hotel overlooks Copacabana so I head out into the dull afternoon, along the swirling grey and cream *calçada portuguesa* between the road and the famous beach.

Instantly it feels like Lispector's world, the one that shows up so frequently in the *crônicas*. In 'Forgiving God' she walks along Avenida Copacabana, imagining herself to be 'the Mother of God who was both earth and the world'. It's a quasi-religious experience – only the reverie is interrupted when she steps on a dead rat. Several of her short stories (including this one) began as *crônicas*. A little further down the seafront is the pristine art deco facade of the Copacabana Palace hotel, the setting for Fred Astaire and Ginger Rogers's 1933 *Flying Down to Rio*. In Lispector's story 'Beauty and the Beast, or the Enormous Wound', the wife of a rich Rio banker leaves the hotel's salon and is awaiting her driver. A beggar asks for money, and the woman's initial revulsion turns into a philosophical reckoning: 'on a physical level they were equal . . . on Avenida Copacabana, anything was possible: people of every sort. At least a different sort from hers.' The story captures what still divides Rio: a gaping chasm between wealth and poverty. It's midweek and overcast, but there are still sellers and hustlers along the strip. Just off the avenida, two homeless women huddle asleep on the ground, oblivious to pedestrians.

Changing direction, I walk towards Leme, where Lispector moved in 1959 as a separated mother of two. *Leme* means 'rudder' – the region is named for the large rock headland that resembles that part of a ship. Clarice felt at home here, at the end of Copacabana. On a wall along Caminho dos Pescadores (Fisherman's Way), sculptor Edgar Duvivier's bronze statue of Lispector sits against the backdrop of the beach, with her faithful dog Ulisses. Read even a little about

Lispector's life, and there will be many references to her as an aloof hermit who avoided socialising, but she liked walking, and browsing the markets with her sons, though it is still a stretch to think of her as a flâneuse. But the city is the beating heart in so much of the work. If the narrative is elusive, working outside of chronology, the places in her work are a dropped pin: Catete, Leme, Cosme Velho, Botafogo. In 2020, a photo of the statue appears online with Clarice and Ulisses wearing face masks.

The moral of the garden

After Floripa's lagoon, there is another unexpected body of water in central Rio. Lagoa Rodrigo de Freitas is close to Rio's Botanical Gardens, where Lispector liked to walk. It appears often in her work, and afforded her the kind of solace that her character Ana initially finds in the short story 'Love': 'The vastness seemed to calm her, the silence regulated her breathing. She was falling asleep inside herself.' Ana escapes the demands of her domestic life, but time passes quickly and the space around her becomes something strange and sinister, a rottenness in each plant and creature. In *Água Viva*, the unnamed narrator is similarly overwhelmed. 'In the Botanical Gardens, I get worn out. With my glance, I must look after thousands of plants and trees and especially the giant water lily.'

Os Tubarões

The weather in Rio is cooler than Florianópolis. More unsettled and overcast, the sky all marbled grey. Before that evening's event, I head to the rooftop bar to take in the view, looking down over the sea. I absently search for 'Copacabana' and 'shark attack' on my phone, and discover there have been several, some fatal. One result has a more sensationalist headline about Recife, where Clarice Lispector grew up. In the twenty years until 2012, a twenty-kilometre stretch of Recife's beaches had fifty-six shark attacks, twenty-one fatal, the highest shark attack rate in the world. In the hotel pool, two men are photographing each other, teeth flashing, jumping upwards in the water. Over and over they repeat this in a bid for the perfect, curated shot. It starts to rain and it's hard not to admire their commitment to this odd choreography. To the right, the waves of the Copacabana darken, forming a crescent all the way to Ipanema, where the event will be held.

Ipanema

The Ipanema venue is Casa de Cultura Laura Alvim, named after the daughter of a famous doctor in the city. It overlooks Ipanema Beach, and a woman at the event says that Laura was the inspiration for Antônio Carlos Jobim's 'The Girl from Ipanema', even though Laura was fifty in 1964, when the song was released. The interior roof is vaulted, and after the event I'm admiring its rainbow shades when an older woman approaches. Her hair is immaculate, her face heavily made up. She proudly declares herself to be a) sixty-eight and b) a huge Bolsonaro supporter ('He's great . . . very good for the country'). I ask another guest about Lispector, and learn that she translated both Oscar Wilde and Jonathan Swift. Despite their shared regard for the epiphany, and her borrowing of 'near to the wild heart' from *A Portrait of the Artist as a Young Man*, Lispector never translated Joyce, and had not read him when her first book was published.

I slip out to the terrace overlooking the sea, and think of 'As You Sleep', another of the *crônicas*. Unable to sleep, Lispector paces a terrace in the middle of the night, listening to and watching the waves. The sea at night is remote, lonely, and its darkness makes her think of all the people she loves, sleeping or socialising. Thousands of kilometres from here, my husband and children are doing just that, and will be easing their frames out of bed for the day ahead. Lispector wrote frequently of her sons in the *crônicas*, and yet she feared the form would lead readers to frame the work as autobiography. The words about her children are some of her least opaque, full of love, but also fear and exhaustion. In Ipanema, the wind is up, raindrops skimming the waves in the bay.

Lusófonos

Spanish is the dominant language of South America, but there are over 250 million *Lusófonos* – lusophone people – in ten sovereign territories where Portuguese is an official language (Brazil, with 210 million, has the largest number of Portuguese speakers in the world). While writing this essay, an email arrives from an academic I met in Santa Catarina to say she wants to translate my essay collection and has found a Portuguese publisher. I wonder how the words will sound in this unfamiliar language – *constelações, sangue, quadril, fantasma*.

One of the essays deals with Ireland's recent abortion referendum, and the translator and I discuss neighbouring Argentina, which recently voted to legalise abortion. Bolsonaro declares that he will never allow this to happen in Brazil: 'I am in deep mourning for the lives of Argentinian children who can now be ripped from their mothers' wombs with the state's full consent. My government and I will do whatever we can so that abortion is never approved in our soil.' The language is strikingly familiar to the polemics heard from Irish pro-life factions arguing against the Repeal the 8th campaign in 2018.

The day after Bolsonaro's tweet, *Diva*, by artist Juliana Notari, appears on a hillside near a museum in Pernambuco state. Measuring thirty-three metres high, sixteen metres wide and two metres deep, it resembles a wound cut into the hill, but is in fact a giant vagina made of concrete and resin. Notari states that it is both, and its aim is to question 'the relationship between nature and culture in our phallocentric and anthropocentric western society'. It provokes ire and derision in right-wing circles, with Bolsonaro's political mentor Olavo de Carvalho suggesting that a giant penis be built opposite. Notari, like Lispector, is from Recife.

Infrathin

From 1967 to 1973, Lispector was one of the few female *crônistas*, writing whatever she wanted within the patriarchal world of Brazil. The form – and the public platform – allowed her to say, and be, whoever she wanted, blurring the lines for the reader. To be categoric, or amorphous; to resist declaring which elements of her writing were fiction and non-fiction. Her work is predicated on the gaps that veer close to one another but don't meet. To me, they embody Marcel Duchamp's concept of the infrathin (*inframince*): something that has an indefinable in-betweenness. Being a visitor to a city is strikingly similar. To be *in*, but not *of* a place.

Corcovado

Statues keep showing up on this trip, and there is one left: one of the most famous, not just in Rio, or Brazil, but recognisable to millions around the world. After the Virgin Mary in Santa Antônio, and the bronze Clarice in Leme, it would be remiss to skip *Cristo Redentor*. Chunky clouds in metal shades crowd overhead as we buy tickets and board a bus to begin the ascent. Moving closer to the sky with each bend, rain rattling the windshield. Visibility is poor and it takes a few minutes to realise we're driving through a cloud. The pressure makes my ears pop. Everyone vigilantly watches for *Cristo*, waiting for him to emerge from the clouds in a suitably biblical manner. The route moves up through Tijuca Forest, now a national park, a massive expanse that spreads out from the urban centres of Copacabana and Botafogo. It's one of the world's largest urban forests, and features in Lispector's novel *An Apprenticeship, or The Book of Pleasures*.

Torrential rain pours down the road in heavy streams as we crowd into the tiny elevator. Through the glass there are only trees and cloud, and we move up through the rainforest. The mountain itself is called Corcovado, which translates as 'hunchback' in Portuguese. It stands at 710 metres high. The hill was originally named Pináculo da Tentação by sixteenth-century settlers, meaning Pinnacle of Temptation, a reference to the final temptation of Christ. In the Bible, the Devil took Jesus to a 'very high place' from which 'all the kingdoms of the world' could be seen, indicating the scale of the dominion Jesus would have if he gave in to Satan. *Cristo Redentor* is impressive, even shrouded in cloud, and perhaps because of the weather it seems possessed of a distinctly religious sorrow.

The fabled view is obscured, with no aerial vista of Copacabana or Sugar Loaf or the favelas. But we are swaddled in clouds, which almost makes up for it. Famous landmarks require a certain kind of procedure: circling, looking, waiting a respectable amount of time before pulling out the camera. A certain kind of behaviour is required with religious monuments too. Tilting my phone upwards, I try to figure out how to capture Jesus and his twenty-eight-metre arm span. Our host points out that at least this photo will be unique: the opposite of a postcard idyll, or sun-streaked selfies. A different kind of memento. I angle my phone up towards the concrete embrace of Christ and click.

Boundaries, circumferences

Since early 2020 the boundaries of the world have become rigid. Everything feels further away, less tangible, than it actually is. If I had made it back to the hills of Lourdes, this essay would not exist. I would not have got to tell you about the Ilha do Bom Abrigo and the *jararacuçu*'s venom; the elaborate shrimp dishes of Florianópolis, holy statues, rainforests and the mysticism of Clarice Lispector. Life's circumferences are small, but intersections happen when we least expect them. In January 2021, K – one of the sisters who drove me to Santa Antônio in Floripa – is studying in Dublin. It is not possible to meet up because of a five-kilometre travel restriction and a ban on home visits. Cafes and restaurants are closed, so we cannot eat shrimp, or find a Dublin barman who knows how to make a caipirinha. I want to apologise for the specific sting of an Irish winter, rue the fact that we're not sitting in the sun in Santa Antônio, looking at the nameless mountain. But we will meet soon, when it's warmer, when the city, like all cities, looks less disconsolate than in the cold, when it is not dark at 5 p.m. When the world has opened up – vast, unknowable – and our collective horizons expand once again. In one of her final *crônicas*, entitled 'Refuge', Clarice imagines herself in a forest surrounded by butterflies; it's an immersive experience, focused on travelling in the mind, embracing the present and finding contentment wherever we can. It's uncharacteristically Zen, an unexpected source of solace in these times when the world is out of sync.

'Each of us is in the right place, and I am perfectly happy with mine.'

Tempo Perdito

A place isn't special if you live there all the time. To the Rio locals, Copacabana is just another beach, a slick crescent of sand. In *Água Viva*, Clarice wants to 'capture the present', which is what writing about a specific place is. Each step, each mile is an act of cartography. The day and time you set out matters: you may get a glorious, sunny view of *Cristo Redentor*, or the statue half submerged in cloud, a melancholic deity. In a small act of Lispectorian significance, I lost my watch in Florianópolis. I retraced the tree-lined path to my door, checked the balcony where I'd had a nightcap to beat the jet lag, but it failed to turn up. Had this happened two days before, I could have lit a candle to St Anthony at the church in Santo Antônio de Lisboa, to ask for its return – but I never saw it again. If the battery has not run out, it may still be marking time, lost near that graveyard by the sea, or on the sands at Jurerê. Four hours behind Dublin until its final tick. Every time we visit a place, a small part of ourselves is left behind, pulsing, pulsing, until we return and all possibility is reset. ■

With thanks to Stefan Tobler for his assistance with some of the Portuguese translations.

CONTRIBUTORS

Jason Allen-Paisant is a Jamaican poet and non-fiction writer based in the UK. He is the author of *Thinking with Trees*, and of the forthcoming memoir *Primitive Child: On Blackness, Landscape and Reclaiming Time.*

Carlos Manuel Álvarez is a journalist and author. He is the editor of *El Estornudo* and regularly contributes to the *New York Times*, Al Jazeera, *Internationale*, BBC World, *El Malpensante* and *Gatopardo.* His first collection of reportage, *The Tribe*, was published in 2017 by Sexto Piso, and will be published in English in 2022 by Fitzcarraldo Editions, in a translation by Frank Wynne.

William Atkins is the author of *The Immeasurable World: A Desert Journey*, which won the 2019 Stanford Dolman Travel Book of the Year, and *Exiles: Three Island Journeys*, which publishes in 2022.

Eliane Brum is a Brazilian writer, journalist and documentary film-maker. She is the author of eight non-fiction books, including *The Collector of Leftover Souls*, as well as the novel *One Two.* She has been awarded more than forty national and international journalism prizes, and has a regular column in *El País.*

Francisco Cantú is the author of *The Line Becomes a River*, winner of the 2018 Los Angeles Times Book Prize and a finalist for the National Book Critics Circle Award in non-fiction. His writing and translations have been featured in the *New Yorker, Best American Essays, Harper's* and *VQR*, as well as on *This American Life.* A lifelong resident of the Southwest, he now lives in Tucson and coordinates the Field Studies in Writing program at the University of Arizona.

Jennifer Croft won the 2020 William Saroyan International Prize for Writing for her memoir *Homesick* and the 2018 Man Booker International Prize for her translation from Polish of Nobel laureate Olga Tokarczuk's *Flights.* She is the author of *Serpientes y escaleras* and *Notes on Postcards* and holds a PhD in Comparative Literary Studies from Northwestern University.

Bathsheba Demuth is an Assistant Professor of History and Environment and Society at Brown University, and the author of *Floating Coast: An Environmental History of the Bering Strait*, which has won a number of prizes. Her writing has appeared in publications ranging from the *American Historical Review* to the *New Yorker.*

Sinéad Gleeson is the author of the award-winning essay collection *Constellations*, and has edited four anthologies of Irish short stories. She is currently working on a novel, and a forthcoming book of essays about music by women.

Diane Grosklaus Whitty's translations include *The Collector of Leftover Souls* by Eliane Brum, which was longlisted for the 2019 National Book Award for Translated Literature; *Activist Biology* by Regina Horta Duarte; *The Sanitation of Brazil* by Gilberto Hochman; and *The Devil and the Land of the Holy Cross* by Laura de Mello e Souza. She spent twenty-three years in Brazil and now lives in Madison, Wisconsin.

Dominic Guerrera is of Ngarrindjeri, Kaurna and Italian descent. Guerrera has primarily worked as an Aboriginal health educator, with a focus on sexual health. His poetry has been published in *Cordite Poetry Review* and *fine print*, and was the recipient of the 2021 Oodgeroo Noonuccal Indigenous Poetry Prize.

Kate Harris lives off-grid in a cabin in northern British Columbia. She is the author of *Lands of Lost Borders: A Journey on the Silk Road.*

Roni Horn's œuvre focuses on conceptual photography, sculpture, books and drawing. Recent solo exhibitions include the Tate Modern, Whitney Museum of American Art, Centre Pompidou, Kunsthaus Bregenz, Hamburger Kunsthalle, Kunsthalle Basel, Fundació Joan Miró, De Pont Museum, Fondation Beyeler, Glenstone Museum, Pinakothek der Moderne, the Menil Drawing Institute and the Pola Museum of Art.

Emmanuel Iduma is the author of *A Stranger's Pose*, a book of travel stories which was longlisted for the RSL Ondaatje Prize. His essays and art criticism have been published in the *New York Review of Books, Aperture, Artforum* and *Art in America*. *I Am Still With You*, his memoir on the aftermath of the Nigerian Civil War, is forthcoming from William Collins.

Kapka Kassabova is most recently the author of the multi-award-winning *Border* and *To the Lake*. Her new book *Elixir* will be published in 2023. She grew up in Bulgaria, was educated in New Zealand, and for the last sixteen years has lived in Scotland.

Taran N. Khan is a journalist and writer based in Mumbai. She is the author of *Shadow City: A Woman Walks Kabul.*

Jessica J. Lee is an author, environmental historian and winner of the Hilary Weston Writers' Trust Prize for Nonfiction, the Boardman Tasker Award for Mountain Literature and the RBC Taylor Prize Emerging Writer Award. She has written two books of nature writing: *Turning* and *Two Trees Make a Forest*. Jessica is the founding editor of the *Willowherb Review* and is a researcher at the University of Cambridge.

Ben Mauk lives in Berlin, where he directs the Berlin Writers' Workshop. He writes for the *New York Times*

Magazine, the *New Yorker* and *Harper's*, among other publications. He is writing a book for Farrar, Straus and Giroux.

Pascale Petit was born in Paris, grew up in France and Wales, and lives in Cornwall. She is of French, Welsh and Indian heritage. Her eighth collection, *Tiger Girl*, was shortlisted for the Forward Prize for Best Collection and for Wales Book of the Year. Her seventh collection, *Mama Amazonica*, won the inaugural 2020 Laurel Prize and the 2018 RSL Ondaatje Prize. Four of her collections have been shortlisted for the T.S. Eliot Prize.

James Tylor is an Australian photographer whose practice explores Australian environment, culture and social history. His work focuses largely on the colonial history of Australia in the nineteenth century, and its continued effect on present-day issues surrounding cultural identity and the environment. He explores Australian cultural representations through the perspectives of his multicultural heritage, which comprises Nunga (Kaurna), Māori (Te Arawa) and European (English, Scottish, Irish, Dutch and Norwegian) ancestries.

Frank Wynne has translated works by authors including Michel Houellebecq, Patrick Modiano, Jean-Baptiste Del Amo, Javier Cercas, Carlos Manuel Álvarez and Virginie Despentes. A number of his translations have won prizes, including the International Dublin Literary Award, the Scott Moncrieff Prize and the Premio Valle Inclán.

Javier Zamora was born in El Salvador. He immigrated to the US when he was nine to reunite with his parents. Zamora was a 2018–19 Radcliffe Institute Fellow at Harvard University, and holds fellowships from CantoMundo, Colgate University, MacDowell, Macondo Writers Workshop, National Endowment for the Arts, Poetry Foundation, Stanford University and Yaddo. He is the author of the poetry collection, *Unaccompanied*, and a memoir, *SOLITO*, forthcoming from Hogarth in 2022. He lives in Tucson, Arizona.